HIGHER LOVE

"When I first met Kit, I thought to myself, 'Wow, there's a lot of hype around this two-time world freeskiing champion.' My first ski run with Kit was Central Couloir off Cody peak, an extremely exposed 'no fall zone' line with a mandatory air at the bottom. On my second outing with her, we skied the Grand Teton. Needless to say, I found out she was the real deal. More than the real deal. She was awesome, in the true sense of the word, a machine in the mountains, intense, calculated, confident but still always had an easy smile to share.

"I quickly realized that Kit could achieve anything she ever set her mind to. It just so happened that climbing the Seven Summits was in her sights…but why just climb? Why not ski them all, too? Watching (and shooting) Kit ski off the summit of Everest is one of the most amazing things I've ever seen and a highlight of my career."

—**Jimmy Chin**, professional climber,
mountaineer, skier, director, and photographer

"When I met Kit, I knew she had what it takes to succeed at whatever she set out to accomplish. I'm honored that my Seven Summits experience prompted her to discover whether she could ski those summits. And I'm thrilled that the answer was 'Yes!' This book not only recounts Kit's challenging climbs and ski descents, it also shares the inspirational philosophy she lives and skis by."

—**Dick Bass**, owner of Snowbird Ski Resort,
coauthor of *Seven Summits*

"I'd been on the summit of Everest four times; I knew that it would be an extreme challenge for Kit to ski it. I had confidence in her abilities and her determination, but there are always unknowns above eight thousand meters. Ours was an autumn expedition to Everest; we were on our own, with no support from other teams. After five weeks of watching Kit and her team prevail as skilled climbers at high altitude, the day finally came to ski the Lhotse Face. When I got the call that she, Rob and Jimmy were safely across the bergschrund, I cried with relief and joy. This book is a whirlwind tour of seven intense climbs and skis and the inner workings of Kit's mind and heart. I'm proud that Berg Adventures could support her achievement by organizing two of her summit expeditions.

—**Wally Berg**, owner of Berg Adventures International

"I was president of The North Face when Kit submitted her proposal for skiing Everest. From the first day we discussed Kit's vision to climb and ski each of the Seven Summits, I was caught by her passion and commitment to achieve a milestone of such significance. This book is an exhilarating story of dreaming big, staying focused and pushing the limits of exploration."

—**Steve Rendle**, Senior Vice President, Americas, VF Corporation

"When I spent twenty minutes on the summit of Mount Everest in 1963, my first worry was: 'how to get down?' It never occurred to me that someone could ski it. Kit asked the question, 'Can it be skied?' and answered by doing it herself. *Higher Love* is about the love of life and the best of both worlds—climbing and skiing."

—**Jim Whittaker**, first American to reach the summit of Mount Everest (1963) and author of *A Life on the Edge*

"Climbing to high places is about so much more than reaching the top. In *Higher Love*, Kit gives you an intimate perspective of the extreme joys and intense challenges that are part of every high-stakes expedition. When you want to do something that no one has ever done before, you have to focus on finding the solution instead of reasons for why it can't be done. That's exactly what Kit DesLauriers demonstrates throughout her adventures on every mountain. This true story will make you laugh, cry and marvel at what people are capable of achieving."

—**Lynn Hill**, first person to free-climb the nose of El Capitan and author of *Climbing Free: My Life in the Vertical World*

"Whether you're a climber, a skier or both, you will enjoy every expedition in this book. In addition to taking you up and down the Seven Summits, Kit takes you to more obscure places like Mount Belukha, the highest peak in Siberia. If you admire the mountains and people who achieve big goals in them, you'll love this book."

—**Phil Powers**, Executive Director, The American Alpine Club

"For most Seven Summiters, the simple, tangible goal is to stand atop the highest point on each continent (and to return intact). For Kit DesLauriers, the top is where the unique challenge begins: to slide back down on a pair of skis. And she was the first person to do it! *Higher Love* is a gripping and reflective account of this odyssey, told by a gutsy, multitalented ski-mountaineering mom. Set your edges and savor the ride."

—**Tom Hornbein**, author of *Everest: The West Ridge*

"When Kit said she wanted to ski off the top of Everest, I didn't think her chance for success was very high, but I changed my mind while watching her surmount every challenge on the expedition. I was amazed at her courage, even enthusiasm, when she put skis on at the summit. I had mixed emotions belaying her around the Hillary Step: awe that she was doing it and concern that something could go dreadfully wrong. At 29,028 feet (5.5 miles above sea level), one small mistake can quickly lead to disaster. In this book, Kit tells the dramatic and sometimes-funny stories of the climbs and ski descents that led her to become the first person to ski the Seven Summits."

—**Dave Hahn**, professional mountain guide,
member of Taos Ski Patrol, summited Everest fifteen times

"*Higher Love* is a gripping, page-turning, real-life adventure. Kit is the heroine of her story as she follows her higher calling with passion, focus and determination. Her experience is an invitation to us all to pursue our dreams and to follow our spirits without hesitation."

—**Carol Mann**, personal transformation coach and author of *Why Wait: Wisdom for Life from Those Who Have Passed Over*

"Our adventure on Aconcagua was a highlight of my climbing and mountaineering career. I will always carry the memories of running down the ridge and catching up with Kit while watching history being made.

The moment she took herself off rappel and proceeded to ski on the steep section was truly inspiring; still today I have the vivid memories of each of the turns [she] made!"

—**Damian Benegas**, professional climber, film specialist, guide for Benegas Brothers Expeditions

HIGHER
LOVE

SKIING THE SEVEN SUMMITS

HIGHER LOVE

SKIING THE SEVEN SUMMITS

Foreword by Conrad Anker

KIT DESLAURIERS

With Doug Wagner

An Archer Publication

An Archer Publication

Copyright © 2018 by Kit DesLauriers

Archer, 453 South Spring Street, Suite 302, Los Angeles, CA 90013
archerlit.com

FIRST TRADE PAPERBACK EDITION

Distributed in the US by Publishers Group West
Printed in the United States
Set in Minion

Publisher's Cataloging-in-Publication data

DesLauriers, Kit.
Higher love : skiing the seven summits / by Kit DesLauriers.
p. cm.
ISBN-13: 9781941729267

1. DesLauriers, Kit. 2. Mountaineering—Personal narratives. 3. Skiing—Personal narratives. 4. Mountaineers—United States—Biography. 5. Mountains. 6. Continents. I. Title.

GV200 .D47 2015
796.52/2—dc23

*For everyone who said they found inspiration in my story
and asked for more.*

*Beyond all else, for my daughters, Grace and Tia, so that you may know
who I was before I became your mother.*

The events and stories contained within this manuscript are true. In the Antarctica and Kilimanjaro chapters, some names have been changed to protect the identities of those involved.

CONTENTS

FOREWORD

by Conrad Anker

ADVENTURE AND EXPLORATION ARE at the heart of the human experience. When we first wandered the globe in search of who and what we are, a hunger for exploration was at the core of our search. What was over the next horizon? What lay across the sea? What would we see from the top of the mountain? Of course, inherent in these explorations was adventure, that happy, soul-enriching, life-affirming offshoot of risk, and soon we were setting out for the unknown to find adventure for its own sake.

But the days of walking off the map are long over. Technology has allowed us to chart the planet with annoying accuracy. With your computer, you can pinpoint your neighbor's lawn sculpture as easily as you can find the headwaters of the Nile. In our overcrowded and overtaxed world, with pretty much every geographical feature mapped, named, and assessed for value, we naturally wonder if we can still find adventure and exploration in the twenty-first century. Even in the mountains, is there anything left to discover?

Long before people started climbing mountains, we were shaped by their presence. Mountains define land. Their immensity, formed by shifting plates driven from the core of the planet, create barriers. Barriers that shape weather, barriers that intimidate people. We fear mountains. The power unleashed by high-country storms and avalanches is the foundation for the many demons and dragons that filled the primitive mind. And water, too, finds its origin in mountains. The essential life force that connects humankind to the spiritual, the river where pilgrims place a drop of water in a newborn's mouth and bring the ashes of loved ones in hopes of auspicious future incarnations.

As a place of renewal and rebirth, mountains have a unique place in the human psyche. Most of the world's religions have a connection to the higher places. Mountains are central to the tenets of Christianity and Buddhism, not to mention the foundation of Greek mythology. The Native American beliefs hold mountains to be sacred, places where there is enlightenment through hardship.

Perhaps it's the connectedness to something timeless and more powerful than mere human existence that draws us to the mountains. They seem so mighty and permanent. They catch the first and last rays of sun, seemingly mystical in the hidden folds of verticality. In the time span of humans, they dwarf us and remind us of our insignificance, yet in the bigger geologic time frame, they are eroding ever so slowly back into the sea. From both perspectives, they're a reminder of life's impermanence.

But despite all this, the fact remains: The mountains have all been charted. So how do we find adventure and exploration in these times when there are no more blank spots on the map? We do it the same way we've always done it—by setting out for the unknown, someplace we don't know. The only difference now is that we search for these places *within*. The demons of doubt and the dragons of uncertainty still dwell within us, and it's in this internal landscape that the elemental human pursuit of adventure plays out. We *can* discover the unknown today. We simply need to locate the blank spots on our own maps and explore them.

In *Higher Love*, Kit shows us her own version of exploration. We're immediately swept into the story with her tale of adopting a wolf—the beginning of one adventure—and then we're plunged into another, her Seven Summits quest. To climb the highest mountain on each continent is a feat unto itself, but to ski them adds a whole other level of complexity and risk. A level that few dare to attain.

Society has placed a glass ceiling on what women can or should be expected to do. For example, climbing mountains is perceived as a masculine activity, yet it has its share of heroines like Kit who break through that perception. As we're taken through Kit's transformation from a competitive skier to a ski mountaineer, she provides us with reasons not to be held back by the labels society has assigned us. And while being a strong-willed woman is often perceived as intimidating, Kit shows us the other side of feminine determination. The grace, balance, and poise that come from unwavering commitment to a goal.

This is how to find adventure and exploration in the twenty-first century.

PROLOGUE

THE LOCAL PAPER WAS open to the classifieds on my lap as I sat in the lotus position on a round Papasan chair, the kind so popular among college students. I wasn't actually looking for anything, considering that my life in Tucson was coming to an end, but I'd scanned the rest of the paper and just ended up in the classifieds out of habit. Within the next ten days, I would graduate from the University of Arizona, get into my '74 pea soup-green GMC pickup and drive ten hours due north to begin a different life in Telluride, Colorado, so I didn't need any more possessions to burden myself with. But as I started to turn the page, one of the ads caught my eye:

Wolf Pups for sale. 5th litter. $200 ea. Must provide references.
Sabino Canyon. Call XXX-XXXX

"Jim!" I said to my housemate across the room. "I think Jere had more wolf pups! Wanna go see them?"

Jim had raised a wolf, and I guessed that this was the same breeder he'd gotten his from. How many wolf breeders could there be in Sabino Canyon?

I read him the phone number.

"Yup, that's Jere," he said. "Wow. So the fifth litter? Isa was from the third litter. I didn't know there was one in between. Yeah, let's go!"

Jim's wolf, Isa, had been a wanderer, a beautiful spirit who had a hard time living in the city, even as relatively mellow a city as Tucson. One day the previous September, she was running alone on one of her regular forays through the arroyos while Jim was at work and she was killed by a car while crossing a six-lane road. Jim had raised Isa for two years since she was a cub, and the loss was devastating to him. He was still in mourning these four months later.

I'd loved Isa, too. When Jim had spent a month in Alaska two summers before, I looked after her. I was living in Telluride at the time, waiting tables at a restaurant and sleeping in my tent in the national forest above town to save money to travel and study in France. I mostly let Isa go free, and she mostly stuck near me. When I wasn't working, I was doing something that Isa wanted to come along for, like hiking or biking up mountains. When she ran off on her own, though, she was prone to encountering porcupines and getting a face full of quills, which I had to learn to pull out because I couldn't afford a veterinarian, not to mention that owning a wolf is illegal in Colorado and I wasn't sure how I'd explain the situation. All in all, Isa was an exhausting amount of responsibility, and I was happy to hand her over to Jim when he came back.

Isa's death had made it very clear to both of us how hard it is on a wild animal to live in domesticity, even a bohemian outdoorsy type of domesticity. It's just not fair to the animal.

When we got to Jere's house, she ushered us to a backyard enclosed by a seven-foot chain-link fence. As we sat on the rocky soil in front of an oversize doghouse, an enormous wolf came up to greet us.

"This is the father, Alf, as in *alpha*," Jere said. "The mama, Nikita, and the pups are inside. Take a look—they're nursing!"

I peered inside at the tiny, seven-day-old animals clambering over each other in an olfactory-driven search for an empty nipple. Wolves' eyes and ears open sometime between two and three weeks of age, like with all canines.

The father sat on his haunches just two feet away, watching our every move. He was 78 percent Minnesota timber wolf, mixed with some Siberian husky and German shepherd, and Jere had raised both him and the mother, who was 100 percent timber wolf. Only mildly cautious with the wolves, Jere stuck her hand into the den and pulled out a couple of pups at a time and set them on the ground in front of us. Alf's attention never wavered, but he also never became aggressive, and I trusted that as long as Jere was there Jim and I would be safe.

I studied the pups' little black noses and the milky covering on their eyes that resembled cataracts. Their midsections were so round and bloated from their just-finished meal of mother's milk that they looked more like hamsters than wolves. One was pure black, and the others were varying shades of gray flecked with black, white, or auburn and often with a black tip on their tails. They all had unique physical characteristics, and I thought I could already sense their unique personalities.

Lost in reverie—it was hard to believe I was actually touching week-old wolf pups—I was visualizing what they would grow up to be when Jere jarred me out of my dream state.

"Would you like to hold one?" she asked as she held one toward me in her palm.

I smiled. "Sure." I took the pup with both hands and held it like Jere had, but I soon handed it back because Alf's close proximity and careful attention were making me uncomfortable.

"Why don't you go over there and sit down with him?" Jere said, gesturing toward the chaise lounges by the pool. "You'll really feel what it's like to hold one if you aren't half-lying on the ground and nervous about the den."

I wanted to hold a different one, though. Something had captivated me about the one with subtle patches of auburn in his coat. When Jere had pulled him from the den and put him on display, he seemed content to be where he was, and I sensed a gentle strength and peace emanating from him.

"I'd rather hold that one," I said, pointing.

Jere smiled. "Are you sure? Can you tell the differences between them? He's not as big, I guess." She reached for him and handed him to me.

I found myself wrapping my forearms around the pup's two-pound body in a protective embrace. "They're all beautiful. I didn't notice much size difference, actually, but there's just something about this one that I liked from the moment I saw him." I carried him to the chaise lounge, where we cuddled while Jim and Jere played with the other pups. Alf cast me an occasional glance, but he stayed put, concentrating on the activity closer at hand.

Within minutes, a previously unknown place in the center of my body began to pulse. The spot was a hand's width above my bellybutton, and it felt warm, like how fresh blood from a wound can be surprisingly warm to the touch. The sensation spread through my body until I found myself inhaling a deep breath and smiling involuntarily. I'd never felt anything like it before. *Is this love? I thought I'd loved before, but this is bigger... Amazing.*

I became frightened of the intensity of my emotions, and from out of nowhere a voice spoke up.

Kit, you'd better stand up and go give this animal back to Jere. You're about to graduate from college and move to Telluride. You have only a few hundred dollars to your name and you want to travel around the world. You have no business holding this wolf.

Guided by the voice, I stood up and began walking back toward the den with the wolf in my arms, and Jere met me halfway.

"I've never done this before and I'll never do it again, since this is the last litter I'll let these animals have," she said. "I can see you're very connected already. If you want to take him home to live with you, you can come back and get him in a week when he's fourteen days old."

She'd broken whatever spell I'd been under. The voice had been silenced.

Jere went on. "I say fourteen days because with the fourth litter, the mom developed mastitis and we discovered it when the pups were fourteen days old. They couldn't nurse, so I consulted a breeder of large canines and a vet and came up with a formula that I mixed by hand and fed them myself. And the socialization of those pups was incredible." She smiled at the obviously fond memory. "I couldn't bring myself to sell them. I gave one to my son and I kept one. You're the only other person I'll ever offer this to, but like I said, I see you have a special connection already."

In the absence of the voice, the truth flowed from me before I could consider the words.

"I'll never live anywhere that a wolf doesn't want to live."

Jere smiled and waited, seeming to know I had more to say.

"I promise I will do everything I can so that he doesn't die for being a wolf in a human's world." I fought back tears and brought the pup up to my lips to kiss the fur of his neck. He nuzzled his head into the nape of my own neck, and the sensation of being fur-to-skin with this beautiful creature was earth-moving.

We walked to the den and Jere put him back in with his mother, Nikita, and the rest of the litter.

On the way inside the house, Jere told me she'd get me the recipe for feeding the pup by next week, and Jim looked questioningly at both of us. I shrugged, barely believing it myself. *Did I really just say I'd love and care for a wolf for the rest of his life? I only have $250 to my name—what am I doing taking on a dependent?*

"I'm thinking of bringing one home with me next week after finals," I said to Jim.

"I told Kit she could take one home at two weeks old and wean him from his mother," Jere said. "I had the most amazing experience doing that with the two pups of the last litter. Like you know, wolves have their social hierarchy established by the time they're three to four weeks old, so I think it's the best way possible if they're going to live with humans…I trust her."

Jim was my roommate, my best friend, and my sometimes lover. He'd seen me care for Isa and care for him during his grief. He knew I hadn't had the slightest intention of bringing a wolf home with me today. He knew I didn't have the money to buy a wolf. And he also knew what boundless love of all things wild lay ahead for me if I chose to live with a wolf. He laughed like he always did when he loved an idea.

"Right on! I'll buy him for you, Kit."

I spent the next week in a daze, going through the motions of taking my exams like a puppet in a play. All I could concentrate on was moving to the mountains with my wolf. Luckily, I'd prepared well throughout the semester, and my finals didn't spring any surprises on me, so that step of my journey was an easy one.

When December 20 arrived, Jim drove me to Jere's house and paid her $200 in cash. She wrote a receipt on a green-lined sheet of paper torn out of a six-by-eight spiral notebook: "Paid $200 cash for one black and white male wolf cub born on Dec. 6 1991." It was really happening—I was adopting a wolf. I had his birth certificate in my hand.

Then she wrote the feeding formula on another sheet of paper and handed it to me: one jar beef baby food, one can condensed milk, a cup of plain whole-milk yogurt, and an egg yolk.

"Are you ready?" she asked with a serious smile.

"As ready as I'll ever be."

When we went to the den, the same story played out, with Alf walking out from his spot under the paloverde trees and settling onto his haunches a few feet from the den. Jere reached in and pulled the wolf pup out and handed him to me. Feeling like a first-time mother, I wrapped my arms around him and cried over the enormity of it all.

As I sat in the passenger seat on the ride home, the tears turned to sobs of sadness for having taken him from his family, sadness that he couldn't be a wild wolf, sadness that people actually breed these animals for a life in captivity. But then came the tears of love, the tears for the commitment I'd made to care for him the way I'd want to be cared for if the tables were turned.

Back home, I dove into my new role with complete dedication. My first task was to find something to wear that the pup could snuggle into for the next three weeks until he could generate his own body heat. From my closet I picked an old, gray wool sweater with the image of a cabin with smoke curling from its chimney stitched into the front. The weave was a little loose, and the collar was stretched out—perfect. I pulled it on, put the pup inside and held a bent arm against the sweater to give him something to sit on.

Then it was time to feed him. I put the formula ingredients in the blender, and when they reached a good consistency, I poured the mixture into a bottle designed for kid goats that I picked up at a feed store. I heated it over a pot of water on the stove until it was wrist temperature and then settled into the Papasan chair and pulled him out of the sweater. Instinctively, he reached for the bottle and suckled the warm formula until he'd had enough. When he was done, I put him on my thigh, stomach down and facing away from me, and gently stroked his back in the direction of his head until he burped. His mother wouldn't have needed to burp him in the wild, of course, but he wouldn't have sucked from a bottle filled with air bubbles in the wild either.

Almost immediately, I discovered his need to urinate after a feeding and rushed him outside. The tricky part was, his legs couldn't support his body weight yet, so I held him upright until he was done. Back inside, I turned him onto his back to clean him with a baby wipe. Again, not something his mother would have done, but I wasn't into *her* way of cleaning him.

And then came the precious hour and a half before I had to start the process all over again. I set up a sleeping bag on the floor of the living room, next to the door so we could get outside quickly when he started to pee, and we cuddled and napped together. I was tired as I got up to feed him every two hours throughout the night, but I loved every minute of it, and Jim helped as much as I'd let him.

The next day I would attend my commencement ceremony, but it was clear that my new life had already commenced.

TWO DAYS LATER, THE pup opened his eyes and began exploring his surroundings with newly sturdy legs and the curiosity of a toddler. He explored me, too, crawling up my body inside our sweater, popping out the neck and clawing his way up my long hair to sit on top of my head— five feet and nine inches off the ground and fearless. He seemed to know he belonged in high places, and I named him Alta, Spanish for *high*.

Fortunately, where we were bound *was* a high place. The next day— Alta's seventeenth day—I packed up and moved us to Telluride, elevation 8,750 feet. I didn't have any money to rent a room, so I parked my truck at the base of the ski resort and set up camp in the back.

At night I would run a power cord from a small ceramic space heater in my uninsulated aluminum camper shell to the nearby condominium building where my parents happened to work as part-time managers to offset their rent. Alta and I slept together in a sleeping bag on the plywood bed I'd made in the back of the truck.

In the morning, I'd use the blender in my parents' kitchen to make Alta's toddler meal of formula mixed with ground-up dry kibble and set down his food bowl on the easy-to-clean linoleum floor. Once he'd finished and we'd gone outside so he could do his business, we would always play, which consisted of a mix of learning about snow, stopping to smell anything interesting we encountered on a walk, and chasing each other. Alta would tire quickly, so around nine I'd put him down for a nap in the closet that my parents let me use and I'd go skiing for an hour or two. When I'd come back at eleven, I'd feed him again, play with him some more, and put him back down for a nap while I went to wait tables at Eddie's Pizzeria for the lunch crowd. It was a good thing that my parents were at their office jobs at the time, because I'd often come back to the condo at two thirty to find Alta chewing on the corner of the carpet or pulling a lamp off a table by its cord.

As the weeks passed, it became obvious that the arrangement couldn't last. My parents grew increasingly unhappy about my leaving Alta at the condo, and justifiably so, since dogs were prohibited there. And even though it was only play, Alta's needle-sharp milk teeth had begun to leave puncture marks on my hands, which were hard to hide while waiting tables.

I didn't know what to do with myself, my freedom, or my wolf, and I worried that I was losing control over Alta's upbringing. I needed to steer his behavior so that he wouldn't be killed for being a wolf in a human's world, but I could see that steering him in *any* way was going to be a challenge. I'd tried to discipline him, but a firm "no" was rarely enough. At the end of January, I took a week off work and went back to Tucson to visit Jim and see if he could help me train my foot-long baby who sometimes seemed to be all teeth.

AS A GRADUATION GIFT, Jim had bought me the book *Of Wolves and Men*, by Barry Lopez, and I'd studied it intently. In it, Lopez tells many stories about the wolf through the eyes of biologists, Native Americans, Alaskan trappers, and observers, and what I took most to heart was the concept threaded through all of them: The wolf is a social animal and depends on cooperation for its survival. The social structure of a wolf pack is dynamic, and the term *alpha*

is a bit misleading because during times of travel or breeding or hunting or play, the subordinate members of the pack may occasionally take the lead. Regardless, the designation of alpha is earned by displaying superior physical prowess or by being socially savvy and forging alliances in the group. In other words, the alpha is the one in the best position to protect the others, and I realized that was exactly what Alta needed from me—I would have to teach myself how to be dominant over a wolf.

When we got back to Tucson, Jim confirmed it for me. "Remember, Kit, wolves are establishing the hierarchy in their pack right about now, and you have to teach him that you're alpha."

"But how?"

"You have to be able to take food away from him. In a pack, a wolf only gets to eat when the alpha lets him eat. So put a bone in front of him, and when he starts eating it, take it away."

Though this sounded logical, it also sounded a little scary, but I didn't feel like I had a choice. So I bought a meaty bone at the grocery store and headed out to the small fenced yard of Jim's new home with Alta following closely and sniffing away. In the shade of the acacia trees lining the yard, I gave Alta the bone.

By now he was seven weeks old and had been weaned, and his meals consisted of dry kibble with some blocks of frozen lamb-and-rice dog food mixed in because I thought he needed to have meat in his life. I'd never thought about taking Alta's food away from him before and it made me nervous. *What if I can't do it?*

Jim stood watch a few yards away, and while Alta was lost in concentration on the bone, I took a step forward and reached my hand in to grab it. In a flash, his mouth curled back to reveal his puppy teeth and he bit me. With a gasp, I instinctively released my grip on the bone and recoiled in pain and shock. All my previous marks from his sharp teeth had been delivered in play, but this time was different.

I'd failed.

"You have to believe you can do it," Jim said. "Try again."

I tried again. And again and again. Sometimes I moved fast, sometimes slowly, and sometimes I sneaked up on Alta from behind, but the result was always the same: He'd snap at me and I couldn't do it. After ten tries, I turned away from Alta and cried.

"Don't break down in front of him," Jim said. "You can't show him that he's won. Let's go inside."

In the kitchen I sobbed into Jim's embrace. "I suck! I can't believe I can't do this! Now what's going to happen to us?"

"You can do this, Kit. You have to. Just take a break and you can try again later."

Between our alpha-training sessions, Alta bore no animosity toward me for trying to take away his bone and acted as if I shouldn't bear him any for biting me. While Jim was at class, Alta and I played and cuddled like usual, and then when Jim got home it was time to try again.

Knowing what was at stake, I'd stand in the doorway and take several deep breaths. I knew the pain of what lay ahead if I didn't get this right. And that was on top of the pain I was in right now—the heart that had opened so completely to this animal was hurting from the rejection. *How could he do this to me? What if I can't ever learn to be alpha?*

But eventually, a shift occurred. When I became stronger in my resolve, telling myself, "Dammit, this is the way it is—I can do this," Alta would let me have the bone. He'd stare up at me as if to ask, "What's next, Mom?" Somehow I'd turned the tide. I'd succeeded.

And then Jim informed me that I wasn't quite there yet.

"Now let's do it with a real piece of meat," he said.

What?! You mean that wasn't good enough? That took me three days of hard, scary work.

But instead of arguing, I just rolled with it. I'd come all the way back to Arizona to ask for Jim's help and there was no sense in doubting him, so we went to the grocery store and picked out a big juicy T-bone.

Back in the yard, it was as if my success with the bones had never happened. When I tried to take the steak away, Alta bit me hard. Maybe the taste of flesh pushed him over the top or maybe I'd just lost my conviction, but whatever the case, my future flashed in front of my eyes. *If I can't consistently do this, then I'll be no better than the people who lock their wolf-dogs up and leave them alone in a house or a yard because they aren't socialized and their owners are scared of them. I swore I'd give him the best life possible, and if I fail at this, then I've failed at that.*

I stomped into the house for a break, and during that cooling-off period I realized I felt a little differently about this latest failed attempt.

I understood that this exercise wasn't a personal exchange between us. It was intrapersonal, not interpersonal. It was about what was going on inside us as individuals, not how we were relating to each other. Alta was driven by instinct, and I had to cultivate the same kind of strong instinct in myself, focusing every bit of my being into the task at hand without a hint of "What if?" anywhere in my energetic bubble. And that's what I did.

When I went back outside, Alta was halfway through the raw T-bone and barely lifted his eyes to me. Drawing on every cell in my body, mind and spirit, I had to stifle the urge to growl with the ferocity I was feeling as I reached in and grabbed the steak. Alta simply pulled back and looked at me.

Jim clapped. "*Yes!*"

For the next few days, I practiced this ritual without a trace of doubt in myself. I scanned my being, and if I sensed any distractions, I turned away from the scene and focused on eliminating them before taking the steak from Alta. I envisioned myself succeeding with complete commitment. After all, Alta's life—and the life I wanted for myself—depended on it. And I never failed again.

Meanwhile, Jim threw himself into his role as Jedi trainer. During a hike in the desert outside Tucson, I wanted to protect Alta from a patch of jumping cholla cactuses that were off the trail, but Jim held me back.

"Let him get stuck, Kit. He has to learn himself. You can't always be there for him."

My first reaction was small-picture: *Oh yeah? Once we go back to the mountains, he'll never have to worry about jumping cholla again.* But then I realized that Jim was speaking in a broader sense and that he was right. Alta was occupying the human world, and he needed my help in realizing his innate independence.

"Aarrgghh, aarrgghh, aarrgghh!" came Alta's cries of pain when the cholla needles inevitably became stuck in his belly. While it hurt to hear him squeal like that, it also warmed my heart that he came running to me for help. I opened the pliers on my multitool, a must for desert hiking, and carefully removed the cactus spines. As we finished our hike, Alta didn't stray from the trail again.

My alpha training would never be entirely over. If I were ever to think I mastered it, that would mean I'd become complacent, and that could bring serious consequences. But we'd achieved the cooperative social dynamic that wolves rely on for their very survival. By the time we went back to Telluride, I'd learned that I can and will fulfill any commitment I make. There was no doubt in my mind that I would succeed in allowing Alta to lead a wolf's life even though he lived in a human's world.

PLAY THE GAME

"**M**Y DAD SAID TO only give ourselves thirty seconds, but there's no way I can write down everything that fast," I said to Rob as I handed him a piece of paper and a pen. "Let's give ourselves a minute."

Dad probably hadn't imagined we'd play "the game" while sitting on the dirty, gray carpet at Logan International's Gate C28 surrounded by throngs of summer travelers. It didn't matter that we were at eye level with dozens of knees rushing by—Rob and I existed in a bubble of new love's bliss, without a care for the chaos around us.

"How does the game go again?" Rob said.

"First we write down everything we want to do in our lives—in one minute. Then we write down everything we want to do in the next five years—in one minute. After that, we write down everything we'd want to do if we had only one year left to live—in one minute. Then we share our lists."

A knot had formed in my stomach at the prospect of sharing my deepest dreams with someone. Seven years after I'd graduated from college, Alta had heard all my hopes and fears, but baring them to another person was new territory for me.

When Dad had introduced the idea of playing this game to us earlier that week, he told us he and Mom had used it as a relationship tool and credited it with helping them to stick together through thirty-five years of marriage and counting. The idea that Rob and I would someday be committed enough to make such serious, long-term plans together seemed like a pretty big assumption. I was twenty-nine and he was thirty-four and we were very much a couple, but we'd met only six months earlier during a ski expedition to Mount Belukha, the highest peak in Siberia. Neither of us had ever been married, and neither of us had thought marriage was in our futures.

Rob had been the cinematographer on the expedition, and I was part of the "talent" crew, although without being a sponsored member of an athlete team, I almost hadn't been. The North Face, one of the companies backing us, wanted its athletes to be a part of the trip, and Rob, who was a team member and a pioneer of American extreme skiing, did his due diligence and found out that I was a nobody in the professional skiing world who lived in the tiny remote town of Ophir, in southwest Colorado. In his estimation, the film would have less appeal with a no-name like me in it than it would if everyone were well-known, and rumor had it he wanted me off the trip.

With a week to go before departure, I was stewing about this development during my fifteen-mile drive to work in Telluride.

"I don't want to go if I'm not wanted," I said to my friend Anne, who was riding with me. "I think I'm going to back out."

"Are you kidding? An all-expenses-paid ski expedition to Siberia? You've *got to go*! Whatever is bothering you, get over it. This is the chance of a lifetime."

I took Anne's advice and flew to Switzerland as planned with Ace Kvale, who was an internationally renowned photographer as well as my regular climbing partner and the person who had dreamed up the idea of this expedition. There we met our mutual friend John Falkiner to ski in Verbier for a few days before it was time to fly to Moscow. The night before our flight, a knock came on the door at John's house and in popped Rob's smiling countenance. He had young Bob Dylan hair and handsome brown eyes, and they seemed to see right into me.

I couldn't believe it. I'd never experienced anything like it. It was like there wasn't anything to hide or any reason to hide it. It was a feeling of total potentiality.

I spent the night trying to make eye contact with him across the dinner table, but he obviously thought Ace and I were a couple and wouldn't look at me. It didn't matter, though—the feeling didn't go away.

A current of electricity kept Rob and me close to each other over the following weeks. As we shared a snow cave with ten teammates, our pinky fingers bravely found each other outside our forty-below-zero sleeping bags. Not most people's idea of holding hands, but it *was* March in Siberia, and under the circumstances, I couldn't imagine a more romantic courtship.

After we got back from the trip, word of our relationship spread quickly. My grandmother called me one day while I was on lunch break from my stonemasonry job and told me of her approaching eightieth-birthday party, and I promised I'd fly to Massachusetts for it.

"Why don't you bring that young man I've heard so much about?" she said.

"But, Granny, we've only known each other for a few months!" I said, looking at Rob, who was visiting from his home in Victor, Idaho.

"I don't care. If he's as nice as I hear he is, then I want to meet him."

I put my hand over the phone. "Granny wants to meet you," I whispered to Rob.

"Only if you agree to meet my family afterward," he replied with a sheepish grin.

And so six months after falling in love in a snow cave, we found ourselves on the family tour, cornered by Dad at the end of a boat dock at the mouth of the Westport River in coastal Massachusetts, where my parents live. He'd never gotten involved in my love life before, but all of a sudden he was giving me relationship advice right in front of my boyfriend.

"After you write your lists and share them," he said, "come up with the items you agree to focus on, both personally and collectively. Then figure out a financial plan to make your dreams a reality."

I liked the idea of making a list and sharing it with Rob, but I felt uncomfortable with the idea of joint economic planning, since we weren't even engaged. Financial matters could wait. Besides, I wasn't sure Dad's suggestion fit with my belief in allowing the universe some space for serendipity.

"Sounds great. Thanks, Dad," I said, just wanting to end the too-intimate conversation.

A few days after Granny's party, we moved on to Burlington, Vermont, to visit Rob's parents, and it was in front of his mother's house on October 1, 1999, that he dropped to one knee, asked me to marry him, and I accepted. It wasn't a quick decision on my part, though—I'd actually overheard him ask my parents' permission the day we left Massachusetts and had given it careful thought. And now, as we waited at the airport for our flight back to Colorado, the idea of playing the game didn't seem so unreasonable anymore. In the end, the fact that my parents were still married after thirty-five years was good enough for us. Besides, I really wanted to know what Rob had in mind for the rest of his life, *and* our lives.

Sitting on the floor, we took turns reading from our lists. When we got to the part about what we wanted to do in the next five years, I was relieved that, like me, Rob hadn't listed having children. And I was surprised by what he did list.

"Denali? Really? You want to ski Denali?"

I'd listed more remote objectives like "ski in Bhutan," and high on my husband-to-be's list was to ski in North America? It seemed like a mundane goal, but I did my best to hide my disappointment, as there were things on my list I hoped *he* wouldn't shun. After all, we were in this together now.

I'd felt a strong pull toward the exotic since being part of a seven-week climbing trip in Sikkim, India, a year before the Siberian expedition. The goal was an obscure and beautiful 20,000-foot peak called Siniolchu, in the Himalayas. It was my first international climbing expedition, and Ace had invited me in part because of my mountain skills, which included being a wilderness emergency medical technician, a highly trained volunteer with San Miguel County Search and Rescue, and a rookie on the Telluride Ski Patrol.

The demanding peak had seen only a handful of previous attempts, and it took us ten days of overland travel just to reach the trailhead at the final village, which was so remote that the youngest children had never seen Caucasian skin before. It was spring in the high country, so instead of easily finding local people wanting several days' work helping us carry our loads into base camp, as I was told is often the case when trekking in that part of the world, we were forced to hike into the hills to find farmers willing to postpone their planting to be our porters. And we needed a lot of them. To carry five weeks' worth of food and fuel, tents, stoves, ropes, and other climbing gear required the muscle of forty porters hauling standard loads of thirty-five pounds.

When we'd rounded up the veritable army we needed, we trekked among blooming rhododendron trees up a valley that revealed itself slowly. The riverbank led us to patches of hardened spring snow that the porters tenuously negotiated in their plastic sandals. In these open areas above the forest, I'd tilt my head so that my ear rested on my shoulder but I could still barely see the summits of the steep glaciated mountains rising the equivalent of ten Empire State Buildings above our little trail of ants. Making an effort to keep my jaw from dropping lest I remind my more experienced teammates how green I was, I mused about how someone picks a peak to travel halfway around the world to climb. *All* the snowy giants in the range looming over us looked like worthy destinations.

There was only one thing missing from the beautiful scenario: my skis. As we gained more and more distance from civilization and its urban trappings and I became more and more relaxed, I settled into a deeply personal mental state that led me to a revelation: I felt lost without my skis. I realized that what I was drawn most to in life was climbing *and* skiing in high mountains—it was a package deal.

The eminently skiable peaks directly above us beckoned me, but we were here strictly for an alpine climb, and it was then that I realized I was different from the others on the trip. While my teammates seemed perfectly content with their climbing objective, I was experiencing a strange feeling of being separated from my highest calling, as if I were a different species from the other climbers. At that moment I made up my mind that in the future, I'd be true to my nature and devote myself to climbing mountains I could ski back down.

When I shared my epiphany with Ace, he smiled the knowing smile of a seasoned climber who has experienced his own moments of clarity in the mountains.

"There's a magical, mystical mountain range in Siberia I've long wanted to visit called the Altai, which means 'golden mountain,'" he said. "Legend says it's the birthplace of skiing."

Most climbers plan their next objective at least as soon as the current one has been achieved, and in our case we didn't wait. As we retraced our steps down the valley of rhododendron trees and raging, newly melted rivers, we planned our Siberian journey for the following year.

Interestingly, much of that conversation had revolved around the same subject that Dad had raised and that I was now wondering about as Rob and I sat on the floor at Logan: Who was going to pay for it?

Several outdoor-industry companies had funded the Siberian expedition as part of Rob's film. To pay for the trip to India, I'd saved for a year and sold my mountain bike—worth more than my car at the time—and had nothing else to sell. I was still a stonemason, and in the same week that Rob had proposed to me, he'd gotten an offer to give up his cinematography and ski career in favor of developing a hotel in Teton Village, Wyoming, for a friend who was the landowner. If Rob did a good job of managing this three-year project, he'd eventually be financially rewarded, but in the meantime the project couldn't afford to pay him a living wage. How could we *afford* to achieve the goals on our lists?

Under the circumstances, it was no slam dunk that we'd be able to attain the kind of independence it would take to see the world, let alone ski it. Dad had made it sound like coming up with a plan for funding our unconventional dreams would be a simple matter, but from where I was sitting, the road ahead was anything but clear.

FINGERPRINTS

A YEAR AFTER MAKING MY list, I achieved both entries in the one-year category: I married Rob and moved to Jackson. But then my progress screeched to a halt. When we returned from a honeymoon in Greece—financed primarily through a Kellogg's miles-for-box tops promotion (really)—we entered a three-year period of keeping our heads down and working like our lives depended on it. The life we wanted required absolute commitment, and we committed absolutely. While I've never fully accepted Dad's suggestion of mapping out precise budgets to accomplish my goals (I got only one "C" in college and it was in economics), I consider myself a realist, and with the opportunities at hand, one thing was obvious: If I could help Rob to be successful in his hotel development venture, that would give us our best chance at the independence we longed for.

When I wasn't trying to help with the project at Rob's makeshift office—a cheap one-bedroom condo where the living room, possibly illegally, became the office and the bedroom was reserved for his father when he visited from Vermont—I'd scrub toilets in the sales trailer or build stone patios for homeowners in the area as I'd done in Telluride. I got up every morning to make him breakfast and a brown-bag lunch because we couldn't afford restaurant meals, ever. We brought in $2,000 a month in income, and $1,458 of that went for the mortgage.

Fortunately, I'd been well trained in living frugally. I grew up in a middle-class family that occasionally fell on hard times. We never got fountain drinks from 7-Eleven—one drink cost the same amount as a six-pack of soda—and we were strictly Nordic skiers, since Nordic equipment was cheaper than downhill equipment. And because it required less precise fitting, three children could get more seasons out of it—being the middle child, I always seemed to have skis that were too long or too short. There was also the fact that Nordic skiing required little to no travel. We could simply duck through the barbed-wire fence around the farmer's fields down the road and push off.

One day when I was on my way out to ride bikes with friends in the neighborhood, my mom pulled me aside. "Please be careful for a little while," she said, looking uncomfortable. "We don't have health insurance and can't afford for anyone to get hurt." Slurpees I could live without, but the idea of not having enough money for emergencies was downright scary.

So the toughest part about my current situation as a struggling newlywed wasn't paying for groceries or car insurance with the $500 left after the mortgage—I knew how to just scrape by. And it wasn't the physical labor, which I actually enjoyed and was used to. The toughest part was that my life's mission had shifted to helping my husband succeed at his new and consuming career—part of his five-year plan from "the list." I yearned for the life of adventure I'd cultivated but abruptly left behind. Soon after our honeymoon, Alta had died at the young age of nine, and I missed my friends in Colorado—I had no friends of my own in this new place. I felt like my fingerprints had been erased, as if the nature I'd promised to honor had been put in a cage. Who was I? I was serving a cause greater than myself, working for *our* freedom, and I didn't understand why that wasn't enough for me. Why was this so hard?

AFTER THREE YEARS WITHOUT a single visit to New England to see our families or more than an occasional splurge on gasoline to drive to Lander, Wyoming, to go climbing for the weekend, we finally made it. We'd saved enough money to buy a home at the base of Jackson Hole Mountain Resort in the summer of 2003. And to commemorate the occasion, we took our first trip since the honeymoon—a celebration of our combined commitment to getting his project done, of our connection, and of the potential to make my own goals a priority again in the near future.

"Where do you want to go?" Rob asked, leaving the destination entirely up to me.

"I want to ski a big mountain in New Zealand," I said, not needing to add that it had been on my five-year game card since that day in the Boston airport.

"New Zealand is my favorite place I've ever been. Let's do it."

In November, we landed in Christchurch. New Zealand's South Island is a land of gentle people and exquisite contrasts: rolling green farmland, rugged coastlines, pristine rivers, and glaciated mountains. We spent twenty days seeing it by way of a rented van that doubled as our hotel room, with a plywood bed in back and crates of cooking gear stored under it. I'd been amazed to find this makeshift "camper" online, but then, what Americans call "roughing it" is a regular part of life for Kiwis.

As for the reason I'd wanted to come to New Zealand—to climb and ski a mountain—we'd decided on Mount Aspiring because the name struck a chord with me and the photos I'd seen of the "Matterhorn of the South" were stunning. The problem was, after driving across the island to the jumping-off town of Wanaka, mountain guides we'd befriended told us that most successful climbs begin with a helicopter lift to the Colin Todd Hut; there are so few days of good weather on the mountain that it's uncommon to get the three in a row it would take to climb it from the bottom and get down below the glaciers before a storm sets in. Since Rob and I couldn't afford to hire a heli-lift, we felt we had no choice but to wait for a good weather window and climb the whole way on our own power.

As it turned out, when we checked in at the guides' office to get a weather report on the fifth morning, we found head guides Dave and Nick scrambling to gather gear, and they offered us their extra seats on a heli-lift to the Bonar Glacier at a very discounted rate. We'd have to be ready by ten, though, because the weather window was so small. While I ran to the grocery store for mountain food, Rob ran to the ATM for the $300 that the flight would cost us, and we made it to the pickup site with all our gear packed just as the helicopter was landing.

After a short uphill ski from the heli-drop site, we spent the night at the Colin Todd Hut and started the six-hour climb to the summit at three the next morning. The weather window did indeed turn out to be small—a storm began to roll in just as we were stepping into our bindings on the summit, which made for an exciting descent. Adding to the drama was the fact that we took the guides' suggestion to try a new variation that entailed skiing over lots of crevasses on the Therma Glacier.

In the end, though the mountain had seen close to a dozen ski descents before ours, on November 5, 2003, I became the first woman to ski down Mount Aspiring.

In addition to coming away with another adventure under our belts, we came away with new motivation to achieve Rob's goal of skiing Denali. After our spicy summit day on Aspiring, we'd stayed the night at the French Ridge Hut with Dave and Nick and their clients, and Nick had suggested that we ski North America's highest peak next. Rob and I traded smiles. The serendipity was impossible to ignore. We had eleven months left to meet the goals on our five-year lists, and Denali was still at the top of Rob's.

So in true explorer fashion, we began plotting the next adventure before the current one was over. By the time we turned in for the night, we'd settled on a $5,000 budget and a date in May for our next expedition: climbing and skiing the highest mountain in North America.

Mount Aspiring marked the beginning of a new era, one in which I focused less on playing the day-to-day support role for my husband, since he was now established in his world, and more on finding my fingerprints again. Besides planning for the expedition to Denali, I began to let myself dream about something else I'd written on my list: I wanted to win something. I wanted to know I could be the best at something.

The previous year, I'd suffered a massive lateral meniscal tear in my left knee while rock climbing on Elephant's Perch in the Sawtooth Range of Idaho. After the surgery, I started a six-month rehab during which I couldn't ski. Working as the caretaker of a home at the base of Jackson Hole Mountain Resort, I spent the winter alternating between physical therapy and lying on the couch looking at the tram going overhead and getting back into dreaming mode so I could find a positive outlet for my mind.

What if?

What if I trained very hard and stayed supremely focused? Was there a chance I could succeed at a freeskiing competition? And maybe win? When I'd toss my I Ching sticks to see what the Chinese Book of Changes had in mind for me, I got the answer: With total dedication, it was possible. I could feel it in my body when I contemplated the question, even before tossing the sticks. It was so far out there for a thirty-three-year-old woman who'd never competed at skiing: so bold, so exciting, so possible.

In June 2003, Rob and I had climbed and skied the Grand Teton in Wyoming for the first time, and it was also the first time I'd done anything physically significant with no knee pain since my injury nine months earlier. By December, after the confidence boost I'd gotten on Aspiring, the question I'd sat on for over a year was demanding an answer: Am I ready to try competitive freeskiing? I didn't need the I Ching sticks to tell me that the answer was, "Yes."

I'd never been afraid to attempt new things. When I was fourteen, my dad asked if I wanted to go downhill skiing (because we could finally afford it), and I imagined it would be like a terrifying amusement-park ride.

As it turned out, skiing immediately became my favorite thing in life. It felt like a dance. A dance I wanted to master. Over the years, I set higher and higher goals for myself until I finally skied from the summit of the Grand Teton for the first time in June 2003, but even with that amazing experience under my belt, one big aspect of skiing still eluded me: competition. The closest I'd ever come was a local banked slalom race in Jackson in March 2002, a few months before my knee injury. I didn't know a thing about freeskiing—why did I think I could compete, let alone win?

Actually, when I looked up the rules of the sport, it seemed like the biggest obstacle might be a technicality I'd have to overcome. To compete at the world level, a skier had to have had a top-ten finish at the national level the previous year. *Aaargh*. I'd just turned thirty-four and didn't want to wait another year.

I called the head of the International Freeskiers Association and asked to compete in the first event, to be held at Whistler-Blackcomb, in British Columbia. I wanted this too much to give up without trying.

"Hi, Adam. I'm not sure if you remember me, but we skied together last April at Snowbird, and I really want to compete on the World Tour.

I know the first event is in two weeks—would it be possible to enter even though I don't have the resume?"

"I remember you," he said. "We skied that run with Rob and you caught air like a guy. I'll give you a bye to get in, but don't tell any of the other competitors."

One obstacle down. How many more to go?

In 2004, the format for each stop on the World Freeskiing Tour was a three-day event. Day one was a judged qualifying run for the skiers who still had to prove themselves as well as a chance for prequalified skiers to make course inspections for the next day. Day two was the first day of the main competition, when at least half the skiers were eliminated. The finals were on day three and were held on the most difficult terrain that a ski resort had to offer, often requiring the competitors to hike to the start zones in areas normally closed to the public. Five judges, who watched the 2,000-vertical-foot ski descents through binoculars, handed out scores based on five categories: control, fluidity, technique, aggressiveness, and difficulty of line choice. The last category carried the most weight, so no one who skied through the main drain of a run would ever advance to day two, and neither would anyone who fell or even made a less-than-solid landing on a jump.

When I got to Blackcomb and competed in that season's first stop on the World Freeskiing Tour, I quickly figured out the unwritten rule of a podium finish. I needed to pick as difficult a line as I felt reasonably sure I could ski without making a mistake, and I needed to ski it fast, with no hesitations.

The combined point score from each day of competition decided who was the winner of an event. Each top finish at an individual event, from first through fifth, held a point value, and at the end of the four stops on the tour, the skier with the highest cumulative score was the overall winner. In addition to Blackcomb, there was an event in France and two in the United States.

I came in eighth at Blackcomb largely because my ski bindings popped off whenever I tried to land a significant air, all of which were bigger than I'd ever made myself jump before. But by the time of the last event, held in Kirkwood, California, on April 5, I'd upgraded my bindings as well as my technique enough to pick up a second and a first. The field of international competitors were an average age of ten years younger than me, yet I was in a close race for first in terms of overall points for the tour. During the final run, though, I faced one of my most difficult mental moments of the tour. Rob was in the crowd of spectators over 2,000 vertical feet below, and I knew how let down he'd be if I got hurt and we couldn't go on our Denali expedition three short weeks later. Now that the Teton Mountain Lodge was open for business, Rob's position had transitioned from developer to property manager and he'd thrown himself back into work with such dedication that he hardly took a day off all winter, including weekends. He *needed* Denali. But with the point scores so close, I couldn't afford to play it safe with my skiing if I wanted to win. How to handle the pressure and stay focused?

At the starting gate, my stomach churned as the possibilities floated across my consciousness. I was staring at the finish line far below when the solution came to me. No amount of worrying or thinking about the Denali expedition would help me at the moment. I had to have a pure belief in myself to ski at the highest level possible. There wasn't space for so much as a single negative thought if I wanted both the title and the Denali trip. I had to be as single-minded as I'd been about taking the bone away from Alta and helping Rob succeed in his career.

I stepped into the starting zone and a rush of heat flooded my body. Each area I was about to ski through was seared into my memory. I'd been visualizing my run since I woke up that morning, and now my brain sailed through the sequences at lightning speed. After the starter said, "Three, two, one, go!" I set off in pursuit of the same pace I'd just seen in my vision.

Stay strong through the steep turns ahead… It gets tighter, so be more technical, Kit. Maintaining my speed for the mandatory traverse to the right, I scanned the zone below so I could hit my entrance to the wide-open face at the right place. *Now down and right to the fall line, open it up and show some big fast turns and pop through those short trees… Now set up to catch air off that rock.* It was hard to see the ground—the takeoff was all white—but I started on the right and landed a little left to miss the bomb holes left by the other skiers. *Stick it!* Capitalizing on the speed from the jump, I tightened my core to stay centered on my skis until I reached the next rock. *It's smaller, so go for it.* After landing, I sailed through the trees above the cliff band and then switched to short-radius technical turns to navigate the rocky section below. *Now straight-line to go faster and get to the left side of the drainage to set up for the biggest air... Scrub just enough speed to land on the right side of the zone without hitting the other wall of rock. The risk of taking this air big enough to land on the other side will score well. Pick up your heels, Kit—just retract. Don't leap too far.* I still wasn't expert at estimating airtime and nearly crashed into the rock wall, but I stayed on my feet with just enough fluidity to continue downhill. *Now keep it together—you have to stay on the traverse back to the middle or you'll end up in the flats shuffling across the finish line... Yes—just a straight line from the finish. Show some aggressiveness. You don't need to make a turn here—just go, and stay stable on both feet.*

When I crossed the finish line I was ecstatic. I knew I'd made a great run, the best of any woman so far that day, and I hadn't even thought about getting hurt. I could have made the last landing a little tighter, a little better, but I'd landed it and done nothing to lose any serious points.

After taking my skis off, tears welled in my eyes as I walked over to Rob, who gave me a knowing smile. There was one woman left to ski, and she wasn't even close to me in the overall point score.

It was official: I was the best at something.

TEN-YEAR WIND AND SNOW

ROB CONSIDERED DENALI—AKA MOUNT McKinley—a rite of passage. He wanted to ski it because of all the rugged North American mountaineers who'd skied it and because he thought it was an experience he should have before setting his sights on skiing an 8,000-meter peak. Ironically, it turned out that I had to be even more rugged than him. And fortunately, during my life with Alta, I'd learned how to be the alpha when I really needed to be.

Day eight of the climb is when things started to get interesting. We were making the move from the 11,200-foot camp to advanced base camp (ABC) after a week of wind and snow unlike anything the climbing rangers had seen in their ten years on patrol. The weather had grounded us for several days, and now we'd made up our minds to go for it because of concern about snow accumulating on the hill above us and because the forecast wasn't getting any better.

At a dangerous exposed section known as Windy Corner, Rob felt confident that we could cross it with skis on since we'd attached climbing skins to the bottom of them. Skins are a strip of material, usually synthetic, that adheres to the base of skis so that in one direction the ski can glide on snow and in the other direction it grips; when skiers use skins in conjunction with special bindings that have a releasable locked-down heel, they can hinge at the toes of the boots and ski uphill. I'd also attached my ski crampons for added security, but my downhill ski still slipped on the blue ice as I crossed Windy Corner ahead of Rob. Falling to the ground, I gasped and instinctively clenched my abdominal muscles to try to hold on to whatever piece of the mountain I could. My right leg was stretched out behind and downhill of my body, which had fallen onto the slick thirty-degree slope, so the narrow uphill edge of my left ski, which remained uncovered by the climbing skin, was the only connection my feet had to the slick mountain.

One of my ski poles was fitted with a scaled-down ice-axe pick, and I swung it into the hard snow as my second point of contact. While the shallow penetration gave me some confidence, it was quickly shattered as I watched one of my water bottles fall out of its pocket on my backpack and tumble end over end into one of the gaping crevasses hundreds of feet below. My heart raced as I unbuckled the waist strap on my pack, pulled it off my back and lowered it to the ground in front of me. After removing my ice axe from its strap on the pack, I carefully swung it so the sharp pick landed as deeply in the snow as the firm conditions allowed. I clipped a carabiner from the pack to the axe so I wouldn't lose the pack, too, and I took my crampons from their exterior pocket. With my ski strap still connecting my ski to my leg, I unclipped the toe of my boot from the ski binding, anchored my ski to the ice axe, and cautiously strapped a crampon onto my right boot.

As I put the other crampon on my left foot, I began to feel safe enough to get angry at myself for having listened to Rob. Though I'd chosen to go along with his idea to cross on skis, my instinct had been otherwise and now I let loose. "Goddamn it! I knew this was a stupid idea. Don't even try it, Rob. Especially not with a sled."

Apparently, I made my point. He put on his crampons and crossed the corner on foot.

With Windy Corner behind us, we were finally moving into the camp that was the gateway to the 20,320-foot summit, and with twelve days' worth of supplies, we imagined we could stay for as long as it took. For climbers who aren't in a big hurry, the norm is to spend two or three days at advanced base camp adjusting to the elevation of 14,000 feet above sea level (ASL) and resting from the push required to get there. It's rare for altitude sickness to set in if a climber follows the rule of gaining only 1,000 feet of elevation a day, and even though almost no one follows that rule precisely, ABC was 3,000 feet above Camp II, so we knew we'd be there for a few days.

Since it was the beginning of the season, ABC, or "14-camp" as we began to call it, was still fairly empty, but it turned out that the Jenny Lake climbing rangers from Grand Teton National Park were working a three-week stint there as the rescue team for climbers on Denali, so we set our tent up near the Quonset hut that served as the rangers' housing and incident command. This put us close to the twice-daily weather checks the rangers posted on a board outside their door, which, during our first few days at 14-camp, often read, "Eat till you're tired. Sleep till you're hungry." Nestled in a snowy basin, the wind wasn't too bad, but above our heads it sounded like a freight train roaring toward the summit, and the clouds ripped across the sky at astonishing speed. We did our best to relax and be patient, stay hydrated, and follow the rangers' advice. Each morning we'd hope for better weather in the afternoon, and each afternoon we'd hope for better weather the next morning. On day four at 14-camp, day twelve of the expedition, I was checking the weatherboard when a ranger walking back to the hut recognized me from our common backyard of Grand Teton National Park and invited me into their hut to listen to the morning-ritual phone call with Jackson, Wyoming meteorologist Jim Woodmencey. The news wasn't good.

"There are eight hundred miles of clouds stacked to the west," Woody said.

"How long does it take eight hundred miles to pass?" I asked.

"Who knows?"

Back at our tent, I shared the grim report with Rob and we decided to spend the forced down time focusing on the snow-block walls that protected our zone against wind. Since we were among the first people on the mountain for the season, we had the pleasure and pain of building each camp from blocks of snow we'd quarry from the mountain. Because the snow on Denali is firm, we used a snow saw similar to a handheld tree-pruning saw to cut into the surface of the glacier in the shape of a square—about twelve inches by twelve inches, since that's about the size of the blade of our avalanche shovel. Once the first block has been pried out, the sizes can vary, but blocks much bigger than a shovel blade tend to fall apart during extraction and they're heavier to work with. When it comes to stacking, like with a good stone wall, one over two and two over one is a good rule to follow. And as for the height and length of a wind barrier, they're directly related to the time and energy available, how many days you imagine using the camp, and how much the wind is going to blow. A decent block wall is almost as tall as the top of the tent and at least two-thirds of the way around it in a horseshoe shape, ideally with the opening somewhere near the tent door.

When we weren't working on the wall or sleeping, we'd pass the time by reading or playing cards, all while keeping an eye on the summit 6,000 feet above and watching for changes in the lenticular clouds that might indicate abating winds.

On day fourteen, we had a decent morning during the one-day break that Woody had forecast, with a high of ten degrees, and Rob and I made a run for it. It was a long shot, especially after such a prolonged period of physical inactivity, but we'd dreamed of being able to reach the summit in one day from ABC, so we headed out at 5:00 a.m. with a stove in our packs. We climbed fast to the 17,000-foot camp, acclimatizing well, and tried to melt snow for water and brew tea on the plateau there. Having full water bottles would be necessary if we were going to climb higher that day, and the civilized treat of a hot drink was sure to be energizing. Instead, the spindrift of snow from the incessant winds kept clogging the fuel port on the stove, and twenty minutes later we still had no flame.

We wandered around the high camp area with intensifying headaches and wondered if there would be a less windy place to set up our tent on our next rotation—it was obvious that climbing this mountain in one push from 14-camp was too much to ask.

After picking a location that looked good for the next attempt, Rob and I walked to the Rescue Gully leading from 17-camp to the glacier below. It looked super steep, narrow, and icy, and although I knew I could descend it on skis when the time came, I wasn't happy about the idea of doing it more than once. Rob wanted to ski it that day so we'd be more familiar with the line after skiing from the summit, but with my headache and the wind biting through my clothes, I could feel my confidence slipping. The altitude was messing with my mind and my mojo, and I told Rob I didn't want to do it.

"OK," he said, "but I want to down-climb it today to check conditions."

In a spirit-breaking moment, I looked at the intimidating face of the mountain above. "I don't care about skiing the mountain. I'm not even sure I want to climb it."

Rob stared at me. "Come on, Kit. Why do you say these things that you and I both know you don't mean? And why are you doubting yourself?"

He didn't say anything more, and I recognized his silence as an opportunity to explain myself and keep the door open for taking another shot at going down the gully, preferably with skis on. "I know myself," I said, "and I usually break down and doubt myself once before I get stronger and resolve to do it." It was my way of saying, "Please don't push me anymore today."

"I know," Rob said. "I've never experienced another mountain that has driven me to say the same thing to myself six times already."

Our words had suggested giving up, but our actions said otherwise, and with our bond renewed we cached our skis and climbed back down the west buttress to ABC.

THERE BUT FOR THE GRACE OF GOD...

"**W**HAAAAAAAAA," LEAD RANGER RENNY Jackson wrote on the weatherboard. "High-wind warning through Saturday. Fifty to seventy mile-per-hour winds above 14,000' ASL. Storms stacked up forever."

Hmmmph. Today had been *entirely* spent in the tent. In fact, I didn't even "get up" until eleven. The spindrift of snow that had accumulated in the front vestibule of the tent was all we needed to see to know what the weather was. Yesterday after coming down from our dry run up to 17,000 feet, I spent four hours building taller snow-block walls around our tent at 14-camp, so I knew we were fortified and I'd decided to just plain rest today. But after so much horizontal time, I was back to the mental space where I was itching to get moving. Plus, if we didn't, our time on the mountain might end up with no summit. "Weather calls for pain," Renny said on the next day's 8:00 p.m. radio broadcast. "Seventy-mile-an-hour winds are expected above seventeen thousand feet tomorrow. Maybe nicer on Tuesday, with snow on Wednesday and Thursday."

OK, Denali, Great One, we don't want to fight. Please grant us safe passage. We need to at least get into position tomorrow. We mean it.

No planes had flown climbers on or off the mountain at the 7,200-foot Kahiltna Glacier starting point since Friday—five days ago. Reports were that forty people were stacked up waiting to fly off the mountain. May is traditionally the cold and clear month, but not this year. It was becoming obvious that we might have to stay longer than planned, so I accepted a handout of food and fuel offered by the team camped next to us, registered as the "Don't Worry Be Happy" team according to the Park

Service stickers on their gear. Like many others, they were turning back even though they'd been on the mountain for almost as long as we had.

Before the trip, I'd researched Denali and learned that in an average year, the success rate for climbers who spend the usual sixteen days on the mountain is only 52 percent, but it rises to 75 percent for those who spend twenty-one days or more on the mountain, so we'd planned for twenty-two. Be careful what you prepare for, though—now it looked like we were headed toward being here for all twenty-two days. At least. And with no guarantees.

Working with the "maybe better for Tuesday" forecast, we climbed to high camp Monday afternoon, pitched our tent and were grateful that we felt better than we had the first time. Rob and I alternated the tasks of melting water for tea in the tent vestibule and building another snow-block wind barrier around the tent. This time, because it was so much colder and drier at 17,000 feet than it had been at 14,000 feet, the snow was harder and it was tougher to force the teeth of the snow saw through it. When we'd finally pry a block loose, the sound it made was like the cracking of a thick slab of Styrofoam.

The 8:00 p.m. weather forecast on the radio called for expected lows of minus-fifteen that night and winds of fifty mph tomorrow, which was a bit of a downgrade from yesterday's seventy mph above 17,000 feet. But during the climb up today, the sky had actually been fairly calm between 14,000 and 17,000 feet, so we were hopeful that the latest forecast was wrong.

I'd arrived at the point of having to believe that any forecast was wrong if I didn't like what it said. I *really* wanted to summit tomorrow.

We left camp on our summit bid at 8:00 a.m. Any earlier would have been suicidal, given the cold. As we climbed, I became worried about my feet. I hadn't felt my toes since strapping my crampons on at camp. Emulating ski racers, I tried to get circulation back to my feet by swinging my legs from the hip down, but it was hard to do with my right leg because we were headed up and left on a forty-five-degree slope.

During the hour-and-a-half climb to Denali Pass, wind gusts dropped us to our knees six times, forcing us to plant our ice axes in the snow to wait it out. During the Siberian expedition where Rob and I had met, Jim Zellers had wondered aloud, "At what temperature do your eyeballs freeze?" Well, this was a new spin on Siberia, and I wondered, *At what wind speed can you no longer take a breath?* However fast it was blowing at the moment was the answer.

I had on a base layer of wool, down pants, soft-shell pants, Gore-Tex shells, and four similar layers on top, with an enormous down jacket over it all. I also wore goggles, a hat, and a balaclava. Most people couldn't fit all this in a *suitcase*. Somehow, though, the wind got through. I was shivering like a little girl who's just gotten out of the bathtub on a chilly night and is waiting for her mother to wrap her in a towel.

When we reached Denali Pass, we met a group of Korean climbers who had left camp just ahead of us and were apparently discussing continuing on to the summit, but we couldn't quite understand them and I wasn't interested in joining forces anyway. While the safety-in-numbers game can sometimes be a help, being a part of a large group can also let the "human factor" influence decision-making. The bigger the safety net of people and resources on hand, the bigger the likelihood that people will choose dangerous decision-making shortcuts and risks they wouldn't normally take. Rob looked toward the summit and then turned to me. "What do you think?"

"Forget it," I said. "I'm not continuing up a mountain where I can't even stand up. Plus, I'm scared of frostbite. I haven't felt my toes since camp."

"Let's take a break behind this rock and rest a minute." Rob led us a little downhill from the climbing route to a shoulder-high boulder that did nothing to stop our shivering but did make me feel like I was spying on the Koreans as they broke their huddle and continued to climb. When they were out of sight and we hadn't regained any body heat, Rob and I agreed to retreat. It just wasn't worth the risk and there would always be tomorrow.

So much for my idea that climbing North America's highest mountain was a mundane goal. Denali was posing more challenges than either of us had expected.

BACK AT 17-CAMP AND finished with the four-hour process of making dinner and melting snow to replenish our water bottles, we laid our heads down for the night around nine o'clock in the waning Alaskan light. I could feel my toes again, but now they were hot, itchy, and extra-sensitive. It was scary how painful it was just to let them touch the fabric of my sleeping bag. I was worrying about what condition they'd be in tomorrow when we heard the crunch of footsteps and some jumbled words in the distance.

"I just fell asleep," Rob groaned.

"*Shit,*" I said as I sat up to listen.

Some of the words became clear through the heavy Korean accent. "Team summit...man fall...twenty meters...above pass...too cold...hit head...won't move...need rescue...have radio?"

I couldn't believe it. After going for the summit in that wind, these guys needed to call in a rescue for their friend who was spending the night alone up high. It could have been us up there if we'd gone for it.

At the time, not everyone who climbed Denali carried a heavy CB radio, but the Park Service recommended it when they took you through the mandatory check-in before you flew onto the Kahiltna Glacier by way of a fixed-wing aircraft. Issues to consider are how to keep the six size-C batteries warm and whether the weight is worth it. "Ounces, ounces, pounds" is a saying I learned as a teenager when having to decide on two or three pairs of socks for a month to be spent in the backcountry. On that occasion, I decided to use only the one and kept the second pair as a clean backup. This time I accepted the free radio loan (batteries not included) and promised Rob I would carry it. Now I rummaged around in the foot of my sleeping bag for the batteries and put them into the radio before handing it out the door of the tent to Rob, who had pulled on his warm layers to go help the Koreans with the radio call. I figured I'd have a better chance of climbing tomorrow, or helping with the rescue, if I avoided putting any pressure on my toes.

In the morning, there was no way we could selfishly try for the summit again with a rescue underway, so Rob took the radio to the edge of the plateau for better reception and called the rangers to offer our help. Our Jenny Lake friends must have started climbing in the middle of the night and been out of range because they didn't answer, but eventually the ranger at Kahiltna base camp did, and she advised

Rob to walk to the top of the Rescue Gully and grab two tents and two stoves from the metal box of rescue gear cached there, then set up the tents and melt as much water as we could. Melting water for the rangers didn't seem like much compared with starting a rescue, but it suited my swollen toes, and it's true that when I get home from a trip like this, the thing I'm most grateful for is being able to turn on the tap and fill a glass with water.

Midmorning, the Jenny Lake rangers arrived at their newly set-up 17-camp, refilled their water bottles, and prepared to climb up to the victim.

"Turn the radio on once every thirty minutes, at the top and bottom of the hour," one of them told us. "If we need any help getting the victim down, we'll ask you then."

Between the radio checks, we continued to melt water and store it in whatever bottles and thermoses we could drum up among the handful of other climbers who were at 17-camp. The members of the Korean team were busy with their assigned task of pulling the thousand-meter rescue rope from its cache and setting it up for the eventual lowering of the victim from 17-camp back to 14-camp. Midday, the wind died down and the snow began to fall so hard that Rob and I would have gotten lost just moving between our tent and the rangers' tents if it hadn't been for the four-foot bamboo wands we'd gotten from the rangers' cache and placed several paces apart along the route.

During the 7:30 p.m. radio check, the request finally came.

"Can you guys come help us haul him across the flats? We're down off the face, but the snow is deep and it's slow going."

Because of the storm, we hadn't even been able to see most of the technical lowering system the rangers had used to get the litter down from Denali Pass. Even though my toes hurt, I was eager to help, so Rob and I immediately headed out with a handful of wands to mark our path.

As we approached the rescue party, the effort the rangers were exerting was obvious from the strain on their faces. Two of them stepped aside to give us a spot on the haul rope attached to the litter, and I felt like a draft horse in winter when I lifted my legs out of the thigh-deep postholes in the newly fallen snow and leaned into the pull. I exhausted quickly and had to rest often. If they hadn't been already, these rangers were now officially superheroes in my book.

As we neared the tent, the victim, who was wrapped in an insulated cocoon and had been lying quietly in the rescue sled, suddenly began talking. "Summit," he said repeatedly, smiling up at us from his strapped-down position. The rangers explained that when they'd found him, one of his hands had been missing a glove, probably for over twenty-four hours, and had now turned purple.

We would later learn that except for his thumbs, all the fingers on both hands had to be amputated.

DAY TWENTY—MAY 22—WE WOKE up suffocating. Literally. Our tent was buried in snow and we needed to dig our way to fresh air. It took about an hour of shoveling to uncover the tent—what a way to wake up.

When we were done we walked over to see the rescue rangers, who were preparing to lower the victim. "Do you guys have a weather report?" I asked.

"Yeah, the mother of all storms is predicted for the next few days. It was so good of you guys to help, but you really should go down."

Yesterday's storm had deposited so much snow that if the forecast for more was right, we really couldn't risk another night up high. We'd been fortunate to be able to dig our way out, but we might not be so lucky the next time. Not to mention that the avalanche risk would increase and that the steep, enormous wall of Denali Pass loomed directly above us.

Rob turned to me. "Let's ski the ridge down, and when the storm lifts we can give it another shot. Maybe we can summit on Monday."

"OK." It was the only option that made any sense.

The new snow had covered lots of rocks on the usually windswept ridge, creating the equivalent of hidden sharks' teeth that often caught my skis and caused me to struggle for balance. Our last time up here, we'd cached our skis at 17-camp and come down on foot with our light day packs. This time we were skiing the whole way, including making tight, technically precise turns down the steep section alongside the fixed ropes (but not clipped in), with *all* our belongings on our backs. We'd summit from 14-camp on Monday or not at all.

THE NEXT DAY WAS Sunday and we woke up feeling like we'd returned to sea level, our well-acclimatized bodies no longer giving us headaches at this 14,200-foot elevation. It was a stormy rest day, and during the 8:00 p.m. weather check the radio crackled until we finally heard, "Light snow likely Tuesday through Thursday. Winds ten to twenty miles per hour." We'd missed Monday? What had they said about Monday? Was there a chance? I suited up and went to the rangers' tent to ask if they'd heard anything more definitive about tomorrow's forecast.

"Same," one said, sounding weary. Was it because of the rescue or was he as tired of the constantly negative forecasts as I was? "Only difference is that the winds may be picking up in a few days, then going back down."

Back at the tent, I pulled a few positive thoughts from some unknown wellspring. "Let's go for it tomorrow," I said to Rob. We'd already given it twenty-one days and were supposed to be at base camp on the Kahiltna the next day, but I figured there were days' worth of climbers down there waiting to be flown out and we'd have to wait our turn if we got there tomorrow anyway. "We can do it in a day now that we're so acclimatized."

"Yeah." He paused. "Trail-breaking will be tough with all this new snow, though. Let's go ask some people that were at 17-camp if they want to go with us."

So with insulated mugs of tea in our hands, Rob and I canvassed ABC and peddled our plan. By eleven o'clock, we had three others on board, and with everyone agreeing to start out at six thirty, we called it a night.

ON REST DAYS, YOU try to eat as much as possible to make up for the higher-altitude climbing days, when it isn't possible to eat "enough," but that night we learned that two Backpacker's Pantry entrées each in one afternoon isn't a good idea. Soon after crawling into our sleeping bags, we started in on the Tums. By midnight, we'd switched to Gas-Ex. And by one, we resorted to splitting a tablet of Vicodin from the medicine kit. There was more than enough to be anxious about without also having to deal with sleep deprivation tomorrow.

THIS TIME FROM THE TOP

ONDAY, MAY 24, OUR twenty-second day on the mountain, we woke to the alarm at five fifteen. In a Vicodin hangover, we looked outside the tent to see incredibly calm, clear skies.

"I can't believe it!" I said.

We scrambled to get ready and were just a little behind schedule when we climbed out of camp at seven fifteen with our three trail-breaking recruits behind us. Sleeping patterns aside, it's hard to get moving early in such cold temperatures.

We climbed fast, weaving in and out of the sun's shadow line as we crested the short section of fixed lines at the top of the headwall. Reaching the 17-camp zone took four hours this time after having taken five hours just days before. We sat for a moment to drink tea as our partners for the day passed us, and I cached the thermos there when we were finished.

Just before two o'clock, we reached the 18,400-foot elevation of Denali Pass and caught back up to them so that we could swap leads breaking trail again. Over the next hour, Rob's pace slowed and the weather deteriorated just enough to be annoying without being dangerous. The sky turned from blue to white. While the visibility diminished to the point where we couldn't distinguish between the snow and the horizon, at least the wind didn't kick up like it had been doing for weeks. Once we reached the Football Field, a plateau at 19,500 feet that's actually much larger than a football field, I ran into an entirely different kind of trouble. While having your husband declare his love for you at the top of his lungs might not seem to be a sign of trouble, that's how it started.

"I love you! I love this life!" Rob said. "Isn't this amazing? *I'm so happy*!!!"

"Yeah, it *is* amazing," I answered. But that went without saying. Though Rob is a positive person, this was a little extreme.

He stood rooted to the mountain looking like he had no plans for moving forward. "Aren't you happy, Kit? What's wrong with you? I love you so much and I'm so happy!"

I gave him a peck on the cheek and searched his eyes for some explanation. He *looked* normal. Because I was spooked by this new attitude, I faked the enthusiasm that I guessed he was looking for and hoped it would get him moving again. "I'm so happy, too! I love you, too!" My heart raced. I'd never seen this behavior in anyone before. I turned away and regarded Pig Hill above us, and then I started climbing into the white clouds that had settled in.

"How can you not be happy, Kit?!" Rob shouted behind me. "I love this! We're about to summit Denali! It's so beautiful and I feel so much love!"

By now the beauty was barely visible. The fog had blocked our views of the summit and the surrounding peaks. When I turned around, I saw that Rob still wasn't moving. I suddenly recalled from my wilderness emergency medical training that euphoria can be a symptom of hypoxia, oxygen deprivation that hinders normal functions like cognition and staying warm. *We should go down right now. If it gets really bad, I have the rope in my pack and I guess I could tie him in to it.* But what if he resisted me? Though he hadn't taken a fall anywhere, he was behaving as if he'd suffered a head injury, and while he wasn't being combative, I was afraid he might.

I walked back toward him along the Football Field. "Rob, I *am* very happy, but we still have a long way to go," I said gently. "It'll probably take us another hour and a half to summit if we keep moving. I think you're having a reaction to the altitude and maybe we should go down."

"*You don't get it!* I'm fine, I don't need to go down. I am just so happy that I need to tell you and I want you to be happy, too. This is amazing!"

I was no longer spooked, I was scared. If I turned around and went down, would he follow me or would he stay up high and maybe even go for the summit alone? Given that possibility, I couldn't leave him. I just hoped I wouldn't have to get the rope out. That would be a clear signal that although our survival depended on cooperation, we'd moved deeply into one-against-the-other territory.

"What's your problem?" he yelled. "Aren't you happy, too?"

I had to make a decision. By now we'd wasted half an hour on this game and it was already four o'clock. If Rob didn't start moving soon, I'd have to figure out how to get him to go down without even trying for the summit first.

Determined to go up if at all possible, I opted for the tactic of climbing toward the summit and seeing if he would follow me this time. And to my tentative relief, once I put enough distance between us, he did. Constantly but discreetly looking over my shoulder, I slowly kicked steps up the snow on the steep section of the summit block, and at the summit ridge I stopped and waited.

At the top of Pig Hill, two of the climbers who'd started the day with us were on their way down from the summit. "My husband is acting really weird and I'm scared," I told them. "Will you tell him he needs to keep moving?"

They looked at each other and then at Rob, who was several paces behind me. "I don't know what you're talking about," one of them said. "He looks fine to me."

There wasn't time to go into detail before Rob would be in hearing range, so the other climbers went on their way and all I could do was stay calm on the surface and hope we'd make it without further incident.

When Rob got there, he started on a whole new soliloquy about our beautiful life, and no amount of hyperbole on my part seemed to satisfy him. So, nervously, I just continued climbing.

At times there were undulations where I couldn't see Rob and I worried for his safety, but stopping anywhere short of the summit would have only meant I'd have to waste precious time while he took a break to rant again. This had become an agonizing pace and we simply didn't have time to stop for this game anymore. So I walked slowly up the ridge, continually glancing back at Rob. Sometimes I paused to wait for him to get closer, but I never wanted to let him get within earshot. Just close enough that he knew I wasn't abandoning him, just far enough to silence his outbursts.

When I reached the top, the poor visibility created the sensation of being inside a jug of skim milk. I could see only as far as the start of the Football Field below. Although I was elated on one level, I was also intensely concerned about us and the recent twist of events. It was seven fifteen and we'd been climbing for exactly twelve hours. We had a 6,000-vertical-foot ski descent ahead of us, and my husband was acting like someone on Ecstasy.

I took my skis off my pack, switched from glacier glasses to goggles, added a down jacket to the layering system under my shell, and generally prepared myself to ski. My plan was to ski off the summit almost as soon as Rob arrived in order to head off another bizarre encounter, but when he arrived at the summit ten minutes later and saw me ready to push off, he was clearly agitated.

"You weren't going to wait for me? I can't believe you! I'm so happy and you're so mad."

"No, Rob, I'm not mad. This *is* wonderful. It's just really late. It's after seven and and we're on top of Denali. We're only halfway—we have to get down."

As he began to make the transition to his skis, the third climber from our original group arrived. He was the last person who would summit that day, and this was my last chance to have someone else try to talk sense into Rob and maybe break the spell he was under.

"Thor, help me," I pleaded out of Rob's earshot as Rob bent over to step into his ski bindings. "Rob is acting crazy and I think it's the altitude. Can you talk to him and tell him how serious this is and how much we need to keep moving?"

When he looked at me as if I were the one whose mental state was in question, I realized how little these other climbers knew us.

"I'm not saying anything," he said. "I have no idea what's going on or who's actually having trouble."

"OK," I said, just barely able to wrap my mind around his viewpoint. I was starting to feel like I was mentally hanging by a thread, too.

Soon after Thor started back down the ridge, we began our descent, which proved only slightly dangerous off the summit block. Wind-slab conditions caused small releases of snow as I made ski cuts down and left, down and left to position myself above the run-out of the Football Field. Normally I have to watch Rob's technique carefully to see if he's having to adjust to difficult conditions, but off the summit of Denali he was clearly skiing in survival mode, although being a world-class skier, his survival mode was equivalent to most people's standard ability.

After descending Denali Pass and returning to 17,200 feet at the entrance to the Rescue Gully, Rob seemed almost entirely normal again, but just in case, I decided not to bring it up yet. The entrance to the couloir of the Rescue Gully held hard blue ice at the top and was every bit of fifty degrees in steepness. We talked about pulling out the rope for a belay, but it was almost nine o'clock at night and decided against it. Besides, it was only me who thought I might want it.

The recent snowstorm had done little to make the conditions at the top of the gully less slick, but this time I didn't have the luxury of backing down and saying, "I don't care about skiing the mountain." I did care and I had to stay strong for both of us. It wasn't over yet and I still felt like I had to lead the way.

When I looked into the couloir, there was a small amount of new snow on top of the same blue ice with the same jagged rocks poking through it as when I'd inspected it a week before. I hadn't even wanted to down-climb it then, and now I was going to ski it. What I do is a lot about risk management, and this was one of those moments.

If I only do it once, then the chances of an error are less than if this were my second time. Maybe I'll use my ice axe for this upper part.

While that thought may have justified the caution I'd shown last week, today I had to face the conditions that were still less than ideal if I was going to make a complete ski descent.

Can you really do this, Kit? What if your ski edge slips on the ice? What if it gets caught up on a piece of rock and you lose your balance? It's a long way down, 1,500 vertical feet before it opens wider to the glacier below, and the crevasses down there would swallow anything.

A few deep belly breaths helped expel some of the doubt, and as if I were observing myself from a distance, I saw clear images of the intimidating lines I'd skied during the World Freeskiing Tour just months before. This objective bird's-eye view helped me assess the risk and realize that if I could do *that*, I could do *this*. So I harnessed the empowered feeling I'd experienced after skiing those lines with authority and sidestepped through the rocks that guarded the entrance to the Rescue Gully.

Once in it, I made myself focus on the move ahead instead of the expanse below. The waning light and the clouds that encompassed us helped me to keep my view on the turn ahead, and I adopted my standard approach to technical moves. *Just do what's right in front of you, Kit.* When an ice bulge in the middle of the couloir felt like it wanted to push me into the overhead rock wall on the left side, I made a careful kick turn, switched the ice axe to my right hand and the ski pole to my left, and sidestepped down twenty vertical feet until I reached a patch of snow that had been deposited on top of the blue ice. After holstering my ice axe and pulling my second ski pole from its special spot on my back, I made a few turns on the "relaxed" fifty-degree angle and backed my ski tails up to the rock wall on the left to wait for Rob.

Rob made it look a little easier than I had, but he took the same level of care, and with bursts of four or five ski turns at a time before resting our burning lungs, we leapfrogged down the rest of the couloir. During each rest, we scanned the crevasse field below for a way to ski through it that would reconnect us to the normal climbing route near the gaping bergschrund, where the glacial ice was separating from the steep mountain. Occasionally, some ski tracks were visible from a group that had passed through earlier in the day, but in the waning light nothing was obvious, so we worked together by shouting things like "Go right!," and "Hole here!" Rob's speech had become as fluid as his skiing by now, and I was no longer worried about the trouble we'd experienced up high.

We carefully navigated the crevasses until we skied over the biggest one, the bergschrund, and from there it was like a low-angle powder field until we got back to 14-camp. It was ten o'clock and we immediately collapsed in our tent for a deep sleep.

On the morning of May 25, our twenty-third day on the mountain, we rehydrated and packed our gear. The pilot won't come to pick up a climber at the 7,200-foot base camp until the ranger on patrol there makes the call verifying that the climbing party is indeed ready. Exit from the mountain is on a first-come, first-served basis, and we wanted to get our names in the queue as soon as possible. A lighter load meant an easier descent, so we pulled the same trick as the Don't Worry Be Happy Team had and gave our extra food and fuel to anyone at ABC who would take it.

Having had experience with skiing rescue sleds during my stint on ski patrol in Telluride, I figured we'd be faster if we put only a little gear in our packs and the bulk of it on one sled, tied the second sled on top of it, and then worked together to ski our load down. Rob agreed, so we attached a rope from the back of his climbing harness to the sled, and as he skied away and pulled the sled behind him, I skied holding the tail rope and pulled tension on it whenever a brake was needed. This technique required great communication skills, because with all the crevasses and side hills to negotiate, we needed more space to get down the mountain than the narrow footpath made by other climbers. Fortunately, by this point Rob and I were a dialed team. We'd been to the top of the mountain in a single push from 14-camp to the summit, navigated the altitude euphoria that had threatened our survival, and successfully skied down. Now, with Rob's mental function fully restored, we simply had to cooperate in order to get to the bottom of the mountain, and that's what we did, making it from 14-camp to base camp, 7,000 feet below and ten miles away, in less than five hours.

Receiving the extra food and fuel from the Don't Worry Be Happy Team had worked out brilliantly for us, allowing us to comfortably stay on the mountain for longer than we'd planned, but giving it all away again on the morning of our final descent didn't turn out to be such a smooth move. It was snowing too heavily for planes to fly into base camp on Kahiltna Glacier, and we'd be staying there for longer than expected. The "ounces, ounces, pounds" mantra had backfired—Rob and I had almost no rations left.

On our second day at base camp, I finally poked my head out of our tent, and good fortune was waiting just outside.

"What's up, Kit?" said one of the guys we'd met at 14-camp. "I haven't seen you in two days!"

"My mom always told me, 'If you don't have anything nice to say, don't say anything at all,' so I'm trying not to, but I'm really hungry."

He laughed and ducked into his tent, and when he returned he was carrying two packages of dried soup mix and two small pieces of chocolate.

"Oh, thank you! Are you sure?"

"No problem," he said with a smile. "Your mom was right, but we've missed seeing you around camp."

Rob and I had been fortunate to climb and ski the mountain in our own personal style, so sitting still at the end of it with almost no food for a day or two was a small price to pay. It was just part of working with the mountain. There were no more endless questions in my head about what to pack on the next climbing rotation, when to leave camp, or whether I should make more water. I was content to read a book or simply stare at the yellow nylon fabric of the tent ceiling and think of almost nothing.

On the third morning at base camp, the mental break ended when it was our turn for a flight back to Talkeetna, but when the pilot arrived he asked us to make one last decision. The new snow on the low-elevation glacier was so wet and heavy that for the Cessna 185 to get off the ground, something—or someone—had to be left behind. The plane could take only one of us and our gear or both of us and *no* gear.

Which do you think we chose?

THE DREAM COMES TRUE

WHEN ALTA AND I drove into Ophir, Colorado, for the first time on a late-April day twelve years before the Denali expedition, I craned my neck from side to side to see the tops of the mountains on both sides of the two-mile dirt road that served as the only western entrance to the narrow valley. They rose 4,000 feet straight up, and even when I leaned over the dashboard of my pickup to see, they could easily hide their summits from me.

Although I'd never been here, this valley with such high walls felt strangely like home, and before we'd even pulled into town, I had an epiphany. "We're either going to live here for a long time or move someplace far away," I said to Alta, who was on the front bench seat next to me. "Like Jackson Hole, Wyoming." It wasn't a plan, just a vision from out of the blue. I'd never been to Jackson Hole either.

We parked outside one of the eight houses on the former silver-mining town's main street. It was a tiny, nicely renovated old miner's cabin where I'd accepted a caretaker's position for three weeks. All I was getting in return for the unpaid position was three weeks of living under a real roof and exploring this beguiling valley at 9,700 feet above sea level on the edge of a national forest in the San Juan range, and I couldn't have been happier.

Alta and I didn't waste much time settling in. I finished unloading the truck before dinner, and by the next morning I had a plan: Every day we'd walk up the Ophir Road and take a right onto the mining road or foot trail that lay just beyond the one we'd taken the day before. Up, up, up we'd go until either I ran out of time and had to go back and get ready for work as a waitress in Telluride or the trail disappeared due to neglect or dead-ended at an old mining site.

I'm continuously creating a map in my mind, and I feel compelled to fill in the blank spots on it. Maybe I have the explorer gene I read about in *National Geographic*. Or maybe I'm just irresistibly drawn to the unknown in general, despite the dangers it so often harbors. Whatever the case, by the end of those three weeks of daily adventure travel, we hadn't missed a single trail in the arc of the valley above town, south to east to north, and I'd gotten the sense of place I was looking for. Another blank spot filled in.

Alta and I also established a new partnership in that time. Because of his wolf's instincts, he often ran ahead of me, but he knew we needed to stick together since we were all that each other had in the world. He didn't want to lose me any more than I wanted to lose him. When he'd been off exploring for a little longer than I was comfortable with, I'd call him and within a minute he'd appear from the forest or from around a bend in the trail ahead with his head cocked and a panting, *What's up?* smile on his face. Each time this happened, I felt like the most fortunate girl in the world to be able to run around the mountains with a wolf who would come when I called him.

Eventually, Alta began coming back to check in with me without being called. When it was on his own terms like this, instead of giving me a questioning look from the path ahead, he'd prance right up to my side and touch his nose to my hand or leg. I always acknowledged his check-ins with a "Good boy" or some wolf-speak—"ararr, ararr, rarr"—and gave him a rub on his head and a pat on the hindquarters to let him know he could go again.

By our last day of caretaking at the cabin, I knew we'd found a home in this valley and I headed for a house on the high side of town that I'd learned was a rental property. As a rule, turnover among renters was almost nonexistent in Ophir because the population was so small—120, to be exact—but I had everything to gain by knocking on the door at 8:00 a.m., Alta at my side. A man in his early twenties opened the door with a surprised look.

"Good morning. What's the chance that you have a room for rent?"

His jaw dropped. "How did you know? Just last night I decided to join the Peace Corps and I'm leaving tomorrow. You can have my room. Your timing is amazing—I've been sitting on the acceptance letter for three weeks now. Come on in, let me show you around."

Looking right at home while he waited for me on the front porch with a view of town and three 14,000-foot peaks to the west of the valley, Alta seemed as content about the prospect of living here as I was.

In the years that followed, we lived the balance between freedom and safety that we'd struck on the trails around Ophir in our first weeks in town. From the moment he'd first climbed to the top of my head as a two-week-old pup, Alta had always sought out high places—it couldn't have been any clearer that it's what he'd been born to do. For him, freedom meant the freedom to go to the highest point he could. And as we climbed the nearby peaks, it was common for him to leave me wondering where he was for as long as a half hour as I scrambled behind him up mountains without trails. It wasn't until I'd reached the saddle between two mountains, or a false summit, or even the summit itself that I'd finally see him again, contentedly sitting on his haunches and gazing into the distance, waiting for me.

The times when he disobeyed my calls—the times when he wasn't willing to compromise in terms of the freedom that was his birthright—were rare. As deeply connected to me as he was, that couldn't always compete with the lure of being where he belonged. He knew his place in life, and sometimes all he could do was follow his heart to that place.

Many years later, while I was trying to decide whether to commit to competing on the World Freeskiing Tour for a second time, I came to understand how Alta must have felt. Ultimately, it wasn't about making a choice—it was a matter of simply doing what I'd been born to do. Just as it had been on Denali.

"Are you going to compete on the Freeskiing Tour again this year?" the man asked me as the quad chairlift carried just the two of us up the mountain on a perfect January morning of powder skiing in Jackson Hole.

I'd just met this friend of a friend less than an hour ago—an hour spent mostly immersed in deep snow with our group of six—and here he was jumping right into my mind.

With only a brief pause to wonder who this omniscient figure was, I let myself dive heart-first into the question I'd been musing about incessantly. Even as I'd been dropping into pillows of waist-deep snow that morning, the question had been eating at me. The first competition of the season was a week away, and because the World Freeskiing Tour is a points series, it's important to earn some at each stop on the tour. If I were to compete again, I wanted to win again, but if I missed the first event, I might as well not show up for the others.

"I don't know," I said. "I mean, what's it all worth? I won last year and proved to myself that I could do it. After all that time and energy, I still barely broke even with all my expenses." The prize money for the women was about half of what it was for the men, and unless you won first place, you took a loss on the deal. The real money was in the sponsorships, and I didn't have any that paid. "What for, then?"

I didn't tell my new friend about the other conversations I'd been having with myself, such as:

Wouldn't it be nice to go out on top?

What if you lose?

Kit, it's pretty pathetic to think you don't want to compete again because you might not win again. Just because you even thought that, you know you should do it.

Maybe you're too old to keep playing around at the skiing thing, Kit. You just turned thirty-five, and even though you're winning and skiing at the top of your game, the sponsors and the filmmakers don't seem to notice you. It's just not sexy to be older than the rest of them and married.

You have to figure this out soon. Sure, you're automatically eligible to compete because you hold the title, but there aren't many days left to prepare, mentally or even logistically.

As we passed two more towers on the Thunder Lift, I continued listening to the voices in my head, and my lift-mate appeared to digest my answer.

"You *have* to compete again!" he finally said. "I've *never* seen another woman ski like you. I'd like to sponsor you."

My brain began to spin like a hard drive and took me back to the years when living my lifestyle of choice had made for hard times. I revisited my days as a waitress and a stonemason in Telluride. I had a fifteen-mile daily commute on mountain roads, and when my truck began misfiring, I realized it needed a tune-up I couldn't afford. I asked the local mechanic to sell me whatever kind of spark plugs the six-cylinder engine used so I could do the work myself, and I borrowed the necessary wrenches and a spark-plug gauge from a neighbor. All set to make the repairs, I became nervous about my ability to do a job I'd never done or even seen done before, and I decided to skip the tune-up and go skiing instead.

Two months later, on a day off in February, I headed outside to load my skis into my truck and found that the snow was up to my waist and blowing sideways. With my ski goggles on, I shoveled a trench to my truck and dug it free. Shivering with my cooling sweat, I slid into the driver's seat and turned the key. Nothing. Not even a misfire. I'd known this moment was coming, though, and as the first ski tracks of the day faded from my imagination, I resigned myself to the task. I opened the hood and attached a tarp to it, creating a lean-to shelter from the storm, and climbed into the engine compartment and taught myself how to change spark plugs so I could go powder skiing.

Then the hard drive spun me back to a campfire moment in the desert after a day of climbing sandstone towers. An impressive twenty-something climber named Sue Nott was visiting our weekend tribe in Indian Creek, and I wondered out loud how she could be so good at the sport. How could she always be on the road climbing instead of working to support herself? And why did she have such a nice truck? Someone whispered her story to me: A friend of her family had seen her talent as a climber and wanted to help her live her dream of being a professional climber, so he sponsored her (and paid for the truck).

From that moment on, I'd dreamed of having someone believe in me enough to sponsor me. More accurately, I dreamed of being *worthy* of sponsorship.

When the disk drive stopped spinning, I was back on the Thunder Lift, and a wave of joy was rushing through me. If this stranger was going to give me money to ski, then what I wanted to do with my life was actually OK. Not just OK—it had purpose. It was worthy of making it my profession.

Instead of sharing these musings, all I could muster was, "Can we put the bar down?" I thought I might pass out and fall off the lift.

"I want you to not worry about money," he said. "Don't sleep in your van in winter just to compete. I want you to buy the plane ticket, rent a car, book a hotel, and don't share a room. Just go out and *win*."

"You're serious?"

He nodded.

"That's amazing. Thank you." It sounded so insufficient, but I had no idea how to properly acknowledge such a gesture. I was still trying to *comprehend* it. "Um...what should I do in return?"

"Do the right thing. If someone asks you to meet with a girls' after-school program, for example, I hope you'll say yes."

That's it? "Of course I would. I'd love to."

It was the stuff of a twenty-two-year-old's dreams, and for the next few hours the thirty-five-year-old's self-protection mechanism didn't allow me to fully believe it would actually happen until he stopped by our house once the chairlifts closed. With my stomach a jumble of excitement and Rob watching in astonishment, the man who was about to become my secret benefactor put a check made out to me for a *lot* of money on our kitchen counter. "Spend it on skiing," he said. Then, reminiscent of St. Nick laying his finger aside his nose, giving a nod, and rising up the chimney, my benefactor walked out the front door, straddled his motorcycle, and drove off, leaving a trail of fairy dust that only I could see.

I WON THAT FIRST event of the Freeskiing Tour at Whistler/Blackcomb a week later, and I was on my way to another win at the second event in February when my health suddenly became an issue. It was a three-day competition at Snowbird, Utah, that also served as the US Freeskiing Nationals, and I was sitting in first place when I woke up on the final day with congested sinuses, a sore, swollen throat, and a severe case of sleep deprivation. I'm not prone to getting sick, but this virus wasn't to be denied. I just *had* to give in and acknowledge that it had taken hold after lurking for the past two days. But what I only slowly realized was that I didn't have to give up. As I lay there, I thought about everything I'd invested into being in that place on that day, how fortunate I was to be the reigning champion, how I was in first place because of the score I'd earned on the first run the day before, how I was competing for the second year because I wanted to and because I'd thought it would be pathetic not to compete just because I was afraid of not "going out on top." And I thought about the positive teachings of my favorite sports psychology book, Chungliang

Al Huang's *Thinking Body, Dancing Mind*, and pictured myself at the starting gate on Mount Baldy and skiing an aggressive, flawless run. Ultimately, I realized I didn't need to be a victim of my virus. I could still give every bit of myself to my ski run that day, mentally and physically. There was everything to gain.

Rob had arrived the evening before so he could be there for the finals, and as I walked over to the coffeemaker in our hotel room, I said to him over my shoulder in a raspy, barely audible voice, "Do you know what?"

He laughed at the sounds I could hardly make and mimicked me in response. "No, whaaat?"

I turned and looked at him. "*I can win this thing.*"

He smiled. "Yes. You can."

Adrenaline helped me to temporarily forget about my condition during my first run of the finals. Luckily, flying down a 2,000-vertical-foot slope without hesitation takes less than two minutes, and I skied it perfectly. The points showed that I'd won the event, but then in a move not uncommon when the skiing conditions are beautiful and the competition stiff, the judges decided to amp up the crowd with a "super final." The top five men and women would head back up the mountain to ski another run, and the score from the super final would be factored into the overall standings.

A wave of exhaustion washed over me, I felt cheated out of my win. I'd given everything I could for three days despite my illness, and I was fatigued to the point of depression. In the grip of the natural cortisol downer that had followed my final-run adrenaline rush, I just wanted to go back to the hotel, lie on the bed, and watch TV.

I tried to rally the other skiers to resist the super final. Though the others had a chance to improve their positions, they could also make a mistake and crash and end up lower in the standings. But while it was clear that no one really wanted to muster the intensity it takes to ski all-out again, one by one I watched them head for the tram to get ready to make that super-final run. There was nothing for me to do but grab a free Red Bull from the competitors' tent and follow.

In finals and super finals, runs are in the opposite order of the standings, which meant I would again go last. As the others chatted until it was their turn, I hung back from the start, which had been moved even higher up the mountain to make the super final a bit of a different course.

When no one was left on top of the mountain but me and the person in charge of counting down the start, I sideslipped into position, buckled my boots a little tighter than normal, and stared into the fifty-foot rock face to the skier's left of the starting gate.

It wasn't a premeditated focal point, but in it I found stillness and I discovered myself appreciating the beauty of the boulder's composition. Before long, though, the sore-throat tightness that had become worse throughout the day vaulted into my awareness. I knew I'd be in trouble if I skied with that thought in the front of my mind, so I repeated to myself what I had said that morning: "I can win this thing." Immediately, I could see past the sickness—I could see myself skiing a winning run—and I knew that if I held on to that vision, the virus wouldn't rule my physical performance.

Just then the announcement came over the radio that the judges were ready, and the starter asked me how I was doing and if I was ready. As feverish chills made me shudder, I moved into position in the starting gate and smiled.

"I *am* ready," I said in the small croak of a voice that I had left, "and I can win this thing."

And I did. After executing some huge high-speed turns and a pair of twenty-foot jumps, I entered the most perilous part of the course with only 800 vertical feet to go. It was covered with hundreds of *punjees*—the tops of ten-foot trees that are almost buried in the snowpack—waiting to ambush skiers crazy enough to venture into this maze on a forty-five-degree slope. The day before, I'd gotten tripped here on a practice run and tumbled to the edge of a sixty-foot cliff, stopping only because I had the composure to grab for the bare treetops every time I flipped uncontrollably, each tree slowing me just enough to stop at the edge. So I thought twice—at least—before attempting it again. This was where I could win it, though, by acing the all-important degree-of-difficulty category, and that was the deciding factor. With the punjees coming at me fast, I made precise turns and pole plants, almost like bunny hops, picking myself up and landing again without touching any of the sharp treetops. Now all that was left was to set up for the finale.

At the top of a towering cliff that was way beyond anything any of us women were willing to chuck ourselves off, I made a swooping turn to the right and three more tight turns down through the rocks to my takeoff. With hands perfectly poised in front, I skied my biggest air of the day—thirty feet—picked an untouched pillow of snow, and landed softly to the deafening roar of the crowd.

It was exactly as I'd visualized: nearly perfect.

BECAUSE OF MY ILLNESS and because I always felt a little out of place at the freeskiing after-parties since I was ten years older than most of my competitors *and* married, Rob and I decided to go out to dinner alone that night at the restaurant on the top floor of the Cliff Lodge. When we walked into the Aerie Lounge, we were seated by the window adjacent to Snowbird owner Dick Bass and his son, Dan. Rob had met Dan at the awards ceremony, and they picked up their conversation where they'd left off and soon incorporated Dick into the mix.

Dick had given a speech at the ceremony, and he proved just as eloquent in casual dinner conversation. He wondered aloud about me, and whenever I could croak out an answer, he drew a parallel between the philosophical approach I take to my sport and the approaches he saw among climbers during his bid to become the first person in the world to climb the "Seven Summits," the highest mountains on each continent.

When we finished dinner, Dick insisted we join him in his private office, also on the top floor of the Cliff Lodge, so he could show us his plans for Snowbird. As much as I wanted to go back to our room and sleep heavily, we joined him around an oblong, highly polished conference table upon which sat a model of Snowbird as he envisioned it in the future. With more tram access to mountains higher and farther away and a summer business centered on body, mind, and spiritual wellness, it was a dream worthy of a man as magnanimous as Dick Bass seemed to be.

I didn't see Dick again before we left, but as we checked out of the hotel early the next day, the clerk handed me a signed copy of *Seven Summits*, the book that Dick had written with Rick Ridgeway. As the competitions of the 2005 season went on into spring, *Seven Summits* was always on my hotel bedside table right next to *Thinking Body, Dancing Mind*. While reading it, I took note of how Dick called himself a high-altitude trekker as opposed to a hardcore alpinist type of climber, and I began to wonder if maybe I could climb *and ski* those same peaks that he'd "trekked."

By the time I finished the book, the idea was speaking to something primal in me. Dick had climbed Denali before he dreamed up the idea of the Seven Summits, and I'd climbed and skied Denali the year before with Rob. I'd written on my life-plan game card that I wanted to climb an 8,000-meter peak, now I was feeling an undeniable pull toward the rest of these high places.

"YOUR PASSPORT SURE WILL BE FULL"

WITH MONEY TO SPEND on skiing, life was different. For one thing, instead of driving our van home twelve hours from Kirkwood, California, like we'd done the year before, this year Rob and I could fly back after the final event of the World Freeskiing Tour and catch closing day at our home mountain in Jackson Hole. After I stood on my last two podiums of the season, one for second place at the Kirkwood comp and the other for winning the overall 2005 Women's Freeskiing World Championship title, I hopped into the rental car and off we sped to the Reno airport.

Indirectly, the money also improved my skiing. I skied better during my second tour than I ever had in my life, and I have no doubt that it's because someone believed in me enough to make that investment. Having a sponsor was like having a constant source of affirmation. I even found myself calling him after a win *before* I called my parents.

On closing day, he hosted an après-ski party, and as Rob and I pulled up to the restaurant, I was tingling with excitement about sharing my success stories of the season with him. But I also felt nervous, like a traitor, because my immediate plans didn't include much skiing. I was sure someone at the party, probably *him*, would ask me, "What's next?" I cringed at the prospect of having to say, "I'm enrolled in a graduate program for a master's in landscape design that starts in August at a school in Massachusetts."

Actually, I'd been enrolled for two years but had deferred my acceptance so I could compete on the Freeskiing Tour. Having been raised to tell the truth, I'd been honest with the admissions officer the year before when I requested my second deferral: I told her I hadn't imagined I could win the first time, and now I wanted the chance to do it again.

After that, I'd be ready. I'd have gotten it out of my system. They believed me because I believed it myself. After all, going to graduate school for landscape architecture had been on my five-year list for six years.

A small prestigious school, the Conway School of Landscape Design seemed to hold the key to my next career and lifestyle move. I wanted to build on the skills I'd developed during my twelve years as a stonemason, when I created outdoor spaces that were in harmony with nature. I loved the art form of building with rocks, and if I became a designer, I could have a profession that fit my values without having to lift all those rocks myself for the rest of my life.

"Why do I feel so nervous?" I said to Rob as we sat in our car in front of the restaurant. "How am I going to let him down?"

Ever since I'd met my husband six years earlier and he seemed to look right into my soul, I'd known I couldn't conceal anything from him. I had the same feeling when he said, "How are you going to let *yourself* down?"

He was right, of course. I realized that I still wanted to ski full time even though I'd achieved my goal and won the Freeskiing Tour twice. I wasn't done, but what was I going to do?

Rob released me from his knowing gaze, got out of the car, and led us inside, where I decided not to mention going back to school. Instead, we simply celebrated the successful end of another ski season and another Freeskiing Tour.

THE MORNING AFTER THE party, I picked up the phone and made an appointment with Carol Mann, a soul reader I'd wanted to meet for years. If ever there was a time in my life when I needed a third informed opinion, this was it.

Never having done anything like this before, I had a hard time deciding what to wear to our meeting a few days later, a concern that turned out to be absurd. After welcoming me into her enclosed porch office in a historical home in downtown Jackson, Carol began our conversation by saying, "Here are my Kit notes." Apparently, once I'd given her verbal permission to tune in to me, she went on to fill page after page of a yellow legal pad with my soul information—how often I've incarnated (and in what genders), why and when I choose to incarnate, what matters most to me. Once again, someone was looking right into me. It couldn't have mattered less what I'd worn.

Her blue eyes sparkling, she jumped right in. "I want to invite you into planetary work, because that's who you are. That's why the small things lose interest for you even though they're great in most other people's view."

Wow. She certainly nailed *that*. Things like having a normal job, planning for retirement, and starting a family had never been high on my list. I felt the urge to confide. "Everyone keeps asking me when I'm going to have kids, and I don't know. I don't even want to think about it right now, but society tells me I should. I'm thirty-five and have been happily married for five years. Is there something wrong with me?"

"Your way of knowing is direct navigating. You will suddenly feel and know that raising a child is an enormous contribution."

Whenever I'd contemplated becoming a parent, I thought that would amount to turning my back on a big piece of myself that I hadn't spent enough time cultivating. Hearing Carol say this gave me some confidence that I was making the right choice. And that confidence seemed to free me to do some direct navigating right then and there. I suddenly felt and knew I would have two children before I turned forty. So there was still time. No need to embrace the pressure that others had been putting on me.

Carol interrupted my musing. "What would you like your legacy to be?"

What? Really? I was already thirty-five, but isn't a legacy something to be pondered at least a *little* later in life?

Actually, Carol was on to something. This was the big question. The issue of having children had been the hors d'oeuvre, and now we were on to the main course: If kids weren't next for me, what was?

"You have an opportunity to expand the scope of your influence. Your soul's essence is balance—balance in body, mind, and spirit. Your soul is part of creating the nature aspect of this planet. This may sound outrageous"—she smiled—"but the job you serve on a big-picture level is planetary park ranger. Not a park ranger for a little park. Your relationship is with the planet."

She'd done it again. Right into me.

"Planetary ecology is the planetary level of balance. Human ecology is the individual personal level of balance. You are involved with both."

The resonance of those words brought me to tears. Actually, I already knew what I wanted to do next, but it was so outrageously big that I hadn't known whether I should allow myself to think about it. Ever since reading *Seven Summits*, though, I'd felt the dream growing, whether I allowed it to or not. Over the months, the term *high-altitude trekker* kept popping into my head. In the book, Dick Bass had made a clear distinction between what he does and what hardcore mountain climbers do, and my mind kept returning to the fact that mountains that don't require elite technical climbing skills should also be skiable. If they aren't too steep for trekkers and the snow lines aren't bisected by the rock and ice that beckon hardcore alpinists, why not? If a trekker could trek the highest peak on each of the seven continents, why couldn't a skier ski them?

Going back to school to get a master's in landscape design would be a perfectly acceptable way to experience and share my connection with the natural world, but I suddenly knew that acceptable wasn't enough for me. The direct navigating that Carol had referred to was already guiding me.

"If you don't access the bigger picture, you are limiting what can come in," Carol said. "Planetary is your scope. Think bigger."

I *did* have a planetary dream that was so big I hadn't dared share it with anyone. It was time to find out what it was like to go after it.

THE DAY AFTER MY session with Carol, the sky in Jackson was a grimy gray, and the mood of the town was a perfect match. Most years this is what April 15 is like, with the ski lifts closed for the season and everyone on a cortisol downer that follows the adrenaline rush of a hundred days spent experiencing the bliss of flying down the mountain on skis. There's still a lot of snow in mid-April, but usually the conditions are changing from winter to spring and skiers switch focus to mountain biking or rock climbing someplace drier and warmer than forty-two degrees. We call it the off-season, and I tended to go through serious withdrawal for a few days. But this April 15, I was consumed by the information Carol had given me and allowing myself the space to think bigger like she'd suggested. Outside my window, the ghost town that Jackson Hole had become overnight was so quiet that I could hear myself breathing as I sat at my computer and opened my mind to the possibilities. *How big is* big *anyway? Is it as big as I thought it was? As big as...*

At over 29,000 feet ASL, Mount Everest is the highest mountain in the world. I'd thought fleetingly about skiing it several years before, but without giving myself permission to access the bigger picture, it had seemed too far-fetched. But now, on April 15, 2005, a day after a soul reader had given me permission, skiing Everest seemed not only reasonable but necessary. *This* is what I was supposed to do next. It was as clear as the fact that getting my master's in landscape design *wasn't* what was next.

As if my fingers were way ahead of my brain, I found that I was Googling information on Everest and the other five of the Seven Summits I hadn't skied yet. On some level, I must have known that if I were really going to tap into the biggest-picture truth of what I sensed was my destiny, I had to think in a way no one else ever had. My mind scrambled for information: When is the best time to ski them? Is it even possible? Is there snow on all of them at *some* time of year? And, almost as important as any of these logistics, could it be done in a short amount of time? Direct navigation had told me I would have two children before I was forty—I had less than five years to climb and ski six more mountains and give birth twice.

Clearly, efficiency was going to be crucial, and I spent the next several hours planning an Everest expedition, since it would be the most complicated one. Not knowing if anyone had ever skied from its summit, I Googled "skiing Mount Everest" and found links to stories about Yuichiro Miura's daring 1970 speed-skiing descent from the South Col (a saddle 3,000 feet beneath the summit) and Megan Carney's 2003 ski attempt. Carney was a highly accomplished ski mountaineer and psychologist from America who'd spent years honing her skiing skills in the French Alps and winning several extreme ski competitions before trying Everest. While she wasn't successful in her attempt to summit, I'd heard stories of how tough she was, and based on dispatches from her autumn 2003 trip posted on the Berg Adventures website, I surmised that once the climbers had been acclimatized were and in position to summit, they just didn't have the right conditions.

When my brain was saturated with information, I walked away from the computer and thought back to my session with Carol. She'd cautioned me to avoid getting caught up in human drama, trauma, and especially melodrama, because whenever I'm around people who don't believe in me, I tend to lose faith in myself. She said that I was highly attuned emotionally and that the downside of that is being susceptible to swings that could knock me off balance. For me to have the greatest clarity, I needed to maintain my emotional balance. "It isn't about you not feeling emotions," she said. "It's about you allowing them to flow through you."

In light of this, I decided to be hyper-careful about sharing my dream with others. This was a private journey, not a public challenge. And I wanted to keep it that way, at least until the journey was completed. The question was, where to begin? Besides Rob, who could I begin to share this dream with who would be only positive and supportive, with no room in their lives for holding on to fear, anger, or hatred? I'd read online that Carney had felt completely supported by Wally Berg, who'd organized her Everest expedition through Berg Adventures. As a woman doing things that most people don't think are possible, I carefully vet whether someone's energy is supportive of me or whether he thinks I'm harebrained. Berg had believed in Carney, and that was a good sign. I picked up the phone and called his home office in Canmore.

"Are you planning a trip to Everest soon?" I asked.

"Yes, for autumn 2006," he said. "We have some people interested."

"Great. My name is Kit DesLauriers and I'd like to be on that trip. I'm planning to ski from the top."

There was a brief pause and I wondered if Wally was Googling me. "I led an expedition in 2003 where Megan Carney attempted the same feat," he said. "I think it's totally doable."

We discussed a few more details, all of them positive, and then I hung up feeling almost numb. It didn't feel real. I'd put the process in motion. I'd allowed myself to think big, and I'd come up with an even more ambitious list of goals than the one I'd been pursuing since Rob and I first played "the game." Yes, I'd wanted to climb an 8,000-meter peak, but now suddenly I was on a course for the top of the world, to try to ski it. And I couldn't believe it felt so right—exciting and comfortable at the same time, as if I'd been walking this path ever since reading Dick's book.

Meanwhile, back on Earth, there was work to be done. Mount Everest was on my calendar for autumn 2006, and somehow I had to fit the other summits around that. So I dug into the handwritten notes, bookmarked pages, and printed articles strewn across my desk and the floor.

First I learned that Vinson Massif, Antarctica's highest peak, can be skied only in late November or early December (Antarctica's summer) because it's the only time that the logistics company flies to that part of the continent. I put it on my calendar for 2005.

Aconcagua, in Argentina, also looked best in late November into December. Given its proximity to Antarctica, I wondered if I could do it right after Vinson Massif. I scribbled a reminder to keep an eye on the snowfall during the Southern Hemisphere's approaching winter season.

Russia's Mount Elbrus, the highest mountain in Europe, was on the North American seasonal calendar and would be best skied in early June just like our big peaks here in the Tetons. *Perfect—how about kicking things off with Mount Elbrus six weeks from now?* Without another thought, I emailed John Falkiner, who had skied Elbrus by the standard southern route and had long wanted to explore the seemingly unskied remote north side. And after the expedition that Rob, John, and I had shared on Siberia's Mount Belukha in 1999, I figured he'd agree that the north side of Elbrus was another adventure we needed to have.

Kilimanjaro, in Tanzania, presented a special problem: It seemed that skiing it wasn't exactly legal. I found YouTube videos of a few people making some ski turns on Kili under the radar, though, so it was possible. But then there was the expense of flying to Africa. I could potentially fly to Tanzania from Russia after Elbrus to keep costs down. I penciled it in for the end of June.

Last on my planning list was Kosciuszko, in Australia. Dick had left it for last in his quest, but that was one thing I wanted to do differently, since, at only 7,000-plus feet ASL, that summit would be anticlimactic. It also didn't have snow on it for much of the year, and if it had a season, it seemed to be August and September. *Hmmmm,* in September 2006 I'd be climbing Everest, so unless Kosciuszko were a stop-off on my way to Nepal—which could cut into my high-altitude focus—it would have to happen in 2005. Note to self: Figure out how to schedule my stonemasonry season so that I have a break between projects to escape to Australia for a secret ski week in early September.

Finally, with a loose game plan in place, it was time to share it with the person I'd promised to share my life with. The one who'd asked, "How are you going to break it to *yourself*?" when I said I might put skiing on the back burner to get my master's degree. I was in my office and he was fixing lunch in the kitchen, just down a short hallway. I took a deep breath.

"Hey, Rob," I hollered. "I have a crazy idea. I think I'm going to ski the Seven Summits."

Silence.

Just when I thought he must not have heard me, he poked his head through the open doorway and smiled. "Your passport sure will be full," he said.

"Do you want to come with me?"

"I don't know, but make sure you invite me for Everest. I've always wanted to ski that one."

RUSSIA'S SECRET HANGING VALLEY

O N JUNE 3, ALONG with John Falkiner and a pesto producer from Zurich named Rolf whom we'd just met, Rob and I stepped off an aging Aeroflot plane after a flight from Munich to Mineralnye Vody, Russia. From there, we would drive to the base of Europe's highest mountain. My Seven Summits quest was officially underway.

Everything had fallen into place: Rob had some unfinished business with Mount Elbrus, and we happened to be about due for our spring vacation when I'd begun planning the summit expeditions. He'd climbed and skied from the lower of Elbrus's twin volcanic summits years before and wanted to go back and ski from the highest point, the west summit. Meanwhile, John had emailed back to say that he had a client from Zurich who wanted to climb and ski Elbrus and that June would work for both of them under one condition: John didn't want to do the standard route from the south. Just the answer I was looking for.

The icing on the cake was that we'd have the same Russian guide who had also helped organize our Siberian ski expedition. Nikolai Shustrov had helped John arrange the Russian travel for his previous Elbrus clients, and during the last trip Nikolai had told John about a cabin he'd heard of on the uninhabited, lawless north side of Elbrus. Legend had it that the hut was ideally situated at 12,000 feet on the rocks at the bottom of the glacier. The west summit is at 18,510 feet ASL, and a summit day of just over 6,000 feet would be an arduous but doable undertaking for us if we were properly acclimatized. Rob and I excitedly agreed to the plan, and thanks to the support of my newfound benefactor, we were able to buy our tickets for Munich.

I can still remember the phone conversation I had with him a few weeks after hatching my possibly far-fetched plot to ski the Seven Summits.

"You know how you told me to spend this money on skiing?" I said.

"Yeah. What's up?"

"Would it be OK if I used the five thousand dollars that I have left over to go to Russia in June and ski Mount Elbrus, which is the highest mountain in Europe? Rob wants to go, too, but he can pay his own way." I hoped that last part might take away from how much I knew I was asking.

"Yeah," he answered. "It *was* for skiing, so that sounds fair."

Wow. "Awesome. Thank you!" I'm sure he could hear the smile on my face. I'd been ready to write a check to return his money, and here he was giving me his blessing to use it to ski a mountain in Russia that he'd never heard of. If he was OK with *that*, maybe...

Just do it, Kit. This is your one chance to ask him. You know he didn't get to be a successful businessman without being clear about what he wants. If nothing else, he'll respect you for trying.

I stood up from my desk chair, where I'd been doing my Seven Summits research, and jumped in. "Hey, so I have another idea I want to tell you about."

"OK."

"Have you heard about the Seven Summits? The highest mountains on each continent?"

"Yeah."

"Well, I want to try to ski them. It seems like no one has ever done it before, although there is a Slovenian guy named Davo Karničar who's been trying for a while."

Pause.

"Cool."

You're halfway there, Kit. Just ask him! If you don't, you won't get any farther than Elbrus.

"Would you be interested in sponsoring me?" I ended the question with a major lilt in my voice.

Pause.

"Probably. Send me a budget and I'll take a look at it. Let's go mountain by mountain, though."

Oh my God. He actually just said yes! I was so excited that I didn't remember hanging up. *Wait—slow down. He said yes to one mountain at a time. It's going to depend on the budget and my success on each mountain. He's a smart guy—of course he wouldn't just write a check for $100,000. This way he can preapprove each expense and stop the funding at any time.*

I felt extravagant, and very nervous, as I sat down and drew up a time line and a proposed budget. When I was done, I was shocked to realize that for fifteen years I'd reported annual personal income on my taxes that was comparable to the amount it was going to cost to book a flight to Antarctica. And Everest would cost twice that.

THE NEXT DAY, I emailed him the proposal, followed up with a phone call.

"What do you think?" I asked, fingers crossed.

"Send me an invoice for what you need to get started and we'll see how it goes. Like I said, mountain by mountain. If you can really be the first one, I think it's cool."

And so there I was in Mineralnye Vody (which means "mineral water") waiting for Nikolai to pick us up and take us to Mount Elbrus. We found him standing just beyond the security gate with his right fist planted over his heart in his countrymen's salute of unity. After hugs and congratulations on our marriage even though it was already five years old, we piled into his hired white van and headed through the gray spring afternoon toward the mountains.

Nikolai was known for planning exceptionally unusual and often pleasant forays into the countryside. Like the time when we came off our climb of Mount Belukha and were weary from weeks of living on half rations while expending 100 percent of our energy. After twelve hours on the bus we would have been ecstatic to stop for a simple sandwich, but instead we pulled up to an unmarked door in the dark of the evening. We didn't even know what town we were in.

Nikolai ushered us through the door and into a long hallway just wide enough for the ten of us to walk single file. Red velvet lined the walls below shoulder height, and long panes of mirrors covered the upper parts of the wall all the way to the ceilings, which were arched and decorated in gold paint. The doorway at the end of the hall was of a curious hobbit size, and just in front of me, Kasha, the other woman on the team, crouched and disappeared into whatever lay on the other side. I gamely followed, and when I stood up to full height again, it was as if I'd stepped into a medieval castle on banquet night. I was in a large room with more of the red velvet and mirrors on the walls, accented by gold-adorned sconces. The mirrors reflected the flickering candles and sparkling crystal goblets that decorated two long wooden tables. The most dazzling sight, though, was what else was on the table: silver platters and tiered trays of beautifully arranged cheeses, breads, fruits, and meats.

After our steady diet of half rations, we all instinctively grabbed for the grapes and the cheese, but Nikolai quickly stopped us. "Ah-ah-ah," he said scoldingly as he shooed our hands away from the towers of glorious food. "Before we begin, I'd like to propose a toast." He poured us all shots of vodka from a bottle on the table. "From America to Europe to Russia we come together. A team this big on the top of Mount Belukha is rare. The friendship we leave with is even more rare."

We greedily downed our shots and moved toward the table, but Nikolai stopped us again.

"There is something else we must do now before we eat." He held open a door that led deeper into this mysterious place and gestured for us to walk through.

Grudgingly, we tore ourselves away from the culinary spectacle and entered a hallway that branched into two changing rooms. In each was an attendant holding a white bedsheet with outspread arms. We looked to Nikolai, who said one word: "Sauna."

In the women's room, Kasha and I got undressed and the attendant draped us in white togas. After we joined the rest of our team in the dizzyingly warm sauna, Nikolai explained that this pre-perestroika men's club was ours for the evening, and though we didn't quite understand our luck, that's not a requisite of adventure travel—we just went with the flow. We alternated between sweating profusely and taking naked dives in the cold lap pool, and when, after an hour, Nikolai determined that the time was right, we returned to the dining hall.

I'd been afraid the spread would vanish while we were gone—could it really have been intended for us?—but there it was. This Roman feast really was all ours, and we reveled in both its bounty and its bizarre nature long into the night.

The spell was broken abruptly when Nikolai announced that it was time to leave. He directed us to our lodging, which was next door, and it turned out to be in sharp contrast with the magical atmosphere we'd just left behind. Inhabited by little more than a sense of foreboding, the building was grim and gray and entirely devoid of furniture on the first floor. In the dark created by the lack of electricity, we climbed the stairs to bedrooms whose windows had been blown out, shards of glass still clinging to the frames. We had the pick of the beds—of course—which were no more than creaky metal frames with mattresses covered with piles of seeds, leaves, bones, and mattress ticking, probably left behind by rats. As we laid our unbelieving heads inside our sleeping bags, all we could do was have faith in Nikolai.

He went on to earn our trust many times over during that trip, and now six years later we were back in those trustworthy hands. Through John's organization, we'd hired Nikolai to guide us to the north side of Mount Elbrus, and three hours after he picked us up at the airport, we knew we were in for another adventure-travel surprise. Near midnight in the darkness of a new moon and at least thirty minutes after we'd passed the last village, our van came to a stop next to a military truck parked on a steel platform under a several-hundred-foot cliff.

"Get out and transfer your bags to the back of the truck," Nikolai said, displaying his knack for not saying more than necessary.

It was hard to see with just the headlights of the van and the truck for lighting, but it wasn't hard to make out the knobby head-high tires and dark green canvas tarp tightly laced over the hoops of the truck bed, both of which said "army" to me.

Even when spoken by a friend like Nikolai, the Russian language can sometimes sound intimidating, and between being told to "get out," the late hour, the army truck, and the fact that I had no idea where we were, I was a little scared.

I grabbed one of my two duffel bags from the van and pulled my down jacket from the top of it and my headlamp from where I always pack it in the zippered mesh pocket. A good traveler always knows where to quickly find a warm layer and a light, and I thanked myself for tending to these details when I'd repacked that morning at the Munich airport.

After efficiently doing as we were told, Rob, John, Rolf, and I joined Nikolai on the small platform and stood shoulder to shoulder with our backs nearly touching the large truck behind us and watched the white van disappear back into the valley as our platform began to rise almost straight up into increasingly cold air. Rob and I traded incredulous looks. We'd been in some unusual places in our lives, but 500 vertical feet in the air atop a hydraulic platform in the Caucasus Mountains at midnight was a new one for us.

When we reached the top of the rock cliff that acted as a natural barrier to the hanging valley above, we were directed to climb into the back of the truck and sit on wooden benches that lined the bed. Any view of the valley that we might have had was obscured by the canvas door that had been zipped shut above the tailgate.

Besides keeping the view out, the canvas door kept the exhaust fumes in, and I soon found myself feeling nauseated. Unwilling to go along for the ride to the point of getting physically ill, I loosened the section of rope between two grommets that held the canvas cover in place behind me and stuck my head out the opening. For the next hour, we bounced along a bumpy, muddy road that sometimes wound between banks of snow that were twenty feet high—a sign that avalanches had crossed the road during winter.

Our destination was the old and largely deserted Soviet military sport camp of Ulla Tau, located in the Hanging Valley. Before our arrival in Russia, we'd agreed as a team to spend some time on neighboring mountains to acclimatize for Mount Elbrus's high elevation, and we'd left the location up to Nikolai. He'd decided on the Adir-Su Valley, to the south of the Baksan Valley, where we were now greeted by a noisy generator and welcoming front-porch lights. Even more welcoming was the warm three-course meal waiting for us inside what Nikolai said had once been the officers' barracks.

Ulla Tau is the same camp where Nikolai himself had lived for many months during his youth while training to compete as a professional alpine climber, at the expense of the former Soviet Union. Channeling the discipline of those formative days, Nikolai set our breakfast call for 5:00 a.m., and after dinner Rob and I retired to one of the small rooms upstairs. It was spartan but fairly clean, with creaky mattresses on twin beds that we spread our sleeping bags on top of. This would be home for the next week.

On our second day, we set our sights on a mountain called Tchotchat far above camp. The rapidly melting spring snow line was close to the valley, so shortly after leaving camp we put our skis on and began skinning. Arriving at a waterfall of snowmelt, we stopped and strapped the skis to our packs and began to make some climbing moves. Carefully placing our hands and feet on wet rock outcroppings, we crossed over low-growing clusters of pink and blue Spring Beauty flowers and then back onto a steep, slippery grass slope that led us back to the snowfield stretching above, seemingly forever.

Because the clouds engulfed us in a warm, wet mist, wearing one base layer was enough on the upper body if we kept moving, but then our heads would get wet, so we put on visors for visibility in the rain, covered by thin hats and the hoods of our waterproof jackets, their empty arms tied to our backpacks. As we climbed farther into the clouds, the temperature dropped enough for snow to not only fall but accumulate. After climbing several thousand feet, we encountered three inches of new wet snow. Because of the clouds, we could hear but not see the small avalanches coming off the cliffs of Tchotchat, and when we reached the bergschrund that guarded access to the summit headwall, it appeared to be dangerously loaded with heavy snow, so we skied down from there.

Each day we pushed a little harder, fueled by the quiet, focused life at Ulla Tau and the chefs' good cooking. After skiing, we'd spend late afternoons reading in bed or practicing glacier-rescue techniques while hanging from the stairs of the barracks until it was time to sit down for borscht with sausage and black olives and cayenne-carrot salad.

On a day that we decided was too rainy to ski, we walked to the camp's "museum" to look at the collection of black-and-white photographs there. Nikolai found someone to let us into the locked building, and inside he told us in his fluent English that there had been seventy to eighty of these mountaineering camps in the Caucasus Mountains during the Soviet era and that about twenty of them were here in the Baksan Valley.

"That is Vitaly Abalakov," he said as I studied a photo hung on the wall painted bright blue. "He was an instructor who invented the Abalakov anchor."

I couldn't believe my ears. The famous technique for creating an anchor in ice that leaves no gear behind had been invented *here*. The Abalakov anchor allows climbers to thread a cord through a V-shaped hole made by ice screws. Anyone who's rappelled on an icy mountain knows how huge a contribution it is to climbing history.

"Who were the students?" John asked as he looked at the graduating-class photos.

"Kids would come here to start their formal mountain-climbing training at age sixteen," Nikolai said. "The cost was heavily subsidized by the government because it was believed that young people who trained at camps like Ulla Tau would eventually make better soldiers. Students from families like mine that couldn't afford it paid as little as forty rubles a month, all-inclusive." He smiled his wry smile. "And if we were late for the morning workout lineup, we had to peel potatoes in the kitchen all day. I was only late once."

Nikolai attained the title of "master of sport" here at Ulla Tau, which had no doubt been a source of great personal pride, but the golden era when the Soviet Union had sponsored people to become professional athletes was gone, and with it went camps like this. Most of them are now closed, and the ones that can still be rented for events are in disrepair. With the stucco peeling off the buildings, exposing the crumbling bricks beneath, Ulla Tau appeared to be "maintained" by a handful of people who seemed to spend most of their time mopping brightly colored paints onto the buildings and not minding if it spilled everywhere.

WHILE THE OFFICERS' BARRACKS had been nice enough at Ulla Tau, there had been no bathing option, much less a Russian *banya* like we'd enjoyed on the Siberian journey five years earlier. We were all lusting for a hot shower when five days later we arrived at the Hotel Itkol, in the village of Terskol, after a short van ride from the bottom of the otherworldly "mountain elevator." Nikolai checked us into our shared rooms in the gray five-floor structure, which didn't look as if it was quite finished being built, and handed us our room keys. With no trace of surprise on his face, he translated what the front-desk clerk had said: "The hot water will be turned on at four p.m."

After the lukewarm showers, which reminded us not to wish for creature comforts while trying to focus on climbing a mountain, we strolled up the valley to a restaurant Nikolai had chosen. On the ten-minute walk, we passed the closed glass doors of a travel agency that had a weather forecast displayed on poster board in the window. High pressure and clear skies had just arrived and were expected to stay for several days.

"Will we be able to get weather updates from the north side?" I asked.

"No," said Nikolai. "This is Russia and we don't have reliable forecasts or good Internet infrastructure even from this village, let alone from the uninhabited north side. We'll just have to pick our summit day the way we always have—by looking at the sky."

By 2005, we'd become accustomed to checking websites for weather predictions, but the Baksan Valley was clearly a step back in time.

Several ski lifts dropped down to the valley floor, creating mini-villages at the base, and at one of them the five of us sat at a picnic table outside the restaurant. In our down jackets, we ordered beer—or *piva*—and ribs and discussed the plan for tomorrow.

Like me, everyone was eager to get on with the journey to the remote north side, so we decided that our second acclimatization tour would be a single day above the Elbrus Ski Resort. After getting our fill of what were easily the best ribs I'd ever had outside America, we headed back to the hotel, where Nikolai arranged to have a car pick us up at eight the next day.

In the morning, the driver dropped us at the end of the road, in the village of Azau, and the five of us promptly became the first in line for the lifts that would take us up to the Elbrus Ski Resort. Taking this standard approach to climbing Mount Elbrus required us to carry our skis in our hands and our packs on our backs while we rode two aging forty-person tram cars streaked with years' worth of oil that had dripped from the cables above. At the top of the trams, we put our skis on, and after waiting in a very short line of eager Russian skiers, some of them in blue jeans, we rode the final lift inside the ski-area boundary, a slow double-seater that completed our mechanical ascent of 5,000 vertical feet in under an hour. I was grateful to reach the top of the ski resort at 12,500 feet ASL at nine thirty on a June day without having broken a sweat, but then, any North American skier would be grateful for a safe delivery from a tram whose midstation was full of crumbling concrete and exposed, twisted rebar. Shouldering our skis, we exited the resort boundary on a plateau and walked through the "Barrels Camp" en route to the mountain above.

Each painted white, blue, and red, the barrels were largely windproof shelters in the shape of gigantic pipes about eight feet across and thirty feet long with one tiny window next to the door on the front. There had also been barrels at our base camp in Siberia, and we had put six people on six bunks per barrel, but the barrel I poked my head into on Elbrus looked like it held the belongings of about twenty climbers. And it smelled as if it were full of sweat-soaked people, yet all the inhabitants were up on the mountain climbing on this rare sunny spring day.

After a quick visit to the obviously well-used outhouse trailer next to the barrels, each of us stepped into our skis, with climbing skins already in place, and began our day above the slopes.

A snowcat—or a "rat track," as the local name for it translates—was parked near the barrels, which prompted John and Nikolai to jokingly suggest hiring it to take us another 3,000 vertical feet up the moderate slope—forty degrees—that lay ahead. They said it would cost less than US$100 for all five of us, but they knew full well that taking the easy way up wasn't our style, nor would it help us to gain the physical acclimatization we'd come in search of.

"It's tempting, but no thanks," I said with a glance at Rolf, who just smiled in agreement.

"OK," Nikolai said, "but remember that the last tram down is at five p.m., so don't miss it!"

Psyched to have a day to ourselves, Rob and I spent the next six hours skinning uphill at a blistering pace. At noon, we'd even foolishly wondered if we could actually make the summit that day, but a few hours later the spot 750 vertical feet below the saddle that divides the east and west summits was looking like a good place to turn around. The slope above began to contour to the west, and that meant that if we continued it would only be for a less-than-ideal skiing fall line and we'd be at risk of not making that last tram down. And there was the fact that in the past hour, we'd both gotten headaches and become noticeably grumpy.

Normally, we would have considered turning around when the headaches kicked in, but that day we treated our reactions to the altitude with uncharacteristic callousness because we knew we'd soon return to civilization after descending from 17,000 feet *and* we had a rest day the next day. And so, for climbing too high too fast, we paid the price of lousy moods and physical discomfort. It didn't help that, due to the strong sun on that southern exposure, the surface of the new snow had become moist—the kind of snow that sticks to the bottom of your skis four inches thick, making every step up and every turn down challenging.

After skiing 2,000 vertical feet from our high point, we met up with Nikolai and Rolf, who were lingering at Pastuckhov Rocks. They'd figured that any time spent at altitude would acclimatize them, so they sat and waited for us. With less new snow at this lower elevation and a slight aspect change, the mountain no longer had the sticky snow but now offered perfect corn—coarse, granular wet snow that's about the best that spring has to offer—for the four of us to blissfully carve turns in. After reentering the resort boundary, we skied under the top lift and the upper tram line and arrived at the midstation by four thirty, where we caught the tram down the melted-out lower mountain to meet John for a *piva* in Azau.

OUR REST DAY HELD more Nikolai-style surprises. During breakfast at the hotel, he warned us not to drink too much coffee or water because once we were loaded into the van at eight o'clock for the drive to the north side of Elbrus, we wouldn't stop until we met the next vehicle in our "shuttle service" at eleven o'clock somewhere in the direction of Mineralnye Vody, on the east side of the massif. "Somewhere" turned out to be on a rural side road, and the next vehicle turned out to be a Russian UAZ jeep with an army-green cab and a body hand-painted in two bright shades of blue. The enthusiastic driver was another Nikolai, a small-framed white-haired man with dazzling blue eyes who directed us to call him Uncle Nik. He was to drive us to the base of the mountain, which he'd climb partway to lead us to his cabin tomorrow.

As we headed through an increasingly beautiful countryside of rolling green hills nearly void of trees, we ate from a flat of wild strawberries Uncle Nik had picked from his yard that morning, served with bowls of sugar and freshly hand-whipped cream on the side. Tiny and ruby-red, the berries were packed several deep in the shallow wooden box, and I marveled at this man who had picked enough strawberries to satisfy five adults and taken the time to whip the cream. As I looked around at the same looks of joy and surprise to be found in a Disneyland commercial, it was clear that everyone was relishing this delicious perk of adventure travel as much as I was.

As we rolled west, with Nikolai seated next to Uncle Nik on the front bench seat and the rest of us sitting on our duffel bags or the wheel wells in the rear compartment, the road turned from asphalt to gravel, and the dachas—weekend farmers' hut-size summer homes—became fewer and farther between. From Uncle Nik via Nikolai's translations—projected over the din of the four-cylinder truck engine—we learned that the area had been full of productive cattle and cheese operations before perestroika. Now the production facilities were crumbling before our eyes.

At the end of the farmland plateau, we reached a police checkpoint that marked the entrance to a secondary road, our route to the north side of Elbrus. After the armed officers allowed us to pass, Uncle Nik explained that permits were required in this area, a sort of nature preserve where hiking and hunting were allowed but homes weren't.

Finally, four hours after starting this leg of our journey, the jeep climbed to the top of the last forested valley, where a young man of about eighteen waved at us from the first driveway we'd seen since passing the guard station an hour earlier. Uncle Nik waved back and turned into the driveway. At the end of it, in a clearing among the birch trees, was a small, bright blue travel trailer, and out of it stepped a mountain of a man, well over six feet tall and as burly as a lumberjack.

Confused, we murmured to each other in the back of the jeep. "What are we doing here?" "Who's this?" "I thought no one lived up here."

"He lives and works here in the summer," Nikolai translated for Uncle Nik. "He keeps an eye on the countryside to make sure no one poaches animals."

They'd picked the right guy for the job. I couldn't imagine a more intimidating enforcer.

"He's a friend of mine," Nikolai translated, "and this was where we arranged to pick up Ramen, the young man who will carry a load to base camp for us."

Nik and Nikolai followed the giant man into his one-room summer home, and we cautiously followed. When the man gestured for us to sit, we tried to make ourselves comfortable on the edge of his bed, since the only other piece of furniture was the table that he and Nik and Nikolai were leaning against. Ramen stood in the open doorway, which let in the only light. Just over my left shoulder on the synthetic-wood-paneled wall was a faded and creased black-and-white poster illustrating the various sex positions of the Kama Sutra. It took some effort to fight back the primal fear that comes with being the only woman in a remote outpost belonging to what looks like a feral man whose only decoration is a sex poster.

The mountain man saw my uneasy smile and addressed me while he poured some kind of liqueur into eight small shot glasses. Translated by Nikolai, he began a toast.

"We are very happy for foreigners to come to the north side of Elbrus. *Chou.*"

Nikolai and the other man looked at us expectantly.

"*Chou,*" Nikolai said. "*Chou* equals 'drink the shot.'"

Green yet clear, the liqueur had the sharp bite of something homemade that I recognized from our Siberia trip, when I'd shared toasts from vodka the locals had made at base camp. What *was* this stuff?

The mountain man continued on about his beloved north side of Elbrus. "It is where the original summit expedition started from. *Chou, chou.*"

This was not a well-aged spirit, and the second shot made my shoulders rise to my ears and my whole body shudder.

"And to the woman who comes to ski. *Chou, chou.*"

That made three shots and it was only three in the afternoon. Everyone looked at me to respond, so from a place of quickly crumbling inhibition, I met the giant man's gaze, thanked him for his welcome, and asked, "How did you make this?"

"This walnut cognac is Uncle Nik's secret recipe," Nikolai translated. "Thirty green walnuts harvested in July. Cut in half. Place with one kilogram sugar. Put in dark place for thirty days. Mix this syrup with three liters alcohol!"

With that and some hearty handshakes, we said goodbye to Mountain Man and loaded back into the jeep, adding Ramen to our crowded mix. Natural spring melting conditions in these mountains above tree line meant that the road had deteriorated to cavernous ruts, and as we pushed on, those of us in the back lurched from side to side, trying not to hit our heads on the ceiling of the jeep as Uncle Nik presumably chose the path of least resistance. As connoisseurs of ski-line choice and with nothing else to do at the moment but backseat-drive, we watched Uncle Nik's driving become less precise as the conditions worsened and, no doubt, the effects of the booze set in, and we called out our predictions on what would happen next.

After he made a couple of lucky saves, Uncle Nik succumbed to the mud and we jeered like football fans whose team has just fumbled. Deeply mired in the ruts, we climbed out and used a combination of tactics to try to free the jeep. Some of us dug with our avalanche shovels, but the mud and water seemed to pour out of the earth for instant refills. Others carried rocks from the tundra hillside to drop into the ruts and displace some of the standing water. Ramen even tried sitting in an open window of the jeep so that it leaned enough for us to pile rocks under the tires. After an hour and a half during which the walnut cognac wore off and left us with headaches, we finally freed the vehicle.

Had someone gotten out and chosen a line through the muck before we headed into it, the whole ordeal could have been avoided, so when, two minutes later, Uncle Nik piloted us into another brown swamp without assessing the situation, we were too surprised to do anything but stare in disbelief. Again, he'd steered into the wrong track, but this time it was far more painful than a fumble. It was more like watching a World Cup skier crash. The standing water rising around us, we climbed out the windows and landed knee-deep in the mud.

John and I resumed the carrying and dropping of rocks in an effort to build a higher track for the jeep to climb out onto from the cavernous ruts. Meanwhile, Rob and Rolf took off walking and disappeared above the slope of low-growing tundra grass.

"Where do those guys think they're going?" John muttered as he prepared to drop another fifty-pound rock into the muddy water.

"Really. They'd better have a good reason for letting us do this ourselves," I said.

Meanwhile, Ramen, Nikolai, and Uncle Nik dumped rocks into the ruts from the other side of the puddle, working as tirelessly and unflappably as if these were exactly the road conditions they'd expected to find.

After thirty minutes, Rob and Rolf reappeared. "We found a bulldozer to pull us out!" Rob said.

There was a rumble from the switchback above us on the road, and I watched incredulously as the gigantic machine came into view.

"Well, look at that," I said.

John laughed. "Look at the brains on them!"

We stepped aside and watched the operator attach a chain to the jeep and pull it to safety. Smirking, Rob sauntered up to us with Rolf by his side.

"How the heck?" John said.

"Well, it's obvious that the road was graded recently," Rob said, "and it's still so soft that the loader couldn't have been far away."

Rolf smiled and shrugged, and I suspected that the pesto maker from Zurich simply hadn't wanted to throw his back out hauling rocks and jumped at the chance to follow Rob. Whatever the case, though, I was grateful that *this* ordeal had lasted only a half hour.

With the jeep pulled free and poised on the road ahead of the water obstacles, Nikolai handed the operator US$50 and climbed back in with Uncle Nik, Ramen, and John. Rob, Rolf, and I balked at the idea of any more delays and instead set out on foot along the more direct line of grass-covered slopes in the waning evening. I pondered the bulldozer's uncanny proximity to the nastiest of road conditions, which weren't replicated farther ahead, and wondered if the bulldozer operator had made those ruts on purpose to be able to make some money on some hapless travelers.

Now that the acclimatization and overland transportation parts of the trip were behind us and we were walking toward the undeveloped remote north side of the mountain, I found myself thinking more about the climb ahead.

Four days of clear blue skies so far—this weather can't last much longer. I mean, how often is there more than four or five days of perfection in a row in early spring? We may have just spent the last best weather day driving around this mountain. Maybe we should turn around and go back to the lift station at Azau to climb the mountain the way we already know and then come back here to no-man's-land and do it this way, too, if we have time.

Ouch! The steep hill we were on was full of tundra tussocks, and they were trying to twist my ankles, which were already compromised by torn and loose ligaments I'd suffered while playing soccer as a kid.

Can't afford to hurt myself now. The south side seemed like an easy climb, and now we've purposefully put ourselves into the unknown and spent a huge amount of effort to do so. It would take a whole day to get back to the south and probably another day to summit. We could do it in a day from the barrels maybe, but we'd want to spend the night up there to start early...

Listen to yourself, Kit. It's like all you care about is the summit! This isn't you. Usually you want to do meaningful things like explore a different route on the way. Chill out. If it's two more days, maybe more, to summit from the south, then just get it done in two days from where you are.

"Relax, Kit. There's no way we'd be able to convince everyone to turn around and go back now," Rob said when I shared a small fraction of what had been running through my mind. "Besides, what if our best weather is only the next two days? We wouldn't want to waste it with all that traveling."

After less than an hour of walking, Rob, Rolf, and I walked down the switchbacks from the hillside and into the camp at the foot of the mountain. The jeep was already parked next to the only building in sight, a deserted sheepherder's three-sided lean-to in a flower-studded meadow alongside a rushing river. Uncle Nik, Nikolai, Ramen, and John were unloading backpacks and skis. Any lingering doubts I may have had about our approach vanished as I threw myself into the chores that needed to be done, like filling water bottles from the naturally carbonated aquifer that poured into the river just below the tin-and-tarpaulin shack. After Uncle Nik reheated his homemade goulash on a camp stove for our dinner, Rob and I wrapped our sleeping bags in our tent to protect against the spring dew that would be everywhere by morning. With my head only feet from the riverbank and facing the snowy twin summits of Elbrus more than 10,000 feet above, I drifted off to sleep without another thought of going backward.

ADVENTURE TRAVEL AT ITS FINEST

REWARMED GOULASH DOESN'T TASTE as good for breakfast as it does for dinner, but when it comes to preparing you to ford the frigid, knee-deep Kyzyl-Su River, fed by Mount Elbrus's milky glacial runoff, it gets the job done.

As we ate, Uncle Nik told us that we were camping in the same spot where Cavalry General George Emmanuel, one of the heroes of Napoleon's invasion of Russia in 1812, had camped in 1829 during the first ascent of Elbrus. Until Mountain Man had mentioned it yesterday, I hadn't even known that the north route was the original summit route.

When we were finished, Rob, John, Rolf, Nikolai, and I got busy stuffing our backpacks to the bursting point. Our gear included twenty-below-zero sleeping bags, sleeping pads, climbing skins, ice axes, harnesses with glacier travel gear, crampons, avalanche shovels and probes, down jackets, shell pants and jackets, base and midlayers of clothing, warm hats, balaclavas, goggles, sunglasses, gloves, mittens, socks, personal first-aid and hygiene items, sunscreen, cameras, trail food for four days, and two liters of water per person for the day. And on the outside of the packs we had to attach our skis and ski boots.

The sun had reached us by the time we were ready to go, but it still wasn't enough thermal radiation to take the chill off as we rolled our pants up to our knees, tied our hiking boots to our packs and forded the river wearing only socks and the plastic shells of our ski boots on our feet for protection against the rocks under the raging water. Our footing was wobbly as we navigated across the hundred feet of rocky river bottom, but after about fifty steps, we arrived safely on the other side. We quickly changed into dry socks and hiking boots and added our ski boots to the monstrous backpacks.

Ski poles helped me to balance the load on my back as I walked past what may have been General Emmanuel's horse corral, now overtaken by mushrooms sprouting from the dirt. Uncle Nik had pointed us in this direction and said there would be a natural place ahead to rest and regroup in an hour or so, and I was grateful for the chance to hike within sight of the others but mostly alone as I adjusted to the enormous weight on my back and picked my way along the grassy tundra hillsides littered with lava rock.

After having climbed 1,000 vertical feet to an elevation of 9,500 feet over the course of an hour, I'd begun to doubt my pace when I came upon a natural flat space the size of ten football fields. While it was obvious that this was where Uncle Nik intended us to regroup, I had to laugh out loud at the language barrier that hadn't communicated the vastness of this extraordinary land feature. John was close to a mile ahead of me on the plateau, and I figured it would take twenty minutes to catch up to him—that's how big it was. When Uncle Nik reached us, burdened by his gigantic orange rucksack full of food, he shared a little more information.

"This was a top-secret airstrip used by the Germans for refueling planes when Hitler invaded this area in 1943 looking for oil," he said in an earnest tone.

Is he serious? Given the unusual dimensions of this meadow on an otherwise-steep hillside, I decided to believe Uncle Nik's explanation for the moment and made a mental note to ask him for more details of the area's history after the climb.

After sleeping in General Emmanuel's camp from the 1800s and snacking in Hitler's private aerodrome from the 1940s, it was time to move on to the hut that Uncle Nik said he'd built by hand—without permission from the authorities—3,000 vertical feet above us. After he gave us a brief description of how to get there so we could move at our own pace, which would be faster on the snow above than he'd be on foot, we skiers set off using our ski boots, skis, and climbing skins to stay on top of the wet snow. The fog tried to move in but gave up, and we spent the day skinning straight toward the perfectly visible northern faces of Mount Elbrus's twin peaks, still over 6,000 vertical feet above and three horizontal miles away.

Six hours after crossing the Kyzyl-Su River, we arrived at Uncle Nik's cabin. From its position at the edge of the glacier and the moraine from which it had receded, it was clear that he had gone to considerable effort and probably taken some risks in perching the twenty-foot-long Quonset-style hut where he had. I made another mental note to ask him to tell us its story. There had to be one.

We set straight to work on outdoor chores to maximize the moments of sunshine that remained: peeling wet climbing skins from skis, finding rocks to stretch them out on with enough sun orientation that they'd dry, and the same for ski-boot liners and gloves wet with the day's sweat. Uncle Nik arrived an hour later to open the hut, and after we'd eaten dinner and settled onto our wooden bunks, we discussed the plan for the next day.

"I know that today was a decent push," John said, "but given that we don't know if the weather will hold, I think we should get up at three and be climbing by four so we have a chance to reach the summit tomorrow. How do you guys feel?"

"I feel great and I agree," Rob said.

"Me, too," I said.

Rolf chuckled. "If that's what you all agree on, I'm in and I'll try my best." Because of his full-time work in Zurich, Rolf didn't spend as much time in the mountains as we did, and he tended to defer to John's suggestions. Rob and I had a long history of friendly skiing and climbing trips with John, and this conversation held out the possibility that this would be the first trip where only some of our team members might summit. It was understood that we'd all stay together if possible, but if not, Rob and I were a team and Rolf, John, and Nikolai were another team.

The next morning, the five of us left the hut at four o'clock and were able to start skiing uphill with our climbing skins immediately. Using headlamps to illuminate our way, I enjoyed the magical predawn hours when it seems as if I have to expend only a small percentage of the exertion required during daylight, or at least that's the mental trick I play on myself. The combination of that psychological phenomenon and the beautiful colors in the sky as the sun prepared to rise made me feel as if all were right with the world.

And then I noticed that the dawning sky had a strong red and orange tint to it. How did the saying go? Red sky by morning, sailor take warning?

After the sun was up and we'd climbed 2,500 vertical feet, the group came back together like an accordion at the spot we'd agreed on the night before: Lenz Rocks, 15,000 feet ASL, the place where the glaciers become more open. As we took a snack break, John offered his assessment of the sunrise colors we'd seen.

"The weather here moves from the southwest, and we're on the northeast side of the mountain. I know it's still sunny now, but with those lenticular clouds starting to form above the summit, we could be climbing into a storm."

So we kept the gear-and-sustenance break to an efficient twenty minutes, pulling the ropes from our packs and tying in to them as we ate, and the five of us set off again to forge the skin trail toward the saddle between the east and west summits, 2,500 vertical feet above.

Unfortunately, what had been firm snow gave way to a wintry surface condition that allowed our skis to penetrate six inches on each step. To make matters worse, the altitude made it harder to get a deep breath. Still feeling very strong, though, Rob and I took over the lead in setting the skin track, which gave John the chance to give Nikolai and Rolf the more frequent small breaks they'd begun to request.

Keeping a steady pace that we didn't think was too fast, Rob and I continued to traverse from our route under the northeast side of the saddle to where the saddle intersects the west summit massif about 400 vertical feet higher. But in the process, we climbed right into the dreaded storm, which had already unleashed its force on the south side of the mountain. Only minutes after we arrived in the windy space of the saddle, visibility decreased to about ten feet, which was about the distance between Rob and me on the rope. It was also around that time that the angle of the mountain increased substantially. It wasn't long before we couldn't get any purchase with our skis and had to stop in the blizzard and take them off, attach them to our packs, and switch to crampons.

"I can't see the others," I said. "Do you think they're coming?" Before Rob could answer, I went on to reassure myself. "I'm sure they are. They probably just made the crampon change before we did."

"Yeah, they'll be fine," Rob said. "There are some crevasses right here. Maybe we're too far to the north still to gain the ridge. Let's keep the rope tight while we step across them. Hopefully, those guys know a better way, because I don't think Rolf will like this."

After we jumped the crevasses, we climbed to a rock rib running up the ridge toward the west summit. With the sense that we were on the correct route, we decided to continue up even though the visibility had become worse and the frigid wind stung every bit of exposed skin. Crevasses aren't usually right next to ribs of rock, but we knew that just a hundred feet to the climber's right of us the fissures covered the entire north face of the west summit. So we took turns leading and orienteering from the second-in-line position, which offers a much better point of view. Before long, though, the conditions undermined my confidence in our strategy.

"It's soooo cold!" I said. "I think we should stop and let those guys catch up, but I'm too cold to stop! What should we do?"

"Let's just keep going as slowly as we can without sitting still and they'll catch us."

After a few more minutes of careful boot and crampon placements on the steep icy summit ridge in total whiteout conditions, I voiced my growing fear. "I'm afraid we're off-route. Sometimes there are rocks, but when we go a few steps without seeing any, then I think we're too far right or left. I think we should wait because John and Nikolai have been on this ridge before."

"Yeah," Rob said, "I remember Dan Egan telling me about when he was caught up here in a storm like this." Dan is a former professional skier who skied and coached with Rob in the nineties. "It snowed five feet with winds over ninety miles per hour, and they dug a snow cave to wait it out. It took him almost two days to get down and he helped rescue fourteen people but more than thirty people died."

"Oh my God."

"John told me he entered way points from this ridge into his GPS the last time he was here. If we wait for them, we can navigate that way for sure."

Forward momentum is a hard thing to resist, especially in the cold wind, so although we'd just agreed to stop and wait, we pushed on for several small bursts until we reached an area that was flatter than the ridge below had been. This change in angle meant a greater possibility of wandering in circles, so after hollering through the wind at each other to stop, we sat on our packs, pulled our heads into our hoods like turtles, and waited. The full impact of the slow-moving storm was upon us, and I berated myself for not stopping sooner. *We could be so off-route in this flat zone that we never see them pass or hear them over the wind unless they're right in front of our faces. John is going to be mad that we've made him wonder about our safety on top of his responsibility to Rolf.* I felt like a child who's made a mistake and is praying fearfully that nothing bad will come of it.

Minutes later, as if appearing from another realm, John emerged from the whiteness with GPS in hand, and my fears dissipated. Then, like fellow apparitions, Rolf and Nikolai floated into view behind him.

"John! Man, we're glad to see you!" I said and quickly steered the conversation away from how long we'd continued without them. "We stopped and switched to crampons when we crossed those crevasses at the bottom of this pitch. Is that what you did?"

"We'd switched just before that," he said, not mentioning the separation.

Reunited with our team, John continued to consult his GPS and navigated us across the flat false summit and up the steep, final summit bump. At the top, the wind pushed me around enough that I had to sit down for my transition to skis, but now that we'd summited together, the conditions didn't bother me. Instead I felt giddy with gratitude for the fact that what might have been hadn't been.

Rolf and Nikolai had also summited but left their skis just below the top bump, so John set up an anchor in preparation for giving them a belay off the icy summit. With my skis on, I lay on the summit and fed the rope for John, who stood in a strong stance, with his crampons still on, to lower Rolf and Nikolai to the safety of the flat section below. Once done, we cleaned the rope from the anchor system and Nikolai pulled it down to him so that Rob, John, and I could ski without a rope in the way.

Six controlled turns and a bit of sideslipping around the iciest chunks brought me to Rolf and Nikolai, and once John and Rob had done the same, we all continued to ski toward the saddle, cutting across a wind so stiff that it blew the straps on our backpacks horizontally to the sides of our bodies. As we retraced our route by skiing back down the north side, though, the winds suddenly dropped off because the storm hadn't yet moved that far. As joyfully as if we'd just outrun the devil, we skied through a succession of snow types, from nasty wind crusts to perfect powder, toward the sunny green meadows 10,000 feet below. A final section of perfect corn skiing assured me that it really was June, not the dead of winter it had felt like at the summit.

We stepped out of our ski bindings where the glacier met the rocky moraine and, after a two-minute walk uphill, were back at the cabin. Uncle Nik had laid an exquisite feast on a plank table outside, including cheeses, sliced meats, and cans of *piva*. What a gem Nik had turned out to be. Adventure travel in the mountains doesn't get any more decadent.

Our celebration proved to be short-lived, though, as the storm eventually made its way to us, forcing us to secure our mountain equipment outside and move the party inside.

After finishing our feast, Nikolai broke out the walnut cognac that Mountain Man had sent along with him, and that may be why we went on to sleep so well that night. By the time we woke to a howling wind that was rocking the cabin, we'd been asleep for twelve hours. Well rested and wide awake, John picked up his travel guitar and played folk songs while Uncle Nik made breakfast.

As we ate, we talked about the bullet we'd dodged by pushing to the summit yesterday. From the new snow and raging wind outside, it was obvious that the storm was big enough to keep us pinned in the cabin at least until tomorrow. Half-recumbent in our sleeping bags, with our heads propped up by our stuff sacks because the bunk beds were stacked so tightly that there wasn't room to sit up on them, we settled into our weather day, warmed by the small stove that Uncle Nik judiciously fed with firewood he'd cached under the beds.

"So how did you get this cabin here?" I asked Uncle Nik.

After Nikolai translated my question, Uncle Nik stood and began a soliloquy in which he would pause only after he'd given Nikolai quite a mouthful to translate. John softly strummed his guitar to provide punctuation.

"The first summit of Elbrus was from the north side in 1829. The Russian Academy of Sciences came here with 200 Cossack soldiers to take the land. Famous physicist Heinrich Lenz was in the summit party, but only the local guide, Khillar Kashirov, made it to the top of the mountain, ascending the rocks to the east summit all alone, and left his hat to mark it. He was paid 200 rubles, but that did not matter—it was in his heart. Forty-five years later, an expedition from Great Britain made it from the south side to the west summit for the first time."

Feeling remiss for not having studied up on any of this history before the trip, I grabbed my journal and began to scribble notes as he talked.

"In the mid-1980s, in the first days of perestroika, there was geological work to be done on the north side of the mountain looking for silver, gold, etc. A tunnel was made all the way through the Black Hills, and I came through the tunnel as part of the rescue team. People were often descending the north side from the south when the weather turned bad or they became altitude-sick. I had the idea to build a refuge here on the north side, but when the tunnel was closed, I listened to a geologist who suggested a different way to get here. The new idea was to use the roads near here that were built in the 1960s for geologists looking for molybdenum and chromoly metals, which these hills are full of."

John stopped playing. "Wait, who built the roads in the first place?" he asked.

"The main roads were built for farmers, and the forks of the roads were built for geologists."

John nodded and resumed playing.

"Back to the story. I dreamed big and decided to build the refuge anyway with a friend. We built it at home to be disassembled and then had a plane fly the pieces to the airstrip we passed on the way up the mountain that the Germans used as a refueling and base station for small planes."

So it really *was* true.

"In order to afford the cost of transporting loads of refuge parts from my home in Pyatigorsk to the airstrip and then from the airstrip up the next 3,000 feet to the refuge location, I assembled a special party of socialites who would never think of climbing mountains but would pay for a unique party on the side of Mount Elbrus at the airstrip. I organized the party tents and all the trimmings, then I used a pilot with whom I had a special relationship to get everybody and everything to the airstrip. The party people knew about the idea and didn't care much that maybe they had paid a little extra to have the materials delivered there. During the party, I paid the pilot two liters of cognac for the two extra ten-minute flights from the airstrip to the refuge location to deliver the materials. It's been here ever since."

Always energetic, Uncle Nik had become even more animated than usual. His eyes sparkling, he brought us up to the present after speaking for nearly an hour.

"I can't legally own the cabin, but it is mine. I am host and caretaker. I climb the mountain many times each year and have for thirty years now. I have come here already this winter and have spent four of the past five Christmases here. This year I had a helicopter drop two boxes of drink plus food, wood, and a special lady to cook. The rest of the group took the road until it was not passable, then they walked two days to the valley and two more days to the refuge before being stuck here for eight days by a hurricane of a storm! A helicopter dropped them a leg of lamb and a ham that saved them. There is a stove here for winter needs, and it's usually put under the bunk, a German alpine troop stove made in 1942 called an Edelweiss."

I hadn't thought of it before, but the stove seemed to sum up Uncle Nik. His providing of it was the gesture of someone who was truly concerned for the climbers who took on the challenges of Mount Elbrus's north side.

As I closed my journal, I marveled all over at our luck in finding this tour guide extraordinaire.

THE NEXT MORNING, WITH a new historical and personal connection to Mount Elbrus, we left the hut after the bulk of the storm had passed and skied back to the site of Uncle Nik's refuge-building society party before walking the rest of the way out. Uncle Nik somehow got ahead of us while we transitioned from skis back to hiking boots, so when we reached General Emmanuel's camp, the jeep was gone. We followed the directions he'd given us earlier to Dzhily-Su, the health-spa camp where he was arranging our next accommodations.

We arrived after two miles on foot down the dirt road, but what we found—piles of junk and trash heaped against the camp's single-story concrete buildings—didn't look much like a health spa to me. Alerted to Uncle Nik's presence by the blue jeep parked outside, Rob and I entered to find him setting up a dining space for us that was empty except for the table, two benches, and the strong smell of cat urine. Nikolai directed us across the courtyard to pick a bedroom from the choices in that wing of the building. The best of the options had a window and twin spring-loaded bed frames with mattresses, but the rusty coils groaned under the weight of my pack. And when I noticed the mouse feces that covered the windowsill and the table between the beds, I made an executive decision.

"Rob, let's make camp by that waterfall we passed after the bridge."

First, though, I wanted to check out the area's mineral-rich geothermal springs. John, Rolf, Nikolai, Rob, and I walked up the road to the first pool, which wasn't crowded because we were sharing the camp with only about fifteen others. The Russian men in the pool were wearing underwear, so I kept my shirt and underwear on as I climbed into the surprisingly cold, bubbling, fizzing orange water thick with particulates while a hatch of some kind of flying insects hovered at eye level. With Nikolai translating, the men told us we were supposed to stay for fifteen minutes to get the full health benefits, but I was lucky if I lasted ten before grabbing my one clean T-shirt and turning it a splotchy orange as I dried myself off with it. Because of the floaties, I didn't feel clean, but I did feel good. And cold.

Back in the cats' dining room, we had three shots of vodka to warm us up. Each one was accompanied by toasts to various things, including Nikolai's translation skills, John's efforts in bringing us back together for another grand adventure, and my patience as the only woman on the trip. Then it was my turn.

"May I give a toast?" I asked host Uncle Nik.

By now some other "guests" had joined us, and all the Russian men in the room grew wide-eyed—perhaps entranced and a little intimidated by this outspoken woman—and stood up holding their glasses. When I began to stand, they stopped me. "Nyet, nyet."

So I stayed in my seat as I raised my glass. "Six years ago in Siberia, I met my husband-to-be, Rob. And so I toast to Russia and thank her for answering my dreams."

Fully drunk after that shot, we dug into the liver dinner that Uncle Nik had prepared for us in the adjacent caretaker's kitchen. Afterward, John picked up his guitar, and a Dzhily-Su man named Rashid with a half a mouthful of gold fillings announced that he was getting married for the sixteenth time in September and asked me to dance. I tried to follow Rashid's lead as he held my hands, but Russian ballroom dancing is hard enough to follow without having to do it in a room barely big enough for the picnic table that everyone's crowded around. When our dance was over, my legs had had enough for the day, and Rob and I left in the waning light to set up our tent in a field of violets and cabin-size boulders at the base of the hundred-foot waterfall.

AFTER A REST DAY at Dzhily-Su's healing waters, Uncle Nik drove the UAZ jeep back over the circumspect roads and the rest of us hiked downriver for three to four hours along a wet and magical *Lord of the Rings*-type trail before dividing up and choosing our own paths of least resistance to reconnect with the road. Rob and I climbed steep mixed-grass hummocks and rocks decorated with wild thyme, irises, and orchids and finally topped out not far from where Uncle Nik was waiting. When the others appeared, we loaded into the jeep and Uncle Nik returned us to the base of the mountain, where the adventure had begun with a flat of wild strawberries just a week before.

One could only hope there would be more guides like Nikolai and Uncle Nik to smooth the way as my journey led me up the five remaining summits.

GOING IT ALONE (AND SICK)

Y OU'D THINK THAT IDENTIFYING the seven highest summits on each continent would be one of the easier things about a campaign to climb and ski them all, right? I mean, compared with striking out at four in the morning, losing your way in blizzards, and watching your husband suffer from hypoxia, looking at a topo map and figuring out which mountains to climb should be as easy as the simplest math problem.

Actually, to figure out the highest peaks on each continent, first you need to figure out what a continent is. I grew up thinking there were seven continents, but it turns out that some say there are only six, and some landmasses within a continental shelf may be separated by an expanse of water, so in some circles those islands aren't considered part of the continent. And to compound the headache, there isn't even agreement among geographers about whether continents should be defined by the tectonic plates they're situated on.

Long story short, there's a dispute among climbers regarding whether the highest mountain in Australia is Mount Kosciuszko, which is on the mainland, or Carstensz Pyramid, which is on the nearby island of New Guinea and not on the continental plate. So when it came time for me to climb and ski one of them, there was all kinds of research to be done to make sure I chose the correct one. In the end, though, there is no correct one—different factions are going to have to agree to disagree on this. For me, it came down to the same thing it had come down to for Dick Bass. His intention was to climb to the top of the highest mountains on all seven of the world's largest continuous landmasses. My intention was to climb and ski those same mountains.

Fortunately, Dick's way of defining the continents gave me a better chance of having some snow to ski on during the Australian leg of my expedition. Even in Carstensz Pyramid's "peak season" of November, the equatorial snow usually amounts to unskiable patches and streaks. Meanwhile, when I'd been penciling potential summit windows into my calendar in April, I read that the ski season in Thredbo, the town at the base of Kosciuszko, runs from July through September, with late August and early September being the most reliable times. So as soon as I got back from the Elbrus trip in June 2005, I began to plan for a trip to Australia.

It felt kind of silly, though—wrong, even—to use my private sponsor's money for a plane ticket to Sydney for the easiest climb of the Seven Summits while I had the most demanding and logistically difficult mountains still ahead. What if I didn't make the summit of Everest? The trip to Australia will have been a wasted $5,000.

I don't want to finish the Seven Summits with the one that's most expensive and holds the least likelihood of success, but I don't want to finish this project with a bottle of Champagne on Kosciuszko, either. All I can do is go with it, I guess. Besides, Kit, it probably wouldn't be a bad idea to start acting like you believe in yourself. That might come in handy when you have to ask for more money to keep the project going. Just visualize success all the way and stay on course.

I took my own advice, and by the time I headed off for the smallest of the summits in September 2005, I was in it with both feet and I no longer regarded this part of it as a potential waste of time and somebody else's money.

I LANDED IN SYDNEY with a nasty sinus infection, which promised to make my imminent adventure in urban driving especially challenging. If the information coming at me takes a natural form like wind, snow, rock, or ice, I'm usually aware of even subtle changes in qualities like direction. In natural environments, I can carry on a conversation with a friend while exerting myself uphill, making constant choices about the climbing route, and filing away mental notes on my surroundings. Drop me in the driver's seat on a city expressway packed with cars and plastered with exit signs, however, and by the time I mentally process the sign I've been looking for, I've often missed my turn and am forced to make a miles-long detour that threatens me with sub-detours. And if the driver's seat happens to be on the right side of the car, well, I'm lucky if I can keep it together long enough to get out of the parking lot. Even with my sense of direct navigation leading me on a quest around the world, that didn't seem to help me much with urban driving.

The morning I arrived in Sydney, it didn't take long to lose my way amid the traffic and general confusion. I'd barely left the airport when I sensed something was wrong. And it's probably no coincidence that it was Mother Nature who brought it to my attention. I had a nagging feeling that the ocean shouldn't be on my right if I was supposed to be driving southwest toward the Snowy Mountains and the town of Thredbo, so I pulled off and consulted my map. Again.

As I stared at the tangle of roads, I really wished I wasn't alone. Rob couldn't take the time off, and he figured that if we were successful on the other six summits, he could always do this one another time. And because I didn't want anyone else to know about my project, I'd had no choice but to do this by myself even though one of the biggest rewards of mountain experiences is sharing it with friends. None of this felt natural. I felt as out of place as a lone wolf—a concept that's greatly misunderstood, by the way. Wolves don't intentionally separate themselves from their packs. Though some wolves strike out in search of a pack of their own, most wolves don't leave unless they're driven out, so the idea that these animals are commonly solitary creatures is a myth. Even Alta wasn't a "lone wolf." Though he'd grown up never knowing life in a traditional pack, we were a pack of two and he couldn't have lived without me any more than I could have lived without him. Now, trying to find my way across a continent alone, I was experiencing an alien feeling and just wanted to get this thing done.

After getting my bearings and turning myself around, I was finally able to relax a little as I headed southwest along the relatively civilized National Highway 31. But between the sinus infection, the eighteen-hour flight, and the seventeen-hour time difference, I was running out of steam. By the time I approached Canberra, which the rental-car agent had suggested would be a good place for a rest stop, I was shaking my head to fend off the hallucinations. I had to keep going—by now I was overwhelmed by the thought of getting off the highway in another city. Even though I'd already been driving three hours, the small-town girl in me thought I'd be better off taking a break closer to the mountains. As it turned out, just passing *by* Canberra was a test. On the way into town on Route 31 there were seven lefts and rights and two roundabouts, and it took every bit of street-navigational savvy I had to keep driving in the right direction.

Just over an hour later, I found what I was looking for: Cooma, the first town on my drive that looked as if it experienced four seasons instead of one or two. Spring was in the crisp, cool air, and the blossoming flowers in planters along the street suggested that while it probably didn't snow at this elevation, it froze enough to give the town a winter season to emerge from.

I sat down at a diner on Main Street for a cup of coffee and then comfortably jaywalked the two-lane country street to a pharmacy. My congested ears were popping from the effects of gaining 2,600 vertical feet since landing in Sydney, and I'd also come down with a sore throat, swollen glands, and an achy body. The pharmacist suggested several products, all of which I bought and promptly took before pushing on to Kosciuszko National Park. No virus was going to keep me from skiing from the modest height of Kosciuszko's summit.

When I arrived at the small kiosk at the southeastern edge of the park, I saw that the fee was twenty-seven dollars per vehicle per day.

"Is there a discount for a week?" I asked the attendant.

"No," he answered from his window.

I only had five days before I had to drive back to the airport, so in the waning light of the early evening I paid the park attendant $135 and drove the last half hour of a travel day that had now lasted for over twenty-four hours.

It was easy to find the aging Thredbo Alpine Hotel across the street from the Kosciuszko Express chairlift, as the town has fewer than 1,000 residents. I parked in the free lot under the shade of deciduous trees showing off their spring splendor, did another throat gargle, and checked in at the front desk feeling like a shell of myself. A room-service dinner was all I could manage while I put my feet up in the wood-paneled room and studied the map I'd brought with me.

Thredbo ski resort offered the closest access to Mount Kosciuszko, and it looked like I just had to ride the Express chairlift, unload to the left, and start walking north-northeast and I'd be at the top in under two hours. I could hike up the ski area and start the trek on foot to be more hardcore, but I felt terrible. I had the kind of virus that takes days to start releasing the pressure, not unlike the one I'd suffered at the freeskiing competition in Snowbird, and just the thought of getting out of bed the next day was cause for dread.

I didn't even know if it was legal to hike up the ski area. If it was, though, the melted-out lower mountain confirmed that the end of the season was rapidly approaching, and the mud at the bottom wasn't inviting.

So just take the lift, Kit. That's what Dick did. And if you really feel strongly about it, you can hike from the bottom the next day once you get the first summit in the bag. Give yourself a break for once. Don't take yourself so seriously. This would be a good time to laugh instead.

The next morning I did just that, laughing out loud as I walked along the flat hilltop after unloading solo from the Kosciuszko Express quadruple chairlift, from which the summit was 1,000 vertical feet and about four and a half miles away. In front of me was a pathway made of steel anti-slip stair treads poking out from the snow for hundreds of linear feet in the direction of Mount Kosciuszko. This was the antithesis of a wilderness experience.

Without glimpses of that man-made addition to the landscape, I might have needed to take a compass bearing to figure out which way to walk from the top of the ski resort, since it was all above tree line and the terrain consisted of unremarkable undulating white hills erratically punctuated by boulders. In the hazy light of that September midmorning, it wasn't at all apparent that I was nearly at the headwaters of the Snowy River. In fact, there was no obvious summit to be spotted at all. Nothing pointy or jagged—just rounded hills in all directions

Once I'd cruised across the three-quarter-mile length of the metal walkway, complete with informative natural-history plaques melting through the snowpack, I skinned uphill to the left until I came to the final summit block, if you could call it that. The angle of this 500-vertical-foot mound was only slightly steeper than I like for climbing with skins on my skis, so it was around thirty-two degrees, which is in the range for a normal intermediate trail at a ski area.

As I zigzagged my way uphill on skis, about a dozen people were at varying stages of hiking the boot path straight up the middle of Kosciuszko. When I topped out, I heard a young man standing next to the summit cairn joke loudly to his buddies about their own summit achievement, "One down, six to go!" I found a place to sit on the leeward side of the chest-high cairn and hid my face in the hood of my jacket to stifle my second laugh of the day. I was also hiding because I didn't want to be pulled into a conversation about what I was doing there all by myself on a ski holiday to the highest point in Australia at the end of the season. And the fact that I lived in Jackson Hole would make the whole thing even more absurd. Who goes to Thredbo on a ski vacation from Jackson? So I made my peanut butter and jelly sandwich last until everyone else had gone back down.

Alone again, my task now was to document myself skiing this mountain. I set up my video camera on its tripod and smiled at the camera before lowering my sunglasses and skiing away. Once out of sight below the camera, I stepped out of my bindings and hustled back up the boot track to the camera with my skis over my shoulder and pressed "rewind" to see how the shot looked. I repeated the process again and again and again using slightly different angles, and my third good laugh of the day was at how foolish I must have looked doing this solo dance all over the top of this mellow mountain oh so gently rounded by glaciers that had disappeared long ago.

After my last lap on the summit, I skied back toward the inbounds area at Thredbo, where some of the trek was so flat that I had to push with my poles and use a Nordic skiing technique to get across it. At the boundary, I worked my way left and over to the T-bar surface lifts of the central spur in search of the steepest and best spring-corn skiing I could find. The slush-bump lines between the trees took me back to my days of skiing in Telluride, and the surface lifts were something I hadn't been exposed to much in my ski life, so I laughed yet again, this time at the novelty of it all. When I noticed skiers pointing their gloved fingers at me doing my fast-paced ski laps on the short runs like I was in orbit around the chairlift, I switched to a different part of the mountain to avoid having to answer the inevitable question: What are you *doing* here? Not even my parents knew I was in Australia.

Sometimes it can take the energy away from a pursuit when people make their plans too public before carrying them out, so when one of my closest friends had asked me if I was trying to ski the Seven Summits, I told her, "Yes, but I'm not admitting it to anyone else but Rob and my sponsor. I need to keep the energy to myself because it's already a long shot. Plus, I don't want to have to explain my decisions to the media." She was really concerned about my safety and I reassured her with what I knew to be true: "Sue, I promise that if at some point something doesn't feel right, like if I get frostbite or injured at all, I won't keep trying. That's the other part of why I'm not talking about it. I don't want the pressure of having to explain myself to the whole world if I don't do it."

There was also the fact that Davo Karničar had been trying to become the first person to ski the Seven Summits for a few years already and if he knew I was gunning for the same thing, he might speed things up and get it done before me. My sponsor wouldn't have been crazy about that scenario either, and so, yes, I'd kept my quest a secret even from my parents.

If I'd been at home, I'd probably have spent the next couple of days resting to regain my health more quickly. If I'd been in Thredbo and felt physically healthy, I'd have hiked the mountain from the base without using the lift. Since I was neither, I decided to repeat the lift-assisted morning treks to the summit for some gentle exertion, followed by more inbounds afternoon skiing, but after three days of this routine, there was no more reason to stay in Thredbo. The lower parts of the resort were so bare of snow and so muddy that even if my sinuses hadn't been packed solid, I probably wouldn't have bothered hiking up from the bottom.

So I checked out of the hotel and drove an hour to Perisher, the other ski resort in Kosciuszko National Park. With a higher base elevation, it offered better skiing, and I spent the rest of my time in Australia enjoying the journey and generally not taking myself too seriously. Lesson learned, finally.

LANDING ON ICE, WALKING ON EGGSHELLS

VERY MOUNTAIN HAS ITS best-weather window for a climb. Sometimes there are a few choices, but in May 2005 when I was creating my summit schedule, there were only two options for flying from South America to the Vinson Massif's Patriot Hills base camp that year: November 21 and December 5. Being in Antarctica during its summer seemed sensible, but the $25,000 price tag didn't. And that was before buying the $250,000 in rescue insurance required by the sole flight operator, Antarctic Logistics & Expeditions. A quarter of a million dollars in fuel was what it would take if the 1970s-era Russian Ilyushin cargo plane had to return, unscheduled, to the continent to pick you up in case of an emergency. The hard cost of the rescue policy was less than $500, though, and having it offered a little peace of mind during an expedition where protection was going to be hard to come by.

Since Rob wanted to go, too, and he would be paying his own way, I bounced the dates off him.

"Well, it might be warmer by December, since it's closer to the summer solstice," he said, sitting on the bench at our front door and lacing his shoes for a run. "But that's probably splitting hairs—it *is* Antarctica. Which one do you want to do?"

I'd become attached to the idea of skiing Aconcagua, in Argentina, right after Vinson, and I plunged into the sell job. "The time for a ski descent of Aconcagua is at the beginning of their climbing season, around Thanksgiving. After that, any snow that's left melts really fast. I'm wondering if I can do both back-to-back. In both cases, I have to fly to South America, so I'd save on airfare if I do them together."

He didn't look up from his shoes, and I took the opportunity to drive my argument home.

"But if we go to Aconcagua in late November and get delayed at all, then I'd miss the Antarctica flight and that would ruin everything. It's *so* expensive to get to Antarctica, and I wouldn't get another chance until next year. So I'm thinking we should go to Antarctica from November 21 to December 5, then I still may be able to do Aconcagua in December if everything goes well on Vinson."

"That makes sense. How much is Vinson?"

I paused and searched for the confidence to say the huge numbers out loud. "The price is $25,500 per person, with $5,000 due at booking. And that doesn't include getting to Punta Arenas."

Rob's eyebrows rose—a significant emotional display for him.

I quickly continued. "I found a guide who lists skiing in the description for a late November Vinson climb. He has two guys signed up and has space for two more. I don't want to be guided but it seems impossible to get to Antarctica without it since all the seats on the flight are taken by organized trips."

"Well, the deposit for both of us won't equal what I alone am going to end up owing, so let's book it. Plus, if you don't get us a reservation now, we may not be able to get on a flight this year, and next year we'll be just coming home from Everest." With Everest having entered the conversation, his eyebrows settled back into place. "Call the guide back and put our credit card down for two seats on the November twenty-first flight and we'll spend your birthday in Antarctica!"

And so, four days before my thirty-sixth birthday, we landed in Punta Arenas, Chile, en route to the coldest and most remote of the Seven Summits. On the same day, a story about our trip—gear-packing for extreme cold, what it's like to do this as a couple—appeared on the front page of the sports section of *USA Today*. The writer, Gary Hook, had also written a piece earlier in the year about competitive freeskiing, focusing on why we do it and who was winning. He'd been fascinated by the fact that I held the women's title over competitors who were usually ten years my junior. When he'd called me at home again a few weeks before the Antarctica trip, he asked what my plans for this winter were.

"Are you going to compete again?"

I took a deep breath and stepped outside onto the deck in hopes of channeling the strength of the towering Douglas firs as I answered.

"I don't think I'm going to compete again this year, but Rob and I are heading to Antarctica to ski its highest mountain, Vinson Massif."

"Really? Has it been skied before?" he asked.

"Yes, but no woman's skied it from the top yet, only from the high camp."

"It's amazing what you and Rob do together. I'd like to write a story on this for the newspaper."

That was it. No mention of the Seven Summits. No sign that he'd read Dick Bass's book or knew that an increasing number of climbers were following in his footsteps. My secret was still safe.

The day after our arrival, Rob and I took our seats at a historical downtown theater in Punta Arenas, a cold and windy seaport of about 150,000 people on the north side of the Strait of Magellan. Along with all the other passengers planning to fly on the Antarctic Logistics & Expeditions (ALE) flight to Patriot Hills[1], we listened to a presentation that described the rules of the Antarctic Treaty that would affect our behavior while in Antarctica. ALE representatives focused on the environmental-protection aspects of our two weeks on the continent and showed us photos of what to expect. For instance, you're not allowed to urinate or defecate whenever or wherever the need arises, because with only an inch of new precipitation a year, this is the coldest and driest place on earth and anything left behind would be there indefinitely. As photos of ALE's toilet solution for Vinson were projected onto the big screen, there were murmurs in the audience. A blue fifty-five-gallon plastic drum, fitted with a seat on top, would be placed at the camps in a central location, and everyone was expected to use it for going number two.

Beyond addressing the leave-no-trace protocol, which also allows the spitting of toothpaste only in designated pee spots marked by bamboo wands, ALE showed photos of the known climbing variations and camp locations on Vinson and alerted us to the enormous potential for flight delays due to bad weather.

"As you can see from the photos, this is a big aircraft that lands on a natural blue-ice runway, so in order to take off from Punta Arenas, we need to know that there are at least eight hours of clear skies ahead so we can get back, too," one of the agents said. "Because the fuel and

---

1   In 2010, Antarctic Logistics & Expeditions relocated its camp to Union Glacier and changed the name to Union Glacier Camp.

mobilization costs are so high and weather down here often doesn't cooperate, delays are common. In fact, the first group of staff to go to Patriot Hills this season waited here in town for ten days, but they got in two days ago. Although it's windy, it's beautiful today, so maybe we can fly this afternoon!"

With that, we all lined up to show proof of our $250,000 in rescue insurance, and the individual groups of travelers were given precise times to meet the gear truck at their respective hotels. The game was on for final packing details, and in two hours we had all our expedition gear ready in the hotel lobby. When the ALE staff members arrived, they weighed each of our bags and put them on a truck bound for the airport, where they were pre-loaded into the cargo plane along with the snowcat and other supplies heading to the Patriot Hills research station. All we had left in our possession beyond our wallets were the street clothes on our backs and the extreme-cold clothing we planned to put on as soon as we got the call that the plane was going to fly. ALE's people would call the hotel of each passenger every two hours with an update on the flight status. If we were in our rooms when the "yes" call came, the hotel would notify us, but when we were out, it was our responsibility to check in with the hotel. As it turned out, the call came at eleven the next morning, and two hours later an ALE bus picked us up, along with the rest of the down-suit-clad passengers.

At the airport, Patriot Hills-bound passengers were escorted from the charter bus through airport security and into a waiting area at the gate. Because it was a private charter flight, we didn't have boarding passes, and we didn't need to have our passports checked because Antarctica isn't a sovereign country. Once the door to the tarmac opened, we were marched outside to stand behind the belly of the cavernous plane designed to hold several military tanks. Like soldiers dressed in combat suits who look out of place in an urban setting, our group of climbers wore mountain clothing and insulated boots in the temperate seaside air, and we responded promptly to orders to walk up the ramp to the plane. Our gear had been packed under cargo netting in the center of the plane since the night before, and by the time the sixty passengers were in the air heading toward Antarctica, we were less than twenty-four hours off the best-case-scenario schedule.

The plane's few tiny windows high above our heads offered little natural light, and each seat on the wooden benches bolted along the length of the plane was delineated only by the military-green lap-style safety belt and matching oxygen mask that hung exposed above it. For takeoff, I positioned myself between Rob and someone I hadn't met yet and purposely away from Tim, the guide who had met Rob and me at the airport upon our arrival. Right away, we figured him for an unseasoned traveler, based on his confusion and elevated level of concern about unorthodox baggage-claim and ground-transportation processes. From the moment we'd booked his remaining two seats on the flight to Antarctica, Rob and I had let Tim know that we didn't want to be formally guided. We hoped this was all that was making him act awkward around us. We were staying at the same hotel where Tim was staying with his two clients from Salt Lake City, Hans and Brian, and when the five of us ended up eating together a couple of times, Rob and I noticed that Tim exhibited signs of being on a bizarre power trip. He nitpicked the packing details and the comings and goings of his clients and even tried to do the same with us.

After an hour with him, our hotel room felt like a sanctuary. "You know, judging by what he said when I asked him, it doesn't seem like he's ever been outside of the States other than to Switzerland for that ski-guide exam in the Bernese Oberland," I said, lying back on the bed. "And he talks about that like it's the raddest adventure in the world. I mean, that's fine, but it's not cool to have such a superiority complex as a guide, especially with that resume."

"Yeah, and did you notice how he barely admitted never actually having been to Antarctica?" Rob said, leaning on an elbow beside me. "It's bizarre that he was able to get the seats on a flight to such a remote place. Let's try not to judge him too much, though. Hans and Brian are mostly ski-area skiers and strong backcountry skiers and probably really need Tim's help on a trip like this, and we all have to be nice to each other. Let's play it by ear, but I think we should just plan to work with him when necessary. It'll be fine."

After the plane took off, a few veteran Antarctic travelers and guides stood up and moved around to a more comfortable spot and I took their cue. I lay on top of the netted cargo pile, using an extra jacket as a pillow, and put in my foam earplugs as a buffer against the din of the massive cargo plane's engine. The ability to be comfortable in the moment and rest whenever you get a chance can be as important to a successful expedition as being able to climb a steep and exposed snow slope.

At the end of the four-and-a-half-hour flight, during which we made our own sandwiches from a cooler for the in-flight meal, we returned to our seats and fastened our seat belts. We didn't need a flight attendant to direct us—we were just drawing on our survival instincts. The landing was smoother than almost any I've experienced on a commercial flight, but when the plane took forever to slow down, the passengers began looking at each other with raised eyebrows. The mile-long stretch of blue ice that is the Patriot Hills runway is a natural formation caused by the wind that blows incessantly around a small outcrop of an adjacent mountain butte, and we all knew that brakes are useless when you're hurtling along its surface. But even accounting for the extra stopping time, I found myself bracing against the ninety-degree backboard of my seat.

Finally, after what felt like ten minutes, the plane slowed and taxied to the drop spot and there were relieved expressions all around. The ramp in the belly of the plane opened to reveal the crisp blue sky of Antarctica, and the cold air rushed in as we happily unbuckled and gathered our backpack carry-ons.

"Many climbers have had their trip cut short by slipping on the ice when getting off the plane," the ALE agent had warned us during the meeting in Punta Arenas, and he wasn't kidding. The angle of the ramp pulled us downhill just enough that it took a careful combination of small steps with bent knees and engaged stomach muscles to stay upright as I set foot on the Antarctic continent. After several dangerous steps, though, we were off the bluest of the ice and onto the dry, squeaky layer of snow that covers much of inland Antarctica.

A full-size snowcat had been waiting for us the way workers wait to unload bags at JFK, and it ferried the cargo and our gear a quarter of a mile to the Quonset huts of the Patriot Hills base camp while we followed carefully on foot. Along the way, I took in the stark blue skies and the white landmass as super-cold air seared my lungs and caused coughing if I inhaled too deeply.

ALE welcomed arriving passengers in its cramped corporate hut with a warm dinner, during which we heard the roster of planned flights from there to Vinson base camp. ALE operated the red fixed-wing Twin Otter plane equipped with skis that would fly us the next two hours into the Sentinel Range of the Ellsworth Mountains, but our group was a quarter of the way down on the list of forty people and our best guess was fat chance that we'd get out that day.

Once the "last supper" was finished, most of us were asked to leave the heated Quonset hut. Only the two passengers on the Ilyushin cargo flight who had bought entire climbing packages through ALE were allowed in the mess tent or any ALE buildings other than the outhouses, namely Jamie, a savvy Seven Summits climber with Everest already under his belt, and his British friend Will. The four of us had become friendly, and they were clearly surprised when Rob and I stood up to leave with the others.

"You guys look like you know what you're doing," Jamie said. "Why are you with a guide?"

"When I was researching this, it looked like all the seats were already reserved so I figured that was the only way," I said.

Jamie smiled. "You just have to know who to ask, and with the right resume, ALE will let you climb alone. But they don't like to do it because if someone needs a rescue, then it falls on them."

Even though the hot meal was a nice gesture, after it was over I felt colder than I would have if I hadn't been allowed inside that warm hut in the first place. Like dogs kicked outside after dinner, Rob and I were looking around wondering what to do next when Jamie and Will invited us into their heated cabin for a visit.

"Where else have you guys climbed?" Jamie asked as he sorted gear and we sat on the edge of one of the two small beds in the one-room cabin.

"We skied Denali last year and Elbrus in June," Rob said.

The conversation seemed to be on a crash course for the Seven Summits, and I grabbed the wheel and tried to steer around it. "We live in Jackson Hole, so we climb and ski there, too. We've skied the Grand Teton, and last year we went to New Zealand and skied Mount Aspiring. How 'bout you?"

"Jamie here has climbed Everest," Will said, "and this'll be the last of the Seven Summits for him. I'm a newbie that he keeps around for comedy."

Jamie laughed. "He is not. Will owns a brand consulting firm in the UK. He's good at whatever he does."

I relaxed. Man, this secret-keeping was more work than I'd expected.

By the time we left the warmth of Jamie and Will's cabin, we were determined to do the climb entirely on our own like they were doing, or as independently as possible even though we'd signed on with a team. We'd already gotten everything we needed from Tim. It was tents, self-cooked meals, and route-finding from here on out. His services were definitely not going to be required.

Out in the cold again, we chose a tent site and began to quarry blocks of snow to protect against the ever-present wind. Two hours later, we settled into winter camping in the Antarctic summer.

WHEN ROB HAD SAID, "We'll spend your birthday in Antarctica," I didn't have any idea exactly where in Antarctica we'd be on November 23 or even whether we'd *be* in Antarctica by then. As it turned out, we began with packing up our camp at Patriot Hills and catching the day's second flight to Vinson base camp, on the Branscomb Glacier. The wind at Patriot Hills was so strong that Rob and I looked like a comedy act fighting a losing battle with the elements as we tried to stuff the tent into its sack faster than it could fly out. We ended up planting our ice-axe shafts in the ground and anchoring two tent loops to them while we stuffed.

In the process, my body became so chilled that I couldn't feel my toes inside my ski boots. *I'm about to try to climb Vinson and I can't even handle the cold at Patriot Hills.* Embarrassed and desperate, I wanted to warm my toes in Rob's armpits like I'd done in our snow cave in Siberia, but I was worried about what the other climbers would think of me. I especially didn't want to look weak in front of Tim. I was starting to doubt myself. *If you break down and need that kind of help now, what will it be like when you get higher on the mountain? Do you deserve to be here if you can't keep your own feet warm before the climb even starts?*

We took seats at the back of the plane, and as soon as it took off I quietly asked Rob if I could warm my feet on him.

He smiled with no hint of condescension and turned sideways so my toes could slither up under his many layers. Fighting to quiet the voice telling me I shouldn't be there, I settled for drowning it out with a different one. *It's OK, Kit. Sometimes playing it safe and asking for help is strength itself. It's OK, Kit...*

After an easy landing on the snow at the 7,000-foot base camp an hour and a half later, we formed a chain and were handing the gear out of the plane and into a pile on the glacier as a woman approached us on foot.

"Welcome to Vinson base camp!" she said. "I'm Margot, the base camp manager." She launched right into the same list of rules that ALE had given us back in Punta Arenas, which made sense because it was her job to enforce them. After showing us where the barrel toilet was and on which side of camp to harvest clean snow for melting into water, she retreated to her small version of a Quonset hut, which was the only structure at the camp other than tents.

With several flights' worth of climbers still behind us, we had our virtual pick of sites, and we spent five hours that afternoon setting up camp. Since it can take four hours to melt enough snow to make water for two people in any winter camping environment, we cut snow blocks with our saws to build walls around our site while the stoves were going.

Tim and his clients set their tent up next to ours, and just beyond the front doors we excavated a kitchen area into the snow so we could be out of the wind when we cooked and ate. As we went about our chores, Tim advised us all on matters of storing gear and dinner prep. There were several uncomfortable moments when he exercised a dictatorship about things that, in my opinion, should have been discussed more openly among the team members, like where to store gear and when to cook dinner.

After the chores were done, the five of us stood outside in the dropping temperatures wearing our down suits and drank tea that cooled off almost instantly, even in our insulated mugs. The tea washed down the personal-size cakes Rob had brought for the occasion from the bakery in Punta Arenas, each with "Happy Birthday" inscribed in icing.

"This is one birthday I'll never forget!" I said before blowing out the one candle in my cake.

"And the last baked good you'll have for a couple of weeks," Rob added.

NATURAL LIGHT SHINES AROUND the clock during the "polar day" period here, but the light isn't to be confused with warmth. The temperatures at base camp hovered around twenty below as we lay in our sleeping bags the next morning wondering why the guys in the tent next door were still sleeping. I'm used to getting going early in the morning, and I was uncomfortable with not having a plan by nine. Rob tried to ease my itch to be moving. "I'm thinking this is a noon-to-midnight kind of a place anyway, Kit." But I wasn't buying it.

Once our neighbors finally woke up around ten, we confirmed that our objective for that first day was to shuttle a load of our gear to the low camp and then ski back to sleep another night at base camp, and we decided to leave at one. When the deadline arrived, though, our teammates still weren't ready, and Rob and I tried to distract ourselves from the cold by watching the professionally guided groups work out their rope systems as they slowly departed base camp. Stop and go, stop and go they went, as is inevitable when people are tied in to the same rope and move at different paces; at any given time, any given climber will find that either the rope behind him has become too taut or the rope in front has become too slack. But they were moving for the most part, and I was envious as I swung one leg at a time, trying to keep the blood flowing and ward off the cold toes that I so dreaded.

Already tied together, about fifty feet of rope between us and the extra coiled over our shoulders, Rob and I had made it clear that we were a team of two, so Tim arranged his rope to join his team of three. Finally, around two, we began the gentle ski with skins up the Branscomb Glacier. In the sun, the temperatures were high enough that while climbing we could strip down to a base layer and a Gore-Tex shell on top, along with a balaclava and a baseball cap and omnipresent gloves, but as soon as a cloud would obscure the sun or I'd stop moving, I'd feel dangerously exposed to the cold and race to put on more layers. Because of the gradual incline, we chose to pull most of our gear behind us on sleds like we had on Denali, and it was in this manner, roped together to protect against a crevasse fall, that we snaked our way the six miles up to Camp I at just over 9,000 feet.

Unlike on Denali, though, even the simple act of peeing was complicated here. When the team in front of us needed to take its first pit stop, I watched as the members veered slightly right off the obvious route. They stayed roped together as the first guide of the season planted a bamboo wand to mark the spot and urinated at the base of it. On down the line they went, with each man shuffling forward once he was done. When it was our turn, Rob did as the others had while I scrambled to think of a way to avoid having to squat before an audience of my male teammates, who were rapidly approaching from behind. I decided to prop my backpack on the snow behind me and use my liter-size Nalgene pee bottle in relative privacy. When it was my turn to shuffle past the bamboo pole, I just unscrewed the top of my bottle and poured the contents onto the already-yellow snow.

Between the logistics of taking a simple pee break and the time it took to adjust clothing layers in the cold, Rob and I spent more time covering such a relatively short and easy distance than we had on any expedition. By the time we got to Camp I, it was already eight o'clock and we still had to make a cache for our high mountain food and fuel. The cold day had given way to a brutal evening, thanks to the shadow of the mountain, and the five of us spent an hour using our tree-pruning saw and avalanche shovels to pry blocks of hardened snow from the glacier.

"That's good enough," Tim declared after he put a couple of blocks of snow on top of the stuff sacks of food and gear that he and Hans and Brian had put in their pit. He removed the shovel blade from its shaft so that it would store more compactly in his backpack and prepared to ski back to base camp. Hans and Brian began to follow suit but looked confused when they saw that Rob and I continued to dig our storage pit. We wanted to bury our supplies like the treasure they were, not with the stuff sacks peeking through the cracks between some hastily piled blocks.

"I've been in the situation where my entire expedition has been ruined by losing a cache that wasn't buried deep enough," I said. "I'm going to cut and stack a few more blocks and we'll catch up on the ski down."

"It's fine the way it is," Tim said sternly. "We'll be back tomorrow."

"Tim, we don't know what the weather's going to do tomorrow," Rob said, "so just a little bit more work and it'll be safer. Really, you can start down. We know how to follow the tracks."

Apparently, Tim didn't trust us, so he stood there and watched as Rob and I finished and tied our empty sleds to our packs. A low-angle one-hour unroped ski back to base camp was a fun reward for the slow climb, but a heaviness had permeated our group dynamics that even skiing didn't erase.

They say tomorrow is another day, but in this case tomorrow was just another day of escalating tensions. After returning to Camp I and digging out our cache, the five of us began to set up a new camp. Rob and I knew from camping in Siberia and Alaska, and from the effort it had taken to bury our cache the day before, that it would take hours to saw and pry enough blocks of hardened polar snow from the glacier to make a decent wind barrier. While we worked, I offered to get the stove going.

"Perfect. Thanks," Rob said as he walked off a line in the snow to mark where he thought the camp walls should go. "And let's put the tent here."

"*No*," Tim said. "We are not starting the stoves until the tents are up."

Rob and I stared at each other in disbelief. It was an unprecedented experience for us that in a nonemergency situation of mountain teamwork, someone would speak in such a dominating way. His delivery aside, I worried about Tim's message. Why *wouldn't* we start the stove to melt water? It was cold and dry and we needed to stay hydrated while we worked. It made no sense to spend three hours setting up camp and then spend another three melting water and making hot drinks and food when we could do them at the same time. When we needed a break from the labor for a minute, we could check the stove, rehydrate, and then go back to work. This guy was not only mean-spirited but flat-out wrong, too, and that's a dangerous combination.

Rob and I tried to shrug off Tim's verbal lashing and continued to work on our tent site until about an hour later, when the sun went over the ridge and the temperature dropped enough that I couldn't take the foolishness of the situation anymore. But when I brought up the stove issue again, Tim shouted the same response at me, and it was clear to me that our guide's inability to operate efficiently in these conditions was threatening the safety and success of our expedition. And so was the rift in our team dynamics.

By the time we got our tents up and started the stoves, it was nine o'clock, and water bottles *still* hadn't been filled. As Rob and I waited for dinner in the dusk, with the sun having gone behind the massif above us, we hopped from one foot to another in an effort to keep the glacier from sucking the heat from the soles of our feet. Meanwhile, Tim sat in his position of power next to the two stoves in the back of the subterranean kitchen he'd designed that fit just two people. Even though there was no wind at the moment or any risk of precipitation, he'd covered the kitchen with a tarp fastened to the glacier at earth level, which made it hard to pass supplies around. We could only guess that Tim didn't trust anyone else to use the stoves, and I felt like I was standing in line for my dinner outside a soup kitchen.

Dinner was finally ready at eleven, and as soon as Rob and I finished eating, we retreated into our tents and vented.

"He's trying to kill us!" Rob said, only half-joking.

"I am not sharing a stove or kitchen with him ever again!" I said, not joking at all. As far as I was concerned, he'd driven the final nail into the coffin. I vowed to continue to keep my mouth shut, but the evening's events had made it easier for me to make a clean break with him if the time came.

Before bed, we smoothed our way toward sleep with a new ritual. The temperatures had just become the lowest we'd ever been exposed to—even lower than they'd been in Siberia in March, which I estimated would make it somewhere around forty below zero—and we carefully spread our 8,000-meter Himalayan down suits on top of our sleeping bags for extra warmth. With the arm of Rob's suit tied in a loose knot around the arm of my suit so that they wouldn't slide off, we fell into a warm and restful sleep.

As usual, though, I awoke in the middle of the night with a full bladder and had to leave our cocoon. I climbed out of my sleeping bag and pushed it out of the way as I carefully peed into my designated bottle. When I finished, I scurried back into my bag, zipped the bottle into its insulated holder and put it on the tent floor next to me. In the morning, I didn't want to get dressed to go out of the tent, so I pulled the bottle back out of the holder, but it was frozen solid. I was reminded of my third-grade teacher, who had a favorite saying she'd employ when students complained: "Life's not fair."

I hoped that wouldn't be the theme of our Antarctic adventure.

"NO ONE CAN MAKE ME LEAVE"

CARRYING A USELESS PLASTIC bottle filled with frozen urine seemed like a cruel reward for my first night ever spent sleeping in a tent at forty below (in Siberia we dug snow caves to protect against that kind of cold). But it paled against the risk of making a mistake while going number two wearing a full down suit and using the treaty-approved barrel system.

The next morning, we found that a few other teams had arrived to be our neighbors at Camp I, also known as low camp, and their tents were a similar hundred paces from the blue barrel that Margot had sledded into position the day before as promised. Just waiting in line to use it was awkward because you had to watch the person on the barrel toilet closely enough to see when he or she was finished while also granting some amount of "do unto others as you would have done unto you" privacy. While Rob and I were playing the waiting game at the circumference of the toilet zone, he struck up a conversation with Phil Ershler, a camp neighbor and professional guide.

"How do you know you're clear to 'go' with two base layers underneath this down suit?" Rob asked.

"Unzip the drop seat on your suit and pull it through to the front," Phil said. "Then reach through your legs and pull all your base layers through to the front also. When your balls hang free, then you're safe."

The emotion on the men's faces when they had to visit that toilet marked the first time in the mountains that I thought *they* actually had it harder than a woman when it comes to relieving yourself. We women are infinitely more used to squatting and making sure nothing's in our way.

Fortunately, though, we'd be leaving the barrel system behind when we left for high camp, because Margot hadn't had a chance to install it above the headwall that separates the lower Branscomb Glacier from Vinson's high camp. That climbing season, the professionally guided groups chose to make two camps below the headwall. This was a more conservative choice than making just one camp, because with the severely cold weather there's an inherent risk in being more than three or four hours from the safety of a sleeping bag in a tent. By using a second low camp, the teams could get right under the headwall to make a shorter "double carry" up to high camp, where the terrain was too steep to haul a sled. Like we'd done from base camp to Camp I, during a double carry climbers usually leave their tent and stove set up and put everything they might not need for the next day or two, such as extra food and fuel, into their packs. This extra gear is carried up to the next camp and put into a cache before the climbers return to their lower camp for the night. The next day, the remainder of their camp gets moved up. Under this plan, it would be at least three more days before these guided groups would be in position to go for the summit.

Not our group. Rob and I felt strong enough to move to high camp in one push and we suggested this approach partly in hopes that Tim would disagree and we could splinter off. But Tim agreed, so the five of us left our sleds behind and packed every single belonging inside or tied it to the outside of our sixty-five-liter backpacks and shouldered the abusive eighty-five-pound loads. I hoped Tim, Brian, and Hans would reconsider and stop at Low Camp II for the night, but as we skinned around the rock rib corner and past the other teams building Low Camp II, our team of five held tight.

Just beyond but still within sight of Low Camp II, the fairly flat Branscomb Glacier ran right into the steep headwall, and the incline of the slope quickly increased to forty-five degrees. Because of the angle, we were no longer able to move with skis and climbing skins on our feet and had to stop and add the ten pounds of ski weight to the packs. The result: The wicked load became downright evil. Even after taking out my crampons, it now weighed more than a bag of Portland cement, my maximum training weight, and I couldn't lift it by myself.

"Aargnnhh," I grunted as I tried to lift it by the straps enough to slide it onto my knee. If I could get it there, I could slide my right arm through the shoulder strap and twist and squat enough to get it onto my back, but I couldn't even get it to my knee. Rob stopped trying to put his own on and came over to help me lift it. While accepting the assistance, I made a silent vow. *I will not take this off until I get to high camp. If I do, I'll need help again, which could be dangerous for both of us on that steep slope.*

Tim continued to lead his clients on their rope team and insisted that Rob and I stay behind him, which was fine with me. I was grateful for *any* distance between us. His zigzag switchback route seemed to change angles haphazardly, going unnecessarily far in one direction before cutting back, so Rob and I occasionally made our own track. We also departed from the program by choosing not to clip into the snow pickets that a guide had placed earlier that day, and this kind of independent thinking was too much for Tim.

"Use the anchors!" he'd yell over his shoulder. "Stay in my track!"

It went on like this, similar to telling your mother "OK" even though you really mean "no way," for the entire 2,000 vertical feet of careful crampon footwork up the steep, icy headwall. When he saw that we weren't carrying out his wishes, he'd give us dirty looks but didn't push it, perhaps realizing that he'd pushed us too far the night before.

When we arrived at the next icefall section of the climb, the surface of the glacier became chaotically crevassed and full of ice that over the years had fractured into large columns called seracs that now threatened to collapse at any moment. Although an icefall is dangerous to climbers because it moves downhill faster than any other part of the glacier, it also has some flatter spots at the bottom of the seracs, and it was just this kind of easier terrain that I'd been holding out for to take a quick pee break. We'd been climbing for three hours since the last break, and my bladder threatened to let loose in my down suit. Even though I stood in a six-by-six-foot area of relative flat, I didn't want to risk being knocked off my feet by Rob's efforts to help me with the ridiculously sized pack. And I also didn't want to go back on my vow. There are only so many times you can ask for help on an expedition like this without losing your sense of strength and confidence, which can be even more dangerous than navigating a steep slope.

As soon as Tim and the others moved ahead, I took bold action: I unbuckled the hip belt on my pack, unzipped the rainbow-shaped drop seat on my down suit, and, in a weighted squat, pulled my down and wool layers through to the front and peed with my pack still on as Rob watched in amazement.

"I can't believe you just did that instead of asking for help," he said when I stood up.

I laughed out loud, as if to say, "Oh yes you can." He knows me well enough to imagine the conversation I'd had with myself.

Once safely out of the headwall and the icefall, we faced a new challenge that was more about mental stamina and less about technically precise climbing and pure strength than the challenges in the sections we'd just finished. An hour and a half of easy but undulating terrain separated us from our high camp, and our pace slowed now that we were exhausted from carrying the single loads up the slope for five hours. Fear also became part of the mix because of the severely cold wind we'd just begun to notice. Something had shifted in the weather as we approached the site of our new camp, probably because we were now on a higher glacier, only 3,000 feet below the summit. The wind cranked up to the point where, to be heard just a body's length away, I had to yell so loud that it hurt my throat.

We dropped our backpacks onto the snow and raced darkness to build a new camp from scratch. I quarried blocks while trying to quiet my anxiety about being caught outside at night in these conditions without a quick retreat. Rob stacked as I sawed, and we worked as hard as we could to stay efficient and focused. Meanwhile, Tim and the other two worked furiously on their site, which was adjacent to ours but close enough to tie the tent guy lines to each other in the middle of camp.

When Rob and I were almost finished with our portion of the horseshoe-shaped wall, we began to set the tent up. Had we done it any earlier, it would have blown far, far away. Concerned about the approaching nighttime temperatures, I took a break to light the stove, but the wind thwarted all my efforts. So I returned to helping Rob with the tent, and when we were reasonably confident that our high camp was secure, we all turned in.

"At least with this weather, there's no other stove option than cooking in the vestibule of our own tents," I said quietly as Rob and I began to unpack.

"Yeah, it's pretty obvious, but just so there's no hard feelings, I'm going to let him know that's the plan. Hey, Tim!" Rob shouted loud enough to be heard over the wind and through the nylon walls. "We have a stove, fuel bottle, and cook pot. It's so nasty out that we're going to cook in here."

We looked at each other with baited breath while Tim apparently deliberated.

"OK."

Relieved, we finished inflating our air mattresses, fluffed our sleeping bags, and settled into our private space. The new autonomy of cooking our own dinner and caring for ourselves reminded me of when Rob and I had first started living together and did whatever we wanted. Even though the storm had begun to rage outside, I was in heaven.

MORNING AT HIGH CAMP brought the realization that while our North Face four-season expedition tent had held up to the harsh winds, it provided only minimal protection from the fierce temperatures threatening our survival. I tried to lie as still as possible in my sleeping bag because when I'd move the slightest bit and touch a piece of fabric that hadn't been warmed by my body, I felt a sharp drop in my core temperature, like I'd just jumped into an icy lake. From this motionless position of relative comfort, I watched Rob suffer through the process of getting dressed because he absolutely had to go empty his pee bottle right that minute. The spot we had designated the night before for urine, toothpaste spittle, and gray water was only a hundred steps from our front door, but that morning the bamboo wand wasn't visible from the tent because of the snow riding the raging wind.

There was no use in our both going out into those conditions, but still I didn't see it coming when Rob said, "Hand me your pee bottle and I'll empty it."

We'd been on several extended expeditions together by now, but dumping each other's bottles was new territory. "Are you serious?" I asked as I searched for it inside the foot of my sleeping bag. *Man, am I glad I got that bottle melted out yesterday, although I guess it is creepy to cuddle my pee bottle all night.*

Rob sat at the entrance to the tent with an outstretched hand, so without asking twice I passed it over. "Thanks."

When he came back from emptying the bottles, he climbed back in just far enough to sit by the tent door and lit the stove to start the process of melting snow to make drinking water. I finally forced myself to sit up and steeled myself to say the right thing.

"I'll do that. You should get back in your bag and warm up."

"I'm already dressed," he said. "It's insane out there. I couldn't see a thing. There is no way we're going anywhere this morning, so you should just stay put."

As I remained curled up in a ball in my sleeping bag, I realized that I'd never had anyone wait on me like this. At home I'm always the first one up in the morning, and in the mountains we always take turns at the stove. Even on an "off" day, if I weren't the one cooking or melting snow, I'd still be doing something helpful like finding the food in the stuff sack and playing sous-chef. By the way, finding things in dozens of stuff sacks can be easier said than done, color-coded though they may be. Inside the sacks are Ziplocs hand-labeled with permanent marker—"tea," "salmon jerky," "powdered milk," "instant rice"—but things keep shifting as the plastic bags get repurposed for new, smaller portions destined for higher camps.

Rob handed me my favorite winter camping breakfast, a bowl of warm instant mashed potatoes with butter, salt, and pepper, and when I thanked him, I meant it more sincerely than he could have known.

"How about I take care of all this tomorrow and you can stay warm in bed?" I said. "I bet this storm isn't going anywhere fast."

"Sounds good. We're both going to have to go out there soon to dig the tent out, though. I could hardly see our wall, it's so filled with drifting snow." He turned his head in the direction of the other team's tent. "Hey, guys!" he shouted. "How are you doing over there?"

"We're fine," Tim answered. "Hell of a storm! How are you two?"

"We're good. Looks like a rest day today, except we should all go dig out camp pretty soon."

"Sounds good. The altitude on my watch is rising from last night, which means the barometer is dropping, so the storm might get worse."

A shift had taken place. Rob had expressed himself like an equal, and for the first time, Tim didn't pull a power play in response. There was hope that we'd be able to climb this mountain together after all.

❖

AFTER TWO DAYS OF waiting out the blizzard and no sign of any other groups, the five of us left high camp for a summit attempt in a haze of thin clouds that belied the static barometer reading. Steadfast cold temperatures and the steady but bearable wind weren't enough to keep us stuck in the tent for a third straight day. A rock outcrop ahead meant we had to either go up a steeper section on the climber's right or take a lower-angle wraparound to the climber's left that meant covering a bit more distance. At the bottom of the steeper choice, I could see the open crevasse.

It could be a waste of energy to try going up this slope, since it looks too steep to skin in this firm snow. Whenever a slope is this steep after a flat zone, you know there are bigger crevasses because the glacier is pulling away from the angle more abruptly. Why is no one talking about the options? Am I the only one thinking this? What if we top out here and it doesn't "go"? Then we have to go around anyway. We should just go around the longer way.

But Tim had already started up in this direction, and I decided to keep my mouth shut long enough to see if he could make it. Without ski crampons, he didn't get very far, though, and then I saw Rob attach his crampons to his bindings and skin past Tim for twenty paces until he slipped, too. I inhaled the cold air quickly and held my breath as I watched Rob slide from higher up, unroped, on his side down through the crevasse field. When he came to a stop without falling into a hole, I breathed again and fought the angry urge to tell him he should have known it was too steep and icy to skin. *That wouldn't serve any purpose, Kit. What's more important than the fact that he didn't get hurt?*

When he was safely back on his feet, my thoughts turned to our next move. *Now we'll have to go around the way I thought we should have in the first place. Damn, it's so hard to communicate with this group. I'm trying to only speak my mind if it's wicked important, and I almost blew it there.*

The five of us proceeded to snake our way around the longer lower-angle section and soon found ourselves in a windstorm that was every bit as intense as what we'd lived through the previous two days. Apparently, we'd begun the day's climb when we were in the eye of the storm. This low-pressure system clearly wasn't done with us.

For three hours, we persevered through low visibility up the gentle twenty-five-degree glacier. The grayish outline to our right that was the west shoulder of Vinson Massif was the only thing we could see that wasn't white. We also weren't getting close enough to it to tell whether we'd covered a decent amount of ground. The wind and the cold bit through the two layers of balaclava on my face, my fingers were frozen inside my down mittens, and I hadn't felt my toes since watching Rob slide past the crevasse.

"This is insane! Let's go down!" I yelled to anyone who could hear me.

"Yeah, we're still only halfway to the top!" Rob shouted back.

The other three agreed.

The wind and the cold were even worse than what we'd endured the day of our first Denali summit attempt the year before, and I was reminded of a well-known mountain-climbing saying: "It's not the summits that will kill you. It's the summit attempts."

Close enough to hear each other, we took off our packs and dropped them on the glacier to begin the transition from crampons to skis for the descent to camp. Trying to expediently remove the crampons and get our climbing skins off our skis and into our packs, unzip our neoprene overboots to reach the ski-boot buckles and put them into ski mode, and click into our bindings while trying to protect frozen fingers and toes was a game of mental discipline we all had to win in order to live. Expletives were cried out all around as we dealt with the pain from the cold, and despite the urgent need for speed, we had to take multiple seconds-long breaks to feverishly swing our arms in an attempt to restore blood flow and sensation.

After a few minutes that felt like hours, Hans, Brian, Rob, and I had our packs on, our ski poles in our hands, and our skis on our feet and were facing downhill, ready to go. Inexplicably, though, Tim had a long way to go. His pack was still on the ground, and he was bent over his ski boots messing with the buckles. And as for his skis, they weren't even on his feet. At minus thirty degrees and with a wind speed of thirty miles an hour, the wind chill computes to minus sixty-seven degrees and it takes less than five minutes for frostbite to set in. After five minutes of waiting for Tim to get his system working, he still wasn't ready.

"What's wrong?" I shouted. "It's too dangerous to wait here any longer!"

He looked up with a vacant stare. "I'm having a hard time getting my boot into ski mode."

Rob's skiing skills are so advanced that he wouldn't hesitate to ski a forty-five-degree pitch with a ski boot in walk mode, and I could see his surprise that Tim was holding us up instead of simply skiing this low-angle slope with one boot more flexible than the other.

"Dude, we're really cold," he said. "We have to go. Just ski with it like that."

Tim just bent over and went back to work.

Hans and Brian looked at us with confused expressions. I was so cold that I was almost beyond shivering, and I knew this amount of exposure could soon turn deadly.

"If he doesn't pull it together quickly, I'm out of here," I said quietly enough that Tim wouldn't hear me. "Anyone who wants to wait for him can, but I can't wait much longer." With that I skied a few feet downhill for emphasis.

When I stopped and looked back, I heard Hans say to Tim, "Let's go. I'm cold. Do you really need to do that?"

Tim didn't move.

"This is way too dangerous," Brian said. "I can't feel my hands or feet."

I took Tim's lack of response as his move in a game of life-or-death chess and skied a few more feet downhill. I was making my position clear: I wouldn't risk my safety anymore for his selfish choices. Showing their preference for preserving their own lives, Hans and Brian skied up beside me while Rob made the move that would pose the least risk for everyone's lives at that critical moment.

He sidestepped over to Tim, reached down and engaged his boots into ski mode then guided Tim's boots into his bindings. When he'd finished helping Tim, Rob skied over to me and said, "There was nothing wrong with his system. I don't think he ever tried his overboots before!" As a pack, the four of us made a few turns then looked back to see Tim finally skiing toward us, his overboot still unzipped.

A quick ski descent on hard snow to high camp at two o'clock meant we were back in relative safety with many hours left in the day for the dance of heating snow for water and systematically drying our gear. No one spoke of the danger we'd narrowly averted, but the knot that had formed in my stomach in response to our supposed guide's inability to make good decisions and move efficiently in the mountains had turned into a fist with an iron grip. Was this the second time I'd felt like he tried to kill us, or the third?

Back in the sanctuary of our tent, Rob and I started our routine. The person sitting closest to the stove would fill our two half-liter water bottles with near-boiling water and hand them to the person at the back of the tent, who by then would have spread the four boot liners and four down mittens on the sleeping bags. Rob was usually the one at the stove, and I was usually the one drying the gear because I'd perfected the technique. It went like this: Put the hot-water bottle into the ski-boot liner or mitten just long enough that the material to be dried would gain enough heat from the water bottle that, when the bottle was pulled out, some of the moisture would turn to vapor. It was an advanced dance skill that involved at least two partners, multiple pieces of gear, and dozens of movements of a water bottle between the fabrics in order to keep the most possible moisture evaporating while the least amount of heat possible was lost from the bottle. By the time I'd done what I considered a good enough job that we wouldn't freeze our feet and hands the next time we had to wear our gear, Rob had served us tea, made our dinner of miso soup with ramen noodles, and refilled our remaining water bottles for the night. Finally, with the day's work done and our gear stowed in the feet of our sleeping bags, we could go to bed.

As I drifted toward sleep, I found myself thinking about the other teams tucked below the headwall at Low Camp II and how we'd just finished our third full day at high camp. The others might not summit if it didn't clear enough tomorrow for them to make their first load carry to high camp. For that matter, we might not summit either if it didn't clear tomorrow. Today was the last day of November, and as ALE had let us know, the plane would come to get everyone at base camp on the morning of December 5, summit or not.

I also found myself wondering why I hadn't heard Tim make radio contact with anyone while we were isolated here at high camp. I'd definitely be looking into that tomorrow.

THE FIRST DAY OF December was a lot like the three days that had preceded it: cold, windy, and stormy. The main difference was that on those days, the storm had stayed outside our tent. On this day, we awoke to find a dusting of snow on everything inside and a film of condensation on the yellow nylon walls and ceiling from our breathing overnight. Horrified at the prospect that the moisture would creep into our survival gear, we began to make a plan.

"We need a whisk broom to sweep the tent out," Rob said. Then he remembered a notecard-size piece of cardboard he'd found in our almost-empty food bag. "Stay inside your sleeping bag while I start with the ceiling on your side. I'll scrape the rime from above your head and off your bag, then you do the same above mine. That way we can keep it out of our sleeping bags."

Once we'd swept from the back to the front of the tent and tossed the grapefruit-size ball of snowy debris outside, it was time to face the facts: Today was the fourth day in a row that was not going to be a summit day. This was at least a four-day storm, and although we had plenty of fuel, we'd brought only four days' worth of food up to high camp. Yesterday, both tent groups had scaled back to half rations, but the provisions we'd come to high camp with had already been light, so even with the cutback we'd run out of some things. Over a breakfast drink of hot water and a single chocolate-covered espresso bean each, Rob and I discussed the options.

"Remember when ALE showed that photo of high camp back in Punta Arenas?" I said. "They pointed out where previous teams had buried a cache of food and fuel just behind here. I know that no one is supposed to plan on using it, and no one is allowed to leave anything anymore, but I think we should try to find it today."

Rob nodded. "We should do it this morning because if we can't find it, we should probably go down as soon as the weather lets up. But I think we should try to ask permission."

"Hey, Tim, we're almost out of food," I hollered over.

"Us, too," he answered.

"What do you think of radioing base camp and asking Margot if we can dig up that old cache?"

"Yeah, we should probably ask first, and I am supposed to check in anyway."

Just as I'd expected.

As we chewed on the espresso beans, we overheard parts of his communication with Margot: "Yeah, we're fine. Sorry…I thought I only had to call if we needed help… OK. Hey, we're out of food, though. Is it OK if we dig up the cache and just take what we need?… Cool, thanks… Yeah, we'll check in tomorrow at eight p.m."

After he got off the call, he updated us. "She said it was OK under the circumstances and that it was minus thirty-five degrees with seventy-mile-an-hour winds down at base camp the past few days. Everyone else is sitting tight at Camp II and they were worried about us, but I told her we were fine."

"Oh my God," I said quietly to Rob. "If it was that cold 7,000 feet below us, I'm glad we had no way to measure it here." Obviously, it had been colder than the forty below I'd estimated.

"No doubt. Well, if we can't find the cache, then at least we know Vern's group has food up here, although we don't want to touch that unless we really have to. They're planning on coming up to use it, I'm sure."

"We'll find it," I said confidently. "I'm not leaving until I make this climb and ski."

"What do you mean you aren't leaving? The plane picks us up at base camp on the fifth in time to get us to Patriot Hills for the Ilyushin plane that night. The dates are what they are."

"Yeah, but I've been thinking… So much money went into this trip and it's only possible at one time of year." This had been on my mind since I woke up and saw that we were in for another snow day. I couldn't leave without summiting. "I could never ask for more money to come back here. It's so expensive. I just realized today that I can stay and climb when the second group is coming through if that's what I have to do. No one can make me leave."

Rob laughed nervously, probably because he knew that when I become this adamant about something, I have a hard time seeing any other perspective. "I'm not staying if that's what happens," he said. "Just relax and let's see."

I'd begun to feel as if my usual technique of visualizing success wasn't enough to get up and down this mountain. The thought crept into my head that I needed to project my intention to the powers of the universe with more clarity, so I did.

I am going to stay here until I climb and ski Vinson Massif.

But Rob's advice also crept into my head, and I could feel myself soften. A little.

But I know he's right—relax and don't even think about another fifteen days at this high camp! Remember to let the serendipity of being in tune with the mountains just happen. Maybe you're at the end of the surprises on this mountain and you'll have success soon. Focus on finding that cache and moving in harmony with what's right in front of you.

We did find the cache that day, and discovering that buried bag filled with instant soups, drink mixes, and a couple of candy bars left behind decades ago by foreign climbers was as exciting as if they'd been gold coins. I could only guess at the nationality of our food benefactors, because the writing on the soup packages looked German or Norwegian or Dutch or—it just didn't matter. Except for the Snickers from 1979, the printing on the labels was faded, but the calories did the trick.

After eating, we rested as the storm persisted through the afternoon. Eventually, we shoveled our camp out again, perversely grateful for something to do.

COMMITTED AND CLEAR

A S ANOTHER DAY DAWNED on Vinson, I felt the alpha rising in me, and I recalled a morning during my time in Ophir, Colorado, with Alta. Our routine was to go for a run on the trails and mining roads early every morning regardless of the season and then do it again when I came home from work. I figured that if he could get enough exercise with me, he'd be content to hang out on the porch for the rest of the day, and I turned out to be right. Until the sheep came through town.

On the other side of 11,800-foot Ophir Pass, sheep graze on the grassy meadows for most of the short summer before they're herded down the pass in September. Although the sheep stay on national forest land, the boundary is adjacent to Ophir and they usually spend a couple of days grazing by the pond on the lower side of town, which could be seen from our front porch. The day the herd arrived during our second year in town, I let Alta's girlfriend, a neighbor dog named Osa, stay inside with him and told my roommates not to let them out while I was at work. The house was home to four twenty-somethings, though, which meant lots of opening and closing of the door, and when I got home Alta and Osa were gone. I called their names and ran down the steps to the basement garage, where I could hear the grinding of tools that told me my housemate Andy was working in his wood shop.

"Have you seen Alta?"

"Yeah, I let them out a few minutes ago."

That's right—Andy wasn't home when I told everyone to keep the dogs inside. "Oh my God! The sheep are still here and they were supposed to stay inside!"

I ran down the dirt road past four more houses until the road took a left, and I stayed on the grassy hill above the pond and above the sheep. When I slowed down to survey the situation, I saw that Alta and Osa were stealthily approaching the sheep, moving from shrub to shrub to close the gap as much as possible before they would be exposed on the 200-foot stretch of grass separating them. Two hundred feet also separated *me* from Alta and Osa, and I likewise tried to close the gap.

Ultimately, I felt like I was cutting it too close, and before I could reach them I bellowed from the bottom of my being.

"*Alta! Osa! Nooooo! Stop!*"

Without taking their eyes off the sheep, they settled onto their haunches. Then they turned their heads and looked at me and then back at the sheep. Then back at me and back at the sheep.

"*Come here. Now!*" To be that loud, I'd had to stand still and use all of my core muscles, but now I began to walk toward them. Osa got up and trotted in my direction, but Alta jumped up and ran at the sheep.

My instincts kicked in and I raced down the unmanicured slope dotted with marmot holes and ankle-twisting rocks. I felt as if I'd never run that fast, even during my days on the high-school track team. From the corner of my eye, I saw the door to the sheepherder's silver travel trailer open and a man emerge. I knew that he'd have a gun and wouldn't hesitate to shoot at whatever was threatening his sheep.

Three hundred sheep had been clustered on the uphill side of the pond, but as Alta approached they began to scatter. I pictured his jaws latching on to a woolly throat, and my legs seemed to fly the last hundred feet. There was no logical way I could have reached him before he'd singled out one of the sheep and attacked, but I did.

To our mutual surprise—his at having been caught, mine at the power I'd harnessed—I jumped on him, growled, and bit him on the ear.

Remorse set in immediately, and I checked to make sure I hadn't drawn blood, all the while avoiding making eye contact with him. Wolves look each other in the eye only during regular interactions; when they fight or discipline each other, they avert their gaze. I wanted it to be absolutely clear that this was discipline.

I dug my fingers into the skin on the back of his neck and grabbed enough of him to drag him uphill. As he tried to wriggle out of my grasp, his razor-close call with death at the herder's hands played out in my mind again. I knew I had to make this lesson crystal clear to prevent him from doing something like this again, and I kicked his haunches so hard that he cried out and urinated on himself. As much as it must have hurt, though, it hurt me more. Without slowing, I growled and kept my right hand on the scruff of his neck and marched him toward the house. The tip of his tail was between his legs and I knew I'd made my point, but my heart was still racing and my entire being was shaking.

Holy shit, Kit. Where did that come from?

My instincts had told me I needed to teach Alta a lesson in his own language, just as I had by taking meat away from him over and over when he was a pup. I believed that any response short of what I'd done wouldn't have prevented him from killing a sheep and getting killed himself, but at the same time, I'd scared myself with my actions.

When we got back to the dirt road through town, I loosened my grip on Alta's neck and we walked home side by side. I'd succeeded, for the moment, in honoring my vow to protect him from harm for being a wolf in a human's world, but I had the sense that we couldn't go back to normal yet. Drawing on both my knowledge of wolf behavior and my instinct, I decided to ostracize him for a while to give the lesson time to sink in. At home, I found the webbing collar that I kept handy for our occasional walks down Main Street in Telluride and put it around his neck. Next I found a piece of rebar in Andy's shop and pounded it into the ground and fastened a long piece of cable to it. After clipping Alta's collar to the cable, I gave him a bowl of water and, without meeting his gaze, growled again to let him know I was still upset. Osa tried to keep him company, but he just sulked and lay down.

The next day, the sheep remained at the pond and Alta remained defiant in his demeanor, so I brought him more water and some food, still without looking at him, and left him on the leash. He must have been miserable—I've often said that if you want to know what it's like for a wolf to be tied up, put a collar on and tie *yourself* up in the yard—but he wasn't willing to negotiate for his freedom yet.

Early the next morning, the sheep were gone and I took Alta off the leash. He responded by looking straight into my eyes, giving me an audible "hmmmmppffh," and climbing up the mountain above our house. Without saying a word, I watched him go. I knew he needed time alone after feeling so humiliated.

For the rest of the day, I could see him sitting up there, and my heart ached with fear of the distance I'd put between us. I passed a lonely night knowing that the place where *he* preferred to spend the night was far from me.

The next day, I went outside and howled a long mournful howl up the mountain. I didn't see any movement, though, and my only panicked thought was "What if he doesn't come back? What if he doesn't want to give up his new freedom?"

Endless minutes later, he finally came prancing back to the house in the happy manner that had inspired one of his many nicknames, Twinkle Toes. ("Wolfie" and "Woo" were other favorites.) Overjoyed, I hugged him and gave him one of his favorite treats, a partially thawed block of lamb and rice, and then led him on a run along our favorite route, to Waterfall Canyon. We'd forgiven each other, and the crisis was over.

Fearful of a repeat of the same agonizing situation, I asked around town the next September about the sheep's expected arrival. I learned that they always came through on a Saturday, and I got my roommates on board with a plan to keep Alta inside on Saturdays until the herd's annual migration had passed—for real this time. Imagine my shock as I stood at the picture window early on a Friday morning and saw 500 head of sheep trudging along the national forest boundary just 150 feet from our house. Adrenaline coursing through my veins, I threw the sliding glass door open and was about to yell Alta's name when I saw him sitting proudly on the edge of the porch, staring at the procession without moving a muscle.

I exhaled through a wide smile and reached my arms around his ninety-pound body for a hug. "Good job, Alta," I said as I sat next to him, and he leaned his shoulder against mine.

Sometimes, particularly in life-or-death situations, I feel like I have no choice but to be the alpha among my fellow humans, just as I'd been with Alta. I'd had to do it with Rob on Denali, and when it happened with Tim on Vinson, the role felt familiar and I didn't shy away from it. After all, with freedom comes responsibility, as they say, and in order to appreciate the great freedom that an Antarctic expedition affords, taking responsibility is critical. Everyone's safety depends on it. In our case, summiting depended on it, too, and on our tenth day on Vinson, I woke up determined to do whatever it took to reach my goal while also making sure we all got down safely.

And the weather seemed to grant me its blessing. From inside the tent, there was no wind to be heard, and when Rob poked his head outside, he confirmed it: The sky was a gentle, misty white. The storm was over.

"Hey, you guys," Rob called to Tim and Hans and Brian in the tent next door. "It looks good. How about we be ready to go at nine thirty?"

Zip, zip, zip of a sleeping bag, a tent door, and a tent vestibule.

"Yeah! Sounds good!" Tim answered.

So far, the moderate difficulty of this climbing route had been very similar to what we'd encountered on the West Buttress of Denali, and today's hazy sky on Vinson had the same overcast character that Rob and I had experienced on our Denali summit day. The thin veil of clouds left over after the four-day storm contributed to an inversion, a condition where the temperature of the atmosphere increases with altitude as opposed to the normal decrease. If the average summer temperature on Vinson from November through March is twenty below zero and we'd just survived forty below, today was our lucky day. It felt like fifteen below or even warmer as we headed out from camp with crampons on our ski boots and skis on our backpacks. I was warm enough for the first time in a week to unzip the neck of my down suit. That said, my face was still 90 percent covered by a balaclava, and our ski boots were wrapped in blue overboots made of 4.7mm neoprene and closed-cell foam insulation.

Putting one foot in front of the other while gliding our skis uphill was the only technical skill required for the first three and a half hours on summit day on the twenty-five- to thirty-degree slope. During the first two of those hours, we made decent progress, but then Tim began stopping often for short breaks, and when he *was* moving, it was at a slower pace than it would take to get to the summit in the expected six-hour climbing window. With me in the lead on the rope I shared with Rob, even at a slow pace I got a hundred feet ahead of Tim at one point and heard the standard sharp scold behind me: "Stay behind!"

Aaarrghh! Is he serious? Why?! At this rate we'll never make it to the top. I wonder if he has any clue. I'm tired of him being a liability, because that's what he is. So many poor decisions, ineptitude with his gear, slow transitions, late starts, and now he may be truly sick.

Wanting to avoid confrontation, I stopped and let Tim lead his team ahead again, and then I started walking slowly as soon as Hans pulled up alongside me. He and Brian were tied in at thirty-foot intervals behind Tim.

"Hey, Tim's really dragging," I said. "At this pace we're going way too slow to safely make the summit. Do you know what's wrong with him?"

"Yeah, I see that, but I have no idea what's wrong," Hans said. "What should we do?"

"I don't know, but we have to do something. How about we try to take some weight out of his pack?"

"I can easily carry more. I'm feeling good." Hans was a strong and experienced mountain climber, the greatest asset among Tim's team.

"Me, too. Will you tell him? He seems to fight me."

"Hey, Tim! Hold up! It looks like your pack is too heavy. What's in it?" Hans bravely inquired. "Can we carry something?"

Tim didn't argue with Hans or otherwise assert himself, and I took this as a sign of an altered mental status. He stopped, took his pack off, and set it on the snow. He dug around in it and pulled out the first-aid kit and the GPS. Being the one with wilderness medical training, I reached for the gigantic red medical kit and stuffed it inside my pack while Hans took the heavy GPS. When we started walking again, Tim seemed only slightly better.

An hour passed this way, with Rob and me getting ahead of Tim's team and having to stop again and again until they caught up. Finally, I motioned for Rob to come stand with me. As he approached, I pulled the rope in so he would remain on belay.

"We're almost to the bottom of the pitch we want to ski," I said quietly, "so if we're going to climb it, then we have to talk about it with these guys *now*."

After climbing above the Branscomb Glacier via the icefall and making Camp II above the Vinson-Shinn Col, the normal route up the northwest side of Vinson Massif trends southward for three miles and an elevation gain of 2,700 feet until it veers left for access to the rocky summit ridge and the final thousand feet of climbing. At least that's what we'd been told and had seen on the map. But Rob and I weren't interested in skiing a route that included a rock ridge as long as there was a more aesthetic option. We'd set our sights on a beautiful north-facing line of snow to the climber's right that steepened into a forty-five-degree passage through some rock walls and continued east right to the summit. Compared with the normal route, this option was more compelling, more direct, slightly more difficult, and a far more logical choice for skiing. Once or twice over the previous week we'd gingerly suggested it to the others, but none of them seemed to care which way they went to the top. The closest thing to a commitment we could get was a response like, "If it looks good on summit day, then maybe."

Now we were at the point where, if we followed the normal route any farther, we'd pass by the logical entrance to our line. Tim was obviously in no condition to attempt any route even slightly more difficult than the standard one, and it was debatable whether he should be going uphill at all at this point. Hans and Brian were relying on him to be their guide in all ways, so the three of them would be sticking together whether they continued up the normal route or returned to camp without a summit. It was time to tell Tim we were going our own way.

"You tell him," I said to Rob. "I'm afraid he's going to try to tell us not to go, and I don't want to be in that position. You're so much better at this type of thing."

"OK." Rob smiled, well aware of his ability to manipulate others into seeing things the way he wants them to.

I watched him work his magic with Tim as I explained the situation to Hans. "Rob and I are going to climb that line and ski it. We'll hopefully see you on the summit. Watch out for Tim—I'm still worried about him. Don't let him make a bad decision that affects you, too." I handed him the medical kit just in case.

"Got it. See you up there," Hans said. "But if we don't make it, don't wait for us. We'll see you here on this football field on the way down or back at camp."

With that, our rope went taut. Rob had veered over to our chosen line and begun to lead up it. The side-by-side dance of the two rope teams was over.

After we crossed the bergschrund that separated the glacier from the headwall and moved onto the steep snow, we stopped to remove the rope and take a quick break.

"How'd you do it?" I asked.

"Do what?" Rob said.

"Talk Tim into letting us go this way without a fight."

"We've earned his respect and he knows he's in no position to argue with us. He just said to be careful and I said, 'Of course.'"

The relentless winds of this polar region had made the snow so hard that the front points of our crampons didn't even make a mark on most of our steps up to the summit. To say it was ice would be stretching the truth, but it wasn't exactly snow either. If it's true that the Eskimos have more than a hundred words to describe snow, this was a perfect example of why so many are needed.

As we leaned into our ice axes to pull a final steep move onto the flat zone a few feet below the summit, Hans and Brian were waiting for us. They'd just traded turns on the small summit perch, which was still marked with a ski pole from the 1979 survey expedition.

"Where's Tim?" I asked.

"He's on the ridge," Hans said. "I think he's still coming this way, but we passed him about twenty minutes ago and said we'd pick him up on the way down if he didn't make it."

"How long have you been here?" Rob asked.

"Only five minutes."

In the distance, Tim's figure slowly approached.

"How's he doing?" I said.

"He left his skis at the beginning of the rock ridge, but I think he's OK," Brian said.

Though the view was partially obscured by the slowly lifting clouds that still lingered from the five-day storm, the continent's highest peaks shone through, and it felt wonderful to be on top of Vinson with Rob and have a real ski descent ahead of us without any more angst about the guide situation. Against a background of unbroken white—it was impossible to tell where the land below ended and the mist began—he took photos of me skiing off the summit before I sidestepped with my skis back up to the flat spot and returned the favor.

We traded cameras with Hans and Brian and took group photos, and then Rob and I stepped back into our ski bindings as Tim approached a full fifteen minutes after we'd arrived. With his camera dangling wild and free in front of the unzipped neck of his down suit and his ski poles in his hands, he looked like an Antarctic tourist. While it was a humorous sight, the fact that he'd left his pack below signified that his condition had deteriorated since we'd seen him last and that he was pushing the limits of safe climbing to be standing there. This wasn't the place anyone in his condition should be, and now Hans and Brian would have to take over as guides and lead him down.

"We're going to film all the way down," Rob told the others, "so even though our line is more direct, I'm guessing we'll probably be back to the football-field area about the same time. Let's regroup there."

I was filled with relief to be pushing off on skis in the other direction, away from the drama, but I was also scared. The extreme hardness of the snow surface showed next to no sign of our having climbed from that direction. If our crampons didn't even leave a mark, how were our ski edges going to hold?

Rob had gone first so he could film me, and I looked down toward the zone on the skier's left where I'd go if I slipped. I forced myself to focus on my breathing and make perfectly controlled turns until I reached Rob. I was pleasantly surprised to find that the snow was like cold Styrofoam with a decent, if thin, edge grip. Rob put the camera in his pack before he skied ahead again, and we leapfrogged like this the whole way down.

It was a different kind of exercise in patience for me, because I'd rarely been filmed skiing, but I was pleased that Rob wanted to document me with his fifty-year-old hand-crank Swiss Bolex, the same camera he'd been using when we met in Siberia. Whenever he said, "Rolling!" I tried my best to turn with powerful angulation that would look good for the camera and keep me safely in control on the forty-five-degree slope. While skiing that steep icy section, Rob had to change rolls of film three times, each with surgical precision inside the dark room of his backpack as we kept our steel ski edges still and wedged into the slope.

When we arrived at the lower-angle section, at least an hour had passed since we'd left the summit, and the other three glided up on cue as if they were having a great ski day.

"Follow Kit!" Rob shouted, keeping the camera rolling.

I led the way, making ski turns around the few obvious crevasses and trying to stay in a strong stance over the frozen-solid waves of wind-redeposited snow that covered the glacier. When the skiing was low-angled and easy, I took in the view, and there seemed to be a ring of clouds below the glaciers as far as the eye could see, but I knew that it wasn't all clouds—I was also seeing the surface of Antarctica. Straight across from us was the alluring pyramidal summit of Mount Shinn, which, though only slightly lower than Vinson, looked like an untouchable island separated by dangerous cold. In fact, the whole continent was strikingly beautiful, yet isolated in a way I hadn't fully comprehended before. It's not just about being thousands of feet across the ocean with no organized rescue options or easy retreat; any peak in the Ellsworth Mountains, and any climbing camp on Vinson for that matter, is an island of isolation, with the passages between them full of extreme-cold consequences.

We glided into high camp at six o'clock after skiing more than three miles and nearly 4,000 vertical feet from the summit. The members of the professionally guided team that had made a carry to high camp during the first day of the storm were now hard at work building snow walls and setting up their tents.

"Congratulations. What was it like to open the route?" a climber asked us.

I'd never thought about the fact that we'd been the first team on the summit for the climbing season.

"It didn't feel to me like we opened the route," I said as I opened my pack and began to toss empty water bottles and other gear into our tent. "It just felt normal except we were really lucky with an inversion today. It was pretty warm compared to the past few days."

Alpine Ascents International guide Vern Tejas, a legendary Alaskan mountaineer, wandered over. "You're the first woman to ski from the summit, aren't you?"

I smiled and hoped that would be enough of an answer.

"We think so," Rob said.

"I do, too," Vern said. "I've looked into it, and there was a woman that used to work as a guide for ALE who skied from this high camp back to base camp once, but I haven't found any reports of a woman skiing from the summit."

During the mandatory meeting in Punta Arenas, ALE had announced that if I were successful, I would be the first woman to ski it. I hadn't wanted the attention then and felt the same now, so I was glad that no one else strayed from camp chores to come talk about it. As a guide interested in the history of the mountains where he worked, Vern wanted to acknowledge what had happened today, which was fine, but that's as far as I wanted it to go. I couldn't afford to let any hubris settle in. We weren't finished yet. There was still a lot of mountain ahead of us.

TIRED, WE WOKE TO beautiful blue skies and calm air the next morning. Without any need to hurry, we began to melt snow for water just as the others were departing for their summit climb at nine. It wasn't until two thirty that Rob and I left high camp on our skis, headed for the icefall with all our gear jammed into huge packs and, not surprisingly, ahead of Tim and his team.

When we stopped to look into the initial technical section of the icefall, I became nervous about the first five-foot drop I'd have to make with crevasses to both sides.

"I think we should rope up here," I said.

"OK," Rob said. "I feel better without the rope myself, but I'll belay you."

Damn him. This is scary. I wished he would take a belay, too, but then, he's a better skier than I am, and actually he was right. I knew I could do this without a rope, too. It was just the what-if with all the little drops, funky icy spines, holes, and wicked firm conditions. It almost felt like my skis could break just landing this first tiny air with all the weight on my back, and then I'd be screwed.

As it turned out, I was proud of the speed with which we moved uneventfully through the icefall even with Rob giving me several simple hip belays as he sat and fed the rope out. When I got through a spicy zone, I stopped and watched Rob ski toward me while I coiled the rope in my hands as fast as I could to keep it out of his way. On the easy sections, we skied at the same time, with each of us holding the rope up out of our way with one hand alongside our ski poles.

It was the first time I'd ever used a rope on a ski descent, and in the end we didn't really need it. We passed the icefall section and entered the steep headwall in less than ten minutes. Since Rob had the extra weight of the Bolex, I stuffed our rope into the top of my pack, which now stood taller than my head when it was on my back. It weighed only sixty-five or seventy pounds now, nothing compared with the beast I'd carried up this pitch but still a heavy load for skiing. Luckily, the headwall had the best snow of the mountain, probably because of the thirty- to fifty-foot-tall seracs in the icefall above that shielded *some* wind and left *some* snow on the surface. Confident about this terrain, I skied right down almost on top of Rob as he filmed me.

"Will you sidestep back up and ski that again?" he said.

What?!

"I want to take still photos, too. That was rad!"

Oh sure, Rob, resort to flattery.

I stayed on the skier's right of the climbing line, far out of the way of the guided teams making their final carries to high camp, and sidestepped up a hundred feet and skied it again for the camera.

After that one extra pitch, I really was done with the technical sections of the mountain, so Rob and I waited comfortably at the bottom of the headwall and watched as Tim, Hans, and Brian down-climbed into view through the icefall. They switched from crampons to skis at the bottom of the icefall and made turns on the skier's left of the climbers. Then we all regrouped and skied to low camp, retrieved our cached plastic sleds, and repacked our loads into them for the low-angle glide to base camp, where we pulled in at seven thirty.

Within five minutes of our arrival, Margot was at our side with the box of red wine and five steaks, one for each of us, that we'd heard she gives to all climbers when they return from the summit. As we drank from our insulated mugs of wine and set up the tents, I could feel some of the pressure that had built up over the past week dissipate. When Rob and I went back for refills, Margot invited us into her hut even though no one was supposed to be allowed in.

"What happened up there?" she asked as we huddled in the one-bunk room. "Why didn't Tim call me for three days like he was supposed to?"

"I have no idea," I said. "We had no idea he was supposed to be checking in regularly from high camp. Thankfully, by then we weren't sharing a tent and the storm was so bad that we didn't see him much. He's a total yahoo."

She let out a belly laugh. "I wondered. I was worried about you guys. It was colder down here than any other time I've done this job, and

I've done it for three years. Minus thirty-five degrees and winds at seventy miles an hour here at base. Well, good work up there, especially you, Kit. Congrats. It's awesome that you got the first ski descent for women!" She raised her mug. "Cheers."

The next day, I lay in bed not caring what time anyone else woke up. I had a headache from the wine, and my toes were swollen from the mild case of frost nip that they'd endured on summit day. Or summit-attempt day. Or yesterday. I guess it could have been a combination of all three. I dusted baby powder on my feet and put them into dry socks and then back into my sleeping bag.

Hans and Brian, still in their beds in the tent next door, were talking excitedly about the start of the ski season back at Snowbird. It was December 4, and they'd been busy that morning using their personal satellite phone to check in with their wives about snow conditions and the details of life back home. And, with no choice but to overhear, I knew that Brian's wife was asking him for suggestions about their car, which wouldn't start. My future seemed a world apart from theirs, and even from Rob's, as I contemplated my next move.

When they were done with the phone, Hans shouted over to our tent, "When are your flights home? What are you doing next?"

I gave Rob a pleading look, and he knew what to do.

"I'm flying home, but Kit's going to climb Aconcagua."

I still hadn't told anyone about the Seven Summits project, and I was clinging to whatever secrecy I could still maintain.

"No way. Really? Are you going to ski it, too?"

"That's my plan," I said, thankful for the tent walls separating us.

"Who are you going with?"

"A friend from the North Face athlete team who works as a guide on the mountain." Rob couldn't go, because of obligations at the hotel.

That was more than even my parents knew. When I'd told them about the Antarctic trip, they asked when they should expect me home.

"Either around December 5 or Christmastime," I said.

"That's a big difference," Dad said.

"I know. Depending on conditions, I might go climb another mountain on my way home, but I won't know until I get back from Antarctica."

They didn't ask any more, probably because they didn't want to worry any more than they already were. Beyond Rob and my sponsor and now these guys, no one else knew what was next for me, and I hoped to keep it on the down-low. Luckily, after the teams that had summited last night returned to base in the late afternoon, everyone was so busy packing that no one brought up the details of our ski descent or asked what was next. Actually, the most immediate next step was to get to Patriot Hills before the Ilyushin and then get back to the mainland, all of which was out of our hands.

At Patriot Hills we faced yet another cold camp setup in front of ALE's heated Quonset hut. This time there was no hot-meal welcome, so once our camp was secure, Rob and I joined the other climbers in a separate unheated Quonset kitchen hut that ALE provided for our use. Each team was allowed to use its own camp stove on the countertop tables and then eat and hang out at the communal picnic-style tables. Now that the climb and ski of Vinson Massif was over, I gave myself the mental space to think in specific terms about my plan for Aconcagua while I ate. I'd purposely kept my thoughts about it vague in order to focus on the mountain I was climbing, but now it felt safe enough to go there. The problem was, from Patriot Hills there was still nothing I could do to become more prepared for Aconcagua and no way to ensure that I'd even arrive in Mendoza, Argentina, on time, so I tried to calm my nerves about how long a delay we might encounter getting off the continent.

Lying down back in our tent, I meditated on how everything could still happen 100 percent on time as planned. But the more time I spent in the quiet of the tent, the more I worried and lost focus. *They did say it's more normal for the flight to be delayed than not. We're supposed to fly off Antarctica on the fifth. I have the sixth to do laundry in Punta Arenas, and on the seventh I have a 7:00 a.m. flight to Mendoza. I haven't even called Damian to let him know we're on time, because being on time for the climb doesn't mean anything when there's still this flight ahead to worry about. I guess I could borrow someone's satellite phone to call him, but someone might overhear—why invite speculation? Besides, it wouldn't feel right to be on the phone talking about the next mountain before I'm off this one. No sense angering the mountain gods by being arrogant.*

To pause the conversation in my mind, I went back into the kitchen tent to sit upright for a change and drink tea and listen to some of the others talk about the upcoming "Ski the Last Degree" expedition to the South Pole that Vern was leading. Vern has the first successful winter solo ascent of Denali to his credit, and as a guide he has climbed each of the Seven Summits several times, even holding the speed record. He was hovering in the kitchen, working on the endless task of melting snow for water, when Phil Ershler asked me, "So, where are you going next?"

Uh-oh. So much for the down-low. When these guys hear that I'm going to do Aconcagua on the heels of Vinson, they'll know exactly what's going on. And they moved in a world where word could spread quickly. Since there's nowhere to hide in a Quonset hut in Antarctica, I faced the question. "I'm going to Aconcagua in a couple of days."

"To ski?" Phil asked.

Vern had moved a few feet closer now.

"Yes."

"What route?"

"I hope to ski the Polish Glacier." It hadn't been done yet, and I knew I might look foolish for thinking I could be the first.

Phil's bearded face erupted into an enormous smile. "Right on! That will be exciting. Good luck!"

My apprehension about sharing my lofty goal with a professional lifted instantaneously, and I reveled in the sense of camaraderie and encouragement that now filled the hut's kitchen.

But then Vern spoke up. "That's very dangerous. No one has done it before. You think you can do it? I know you just skied Vinson, but the Polish Glacier is way more serious. Be careful."

Oh, I will. I'll be more careful about what I say.

Just then an ALE employee came into the tent. "The Ilyushin is in the air. Winds calm to nil. Light haze. Be ready to go at eight p.m."

The plane arrived on time, but boarding was delayed until nine because a team of Yugoslavians were still skiing overland from Vinson Massif to Patriot Hills. They radioed in updates that had us expecting them any minute. I refrained from making judgments by reminding myself that if I'd stayed too long on the mountain because, as I'd said, no one could make me leave, it could have been me holding up this group of adventure travelers sitting on the uncomfortable wooden bench seats around me. Wouldn't I have wanted them to wait for me if the penalty for missing the flight was to spend at least two more weeks at Patriot Hills?

Just before 5:00 a.m., the plane landed at the Punta Arenas airport in total darkness. I felt like a boat passenger stepping onto a dock I couldn't see because of the thick harbor mist. After silently filing across the tarmac, we climbed aboard two waiting buses that took us back to our hotels.

I COULDN'T HAVE SLEPT in on December 6 if I'd wanted to. With my dirty clothes in the coin-op wash by ten o'clock, I found a pay phone and called my guide in Argentina.

"Damian! How are you? Are we still on?"

"Kit!" It sounded like "Keeeet" because of his accent and his emphasis on *everything*. "I thought you would have called me before now. You still want to climb and you will be here tomorrow?" He sounded surprised and I suddenly feared that he'd given up on our plans. Damian is a logistical wizard on his home mountain, and there was no question that I needed his help.

"Yes, I do. Sorry, I couldn't really call from Antarctica, and I guess I thought no news was good news. Plus, I was waiting to see if the flight back to Chile would happen on time. I have a seven a.m. flight tomorrow from Punta Arenas through Santiago and I'm supposed to arrive in Mendoza at one p.m. I hope it's still OK with you."

"Yes. Yes. I'll try to get everything together, but we'll still need to get the permits after I pick you up."

I was on schedule. Vinson had gone off without a hitch and I was 99 percent sure I'd told Damian to expect me on December 7 unless he heard otherwise from me. I hoped I hadn't totally screwed up my chances on Aconcagua by not borrowing a phone to call him. After being incommunicado for two weeks in Antarctica, I really needed his help in organizing the next climb. And I needed a partner.

SWITCHING PARTNERS

I MIGHT AS WELL HAVE carried a big greeting sign that said "Kit DesLauriers–Aconcagua" as I dragged my gear through customs and into the meeting area at the Mendoza, Argentina airport. For a change, being conspicuous would have been in my favor, since I had no idea what Damian looked like. At thirty-seven, Damian was an accomplished and internationally acclaimed alpine climber as well as a guide on his "home" mountain of Aconcagua and a member of The North Face athlete team. I'd become a member of The North Face team in January, but we'd never met in person before and I must not have focused on his photo when I scanned his Benegas Brothers Expeditions website, because I was taken aback when a sparkly blue-eyed redhead of obvious Caucasian descent hugged me in the meeting area.

As Damian whisked me into a taxi and peppered me with questions and information on the way to my hotel, there was no mistaking the Spanglish accent or the enthusiasm I'd heard when we spoke on the phone. "So, Keeeet, tell me about Antarctica. Did it go well? I've never been there. We'll check you into your hotel, then I'll go finish the food preparations for our trip with my girlfriend, who will be coming to base camp with us. She's working as a porter above base camp this season. You'll meet her at dinner tonight. Tomorrow morning we'll go to the Department of Renewable Resources to buy our permit, then leave for the mountains at three. Is there anything special you need to do in the city this afternoon?"

"Actually, I could use some flip-flops because my toes are swollen from the cold in Antarctica. And is there any chance we can go to dinner early, because I'm bone-tired and don't want to get sick."

Damian walked alongside me on the sidewalks of Mendoza to the gigantic urban version of a drugstore and waited while I bought a pair of flip-flops and some dark chocolate bars for high mountain food. My other request met with a different fate, though. When Damian came to get me at my hotel for dinner, it was quarter to ten and I was already in bed, but I powered through my fatigue and got dressed for dinner with him and his girlfriend, Eliana. I wanted to get to know them a little before we climbed the continent's highest mountain together, and apparently in Argentina dinner at ten isn't considered late. Though red meat late at night wasn't what my immune system was asking for, any shared experiences were worth their weight right now.

I'd been put in contact with Damian by his twin brother, Willie, whom I'd called that summer for information about skiing Aconcagua. Willie was also a member of The North Face athlete team, and he'd been the guide for a November 1999 attempt the team had made to ski the Polish Glacier on Aconcagua. Rob and I had been invited on that trip, but Rob declined in favor of shaking hands on the multiyear project to develop his first hotel. We'd known each other for only six months at the time and were madly in love, which I suppose is why he felt at liberty to ask me to make the same sacrifice.

"I'd like it if you didn't go on the Aconcagua expedition, either," he said. He was slated to film the trip, and I was going to be a skier this time, not just the medical and rescue resource.

Wait—you're asking me to stop doing what I love to do?! I know it was love at first sight, but you know I like to travel to mountains. I mean, we just met on a ski expedition in Siberia! Now you want me to turn down a paid trip to Aconcagua just because you did? "That doesn't seem like a fair thing to ask."

We were sitting on his mother's couch in her living room, which was used mostly for Christmas celebrations, the same ones pictured in Rob's childhood photo albums open on our laps. I felt like a 1950s bride, but we weren't even engaged. Rob stared at the pictures in front of him and nodded as if he understood my position, so I continued to try to grasp what I thought he was getting at.

"If I agree, what kind of a commitment are you going to make to me?"

He just smiled coyly.

It was later that afternoon, on his mother's front lawn, that he got on one knee and asked me to marry him, and within days Rob and I declined the Aconcagua trip together. I realized that Rob was about to make a huge transition away from his ski career into his second career as a hotelier largely so that we, as spouses, could have a stable financial future. He wasn't asking me to stop doing expeditions forever, but since he couldn't take part in the next one we'd been invited on together, he wanted me to show some solidarity and pass as well. When I understood this, I was happy to make the same sacrifice he was making for the sake of solidifying our partnership. I knew that someday I'd go to Aconcagua to try to ski it, when the timing was right and with or without Rob.

I also knew that Willie thought it was possible to ski or he wouldn't have guided that group in '99, which did go on to climb the Polish Glacier but not ski it. So in July 2005, just home from our ski on Mount Elbrus, I called him.

"Willie, I want to ski the Polish Glacier. When you guided that group five years ago, it was over Thanksgiving, right? I'm thinking of trying for this December. What do you think?"

I had to sit down to focus on his words. It was a struggle to understand his accent, but this is what I thought I heard: "Ahh, Keet. This is a very big snow year. Best in twenty years. The Polaco is difficult and still has not been skied. But for conditions, this would be the year to do it."

Willie was already winning my heart with his supportiveness.

"Yes, we opened the mountain in ninety-nine," he said, "so early, in fact, that the Plaza de Mulas base camp was still closed from winter avalanches, so we went around from the other side. The *penitentes* form quickly, so you might even want to go earlier than Thanksgiving, but then again, there won't be base camps set up before the third week in November." Sometimes as tall as a person, penitentes form at high altitudes in the Andes when the strength of the sun morphs the snow into thin blades of ice that reach for the sky.

"Well, I'm actually thinking about going to Antarctica in late November," I said, "then to Aconcagua immediately afterward, like December 6. Do you think that would be too late? Will you help me?"

"My brother Damian knows the mountain as well as I do and he will help you. He is down there much more than I am these days. I think you should go as early as you can, Keet."

And so here I was, settling into a corner table with Damian and his girlfriend, about to taste Argentinian beef—which Damian assured me was the best in the world—for the first time.

AFTER BUYING OUR CLIMBING permit the next day, Damian, Eliana, and I piled into a hired van with our gear for the afternoon trip through dry upland country and vineyards into the mountains and eventually arrived at the deserted ski town of Penitentes, where we checked into an almost-empty hotel and I finally caught up on my sleep.

After getting up at nine thirty the next day, I found Damian in a gear room beneath the hotel sorting through our food and equipment. We pulled out only what we'd need access to during our overnight trek to base camp, and the rest went into carefully weighted duffel bags for the mules that Damian had rented through an outfitter. Don Andres, a seventy-two-year-old expedition outfitter and lead snow-safety employee for the Penitentes Resort, then drove us to pick out the mules, and a vaquero herded them to meet us at the nearby trailhead.

It takes most people three hours to hike the moderate uphill trail to Confluencia Camp, located at 11,000 feet ASL, but it took us only an hour and a half. Our speed was probably due to our high levels of fitness as well as my lingering acclimatization from having been on the summit of Vinson Massif just seven days before. Along the way, Damian had been greeted a dozen times by rangers and others who seemed to make their living on or around Cerro Aconcagua, and I felt like a groupie of the mayor of Aconcagua as I was introduced to them. After my experience on Vinson Massif, it was a welcome change to be on a mountain with a guide and colleague who was fast becoming a friend *and* who had a lifetime of experience and the relationships to prove it.

The next morning, we finally got on a mountain-esque schedule when we began our ten-mile hike at first light in order to reach the Plaza de Mulas base camp, at 14,100 feet. As it turned out, we hadn't needed to go so early, because this time we covered an arduous trek that takes most climbers eight hours in just over five. That included stopping to chat with more of Damian's mountain friends who were on their way off the mountain and happy to offer condition reports from up high.

When we arrived at Plaza de Mulas, I felt like I was early to a gold rush. About two hundred people were already there in various stages of climbing or working for the season in support of the climbers, and Damian told me the number would soon swell to five hundred. There was a medical tent as well as large-scale canvas-and-nylon kitchen tents everywhere with outfitters' names on the outsides. Our kitchen tent was labeled "Fernando Grajales Expeditions" and was ideally situated next to the glacier; water was siphoned straight from the melting ice into storage barrels where we could fill our water bottles. Though the mules had carried our duffel bags and skis this far, it was our responsibility to carry them the rest of the way because the slopes became much steeper from there; switchbacks were visible in the dirt and melting ice above camp. We rearranged glacial rocks to make room for our sleeping tents, and inside mine, just before the eight o'clock dinner call, the temperature was eighty-five degrees. No wonder the glacier was melting and reports said there was no snow to ski on the normal route.

We were the first clients of the season for the Fernando Grajales camp, and although the dining tent, even larger than the kitchen tent, had already been set up, it was entirely empty and needed lots of work. According to Fernando Grajales custom, the uneven ground needed to be leveled enough to accommodate a wooden floor, so after breakfast in the kitchen with Lily and Santiago—the camp staff—the five of us built pallets from the bundles of wood carried up on mules. To level the pallets, we used a pickax to remove hard dirt in some places and a shovel to build it up in others.

Having been a professional stonemason for twelve years, my interest lay less in the installation of the floor than in how to solve the problem of the loose rock on the downhill slope that served as the entrance to the dining tent. This was the beginning of a two-month season for Lily and Santiago, who had to carry the clients' meals at least twice a day from the kitchen tent to the dining tent, so I offered to build stone steps to the entrance.

Four hours later, I'd finished two sets of four steps and was eating lunch in the kitchen tent when Lily offered me a Sprite and, in broken English, explained that the soda was a gift to thank me for my help, since clients don't usually work and soft drinks are available only for purchase at base camp. It was suddenly clear to me that I was being treated as a client. Much preferring to be treated as part of a pack, though, I resolved to try to bridge the gap.

AFTER BREAKFAST THE NEXT day in the dining tent, Damian laid out our schedule over our morning tea. We would carry a load to Camp I that afternoon, December 12, which was at 16,500 feet and would take an hour to get to, he said. The following day, we would carry another load up to Camp II and leave it there at 18,200 feet before going back to base camp. December 14 would be a rest day, and then we'd begin our first summit attempt, sleeping at Camp I on the fifteenth, Camp II on the sixteenth, Camp III on the seventeenth, and possibly summiting on the eighteenth.

"Sounds good to me," I said. "What time should we leave?"

"Even though it's a straightforward hike, the trail is steep with loose rock," he said. "Two thousand feet will take us an hour, maybe a little bit more. So with three hours round trip, we'll leave after lunch."

Now the question was how acclimatized I was. Our stash of group gear included a pulse oximeter and a blood-pressure cuff for measuring our oxygen levels and vital signs, and while sitting in the dining tent reading my book and drinking tea to pass the time over the past couple of days, I'd become obsessed with my vital statistics. Today, even though I felt good, my numbers didn't show that I was any more acclimatized to the elevation than Damian, who had been in Mendoza for weeks. My resting pulse, usually in the fifties at home, was in the high eighties, my oxygen saturation, or "O-sat," was in the low eighties, and my blood pressure was often as high as 145/96. Regardless of my numbers, though, I felt ready, and we left that afternoon per Damian's plan.

I carried my ski boots, neoprene overboots, crampons, ice axes, harness, helmet, goggles, gloves, socks, ski-boot heating system, extra down jacket, and a couple of base layers. I knew my pack had weighed twenty kilos before adding food and water, since Damian insisted we weigh them on Fernando Grajales' camp scale before heading out in order to make sure no one was carrying too much. Twenty kilos equals forty-four pounds, so when I added six more pounds for my day's food and water, I was at a manageable fifty pounds. Damian and Eliana shouldered thirty kilos each when fully loaded, which equaled sixty-six pounds. I was thankful I'd paid the extra cost for Eliana to help us. Otherwise, Damian and I would have had to carry at least eighty pounds each or make two trips.

For all his attention to detail, though, part of Damian's load seemed excessive. Namely the plastic toilet mounted on a light metal frame that was strapped to the outside of his pack.

"Keet, you'll see," he'd said when I laughed incredulously. "There are piles of shit all over this mountain. People just put a rock on top of it and call it good. I talked to some other guides and they agreed that if I bring this seat up to Camp I, they and their clients will put plastic bags under it, poop in the bags, and carry it back to base camp."

It was one man's approach to a large problem that's regulated on mountains like Denali, and I supported his efforts. But that didn't mean I could help laughing as I walked behind him and his toilet in transit.

When we got to Camp I, Damian set up the toilet a few strides away from the tent sites. He piled rocks to anchor the frame in place and then stashed the seat just under it in hopes that the wind wouldn't carry the whole contraption away. While he worked on his project, Eliana and I mounded heaps of rocks on top of our gear cache, and when our chores were finished we retreated back down to base camp for the night with our empty packs.

The next day we upped the ante by packing moderate loads that included my skis to Camp I, where we ate lunch and then added the cached gear to our packs for a hike to Camp II, aka Nido de Condores, or Flight of the Condor. I felt really good for the second part of the day and kept going ahead at my own pace with only a couple of two-minute stops for a sip of water and a GU energy gel.

On December 14, though, back at Plaza de Mulas, I really began to feel the downside of spending so much time alone. This was such a different journey without my normal tent and climbing partner. I missed Rob even more than usual and wished he were there to talk to. I settled for making the forty-five-minute walk across the glacier to the Refugio Plaza de Mulas to use the pay phone to call him.

After talking for a few minutes, I told him about something that had happened that morning. "While I was walking around the base camp asking for a charger for my iPod, I went to a communications tent to pay twenty bucks to use their Internet to check the weather forecast," I told him, "and as I was leaving, I heard someone say behind my back, 'That's the girl who thinks she's gonna ski the Polaco.' It really hurt to hear them doubt me like that. I feel so alone."

"You're tough, Kit," Rob said. "You know you can do it and it doesn't matter what they say. Try not to let it bother you."

"It's just so hard being alone. Damian is being super nice to me, but still, he has Eliana and I have no one to really talk to. I miss you."

"I miss you, too. You'll be fine. You can do it,"

It was good to hear his voice, but after we hung up, I felt lonelier than ever.

As for the weather forecast I'd read online, it looked like the next decent summit day would be the eighteenth, after which the weather was expected to deteriorate again. Between now and then, the winds at the summit were supposed to drop from an average of forty-five mph to thirty mph, and temperatures were supposed to increase from "extreme cold" to five below. Factoring in wind chills, I estimated that the air would feel like negative thirty, which concerned me. I shared the numbers with Damian.

"That's the way the summit of Aconcagua is, Keet," he said. "That's as good as it gets. It's always windy up there."

So with the goal of summiting on the eighteenth, Damian and I climbed from base camp to Camp I on December 16 and quickly settled into the tent to rest, read, and melt snow for water so we could hydrate. The next morning, I realized I had my first real headache of the trip and began to wish I'd taken a real rest day at base camp instead of a fast-paced hike to the Refugio. As we started our climb to Camp Nido, the frigid, dry wind was searing my lungs, so I protected my nose and mouth with a balaclava. It even hurt to drink cold water.

After our blustery two-hour climb, Damian chose a flat spot for our tent on the outskirts of what had already become a burgeoning camp dotted with the tents of dozens of climbers all gunning for the normal route. Damian and I worked together in the constant wind to set the tent up. When we were done, I obsessed over the oximeter again. O-sat, 76ish.

Pulse, 86 to 90. Blood pressure, 124/82. Still not great. I had a headache to boot, and the winds were cold and strong. I tried to turn my thoughts to the positive. This is a big commitment. I want to do it right. My numbers aren't what I'd like, but if I can relax I should be all right.

As if he'd read my mind, Damian invited me to the rangers' hut for tea just then, and I jumped at the opportunity for camaraderie. As it turned out, though, the hut was so crammed with men and gear that someone had to stand in order for me to sit. Still, I was much happier to have too little space than to have too much. I began to believe that things were going to be OK.

ELIANA HELPED US MOVE from Nido to Camp III at noon the next day, which was perfect timing because it was only a two-and-a-half-hour climb. Our Camp III was a deviation from the normal Camp III, aka Camp Colera, since it sits halfway between the regular climbing route and the Polish Glacier. Damian said he and Willie had been the first to establish a high camp here and had named it Plaza Don Benegas after their father, a Patagonian who had married an American. "Willie and I were born and raised in the wild heart of Patagonia listening to our dad's stories about climbing adventures," Damian said. "Our mom was way into horses and taught us English, so we speak both languages, but neither one very well!"

The last fifteen minutes from the main route over to Plaza Don Benegas had the only technical climbing I'd encountered so far. Three body lengths of rock that required me to use my hands as well as my feet, which is the definition of fourth-class climbing, gave a little spice, but it still wasn't enough to need a rope for.

In the howling wind, Eliana helped us set our tent up and then left to go back to base camp. Damian and I immediately set about melting water from a patch of snow we'd harvested amid the rocks a few hundred feet away. We used the same stove as we had at Camp I and Nido, but for some reason it wouldn't burn strongly or stay lit now. When the flame went out or just barely sputtered, the fumes from the incomplete combustion of the gas made my head spin enough that I worried about carbon monoxide poisoning.

I'd volunteered to do the first round of snow-to-water alchemy, but Damian quickly asked me to switch with him. I went to the back of the tent and tried to organize my gear for the summit push the next day. Instead I was interrupted by the need for fresh air when the stove fumes made me nauseated, so I found myself unzipping the back door and sticking my head out every few minutes. The smell didn't seem to bother Damian.

"You know, when I was on Denali last year," I said, "there were some doctors doing a study on carbon monoxide poisoning, and the results showed that about half the people who feel altitude-sick actually have carbon monoxide in their blood from cooking in poorly ventilated tents."

From his position in the front of the tent, Damian tried to poke the jet clean, but the fix didn't last long and I went outside with the stove and carefully cleaned the fuel orifices. Then I looked at the bottle of fuel lying amid the rocks. It was a disposable soft-plastic water bottle, and I could see white things floating in it that looked like jellyfish. In North America we use white gas, which is clear fuel—it's not white and it doesn't have floaties. But this obviously wasn't North America.

"Damian, where did you get this fuel? I've never seen fuel stored in a bottle like this."

"The rangers gave it to me," he said from inside the tent.

When I finished cleaning the stove, I put it back in the front of the vestibule and returned to my spot at the back door within easy reach of fresh air. Slowly but surely, we finished the task of melting snow for dinner, breakfast, and our climb to the summit the next day.

RACING THE DEVIL

THE STIFFNESS OF MY ski boots made each step across the rocky sloping traverse easier on my ankles but harder on my knees. As the first warm colors of light crept across the dark morning sky, the dirt and rocks under our feet began to change to patches of ice, and Damian and I stopped to put our crampons on by the light of our headlamps.

While traversing is often easier than climbing uphill because little to no elevation is gained, the section from Plaza Don Benegas to the Polish Glacier was a glaring exception. As we moved east at the 20,000-foot elevation, the patches of ice on the ground morphed into penitentes, and we carefully weaved among the waist- to shoulder-high blades. A single misstep could snap an ankle, even in a ski boot. The tails of my skis hung below the sides of my pack, and when they scraped the ice they threatened to throw us into the daggers, but by using our trekking poles like canes, we made slow but sure progress.

After an hour and a half, we reached the end of the penitentes but met up with a new challenge: a sloping bulge of rock that blocked easy access to the glacier. Still wearing crampons, Damian moved across the smooth rock on a short but tenuous traverse, and I followed.

Ten minutes later, our first moves onto the Polish Glacier showed us light, dry powder that was good for skiing, which meant it was difficult to climb, with each step sinking deeply into the snow. At high elevations, the wind nearly always affects surface conditions, and once above the shelter of the rock bulge, we quickly discovered that the Polaco was no exception. A windblown crust on the snow supported some steps but not others, and as I struggled to free my legs from the thigh-deep postholes, I wished for almost any snow condition that was more predictable than this one.

After the initial traverse onto the glacier, the snow's changing consistency was making for a slow climb, and we were forced to zigzag along the right side of the Polaco to find the easiest route. Although the weather was favorable, just as the forecast had said, I noticed that our pace slowed even more when Damian took the lead. I made a mental note to double-check our pace the next time we swapped leads to see if my perception was accurate or if he'd just encountered an unlucky section of snow. There was always the chance that I wasn't thinking clearly at this elevation, which was about the same as the summit of Denali, with over 2,000 vertical feet still to go.

I got out an energy gel and the water bottle I'd stored in my jacket pocket and drank and ate during pauses in Damian's steps. On a high-altitude summit day that's expected to take over twelve hours, it's common practice to eat light and on the go. Twenty-one thousand feet is no place for a full-course picnic. In fact, eating while moving is part of having a successful day, since speed often equals safety. But after three hours of going slower than I'd expected, I began to wonder if Damian was feeling OK. I was feeling OK at best. *Hmmm, if I'm seeing this clearly, something's not right with him. He's not acting or moving like the accomplished mountaineer that he is. Is he altitude-sick? Or carbon-monoxide poisoned from the stove?*

Again, I took over the lead. "Good job," I said, since it's proper etiquette to acknowledge the herculean effort required to break trail, regardless of the speed being made. There was a pallor on his face that I hadn't seen before. "You should eat and drink something. I just did and it feels good."

When we reached the next logical stopping point, Damian was several switchbacks behind me in the boot pack. I walked to the rocks on the right side of the glacier and hoped that going off-route for a break like this would inspire him to open up and tell me if he wasn't feeling well enough to continue.

"Damian, do you want to call it and try again later?"

"OK." He stared at the route above and then calmly continued. "Keet, you should leave your skis here. And we can leave our harnesses and ropes here because we don't need them to get back to camp or back up to this point."

My heart lifted. He knew he wasn't feeling right. And considering that I felt so far from 100 percent myself, turning around was fine with me.

I moved quickly to make a pile of gear to stash and protected it with just enough rocks to ward off damage from wind or a hardy alpine bird but hopefully not enough to alert a passing climber to a tempting pile of gear left behind at 21,000 feet. For the most part, climbers are respectful and honest people, but this mountain meant a lot to me, and why not exercise some risk management?

"We should just go down over there on the rocks and stay left of the penitentes below," Damian said.

I wasn't psyched about the consequences of wearing ski boots on a steep, loose downhill of rock and ice when we could have descended on snow instead, but avoiding the penitentes seemed logical.

Running over sliding scree fields, we both stumbled more than once before making it back to Camp III.

"Let's rest and try again tomorrow," Damian said when we got there.

I agreed and sat on the rocks outside our tent to make tea while Damian decided to walk the five minutes down to the other camp that we'd just noticed was set up below ours. When the tea was ready, I took a cup to Damian at the neighbors' camp. They were packing up to go down the mountain, and after a short visit I left them to their task.

"Go ahead, I'll be right there, Keet," Damian said.

After a restful hour back in our tent, he hadn't arrived yet, so I went back out to look for him. I found him sitting on a rock halfway between the now-empty lower camp and ours.

"What are you doing?" I asked. "Have you been here this whole time?"

"Yeah. I threw up for a while."

We walked slowly back to camp and said nothing more. In the tent, Damian fell asleep within a few minutes, and I thought about the sequence of events that could occur if we stayed the night at Plaza Don Benegas and Damian came down with high-altitude cerebral edema (HACE), a condition in which the brain swells with fluid due to the physiological changes that occur at elevation. I knew enough about altitude illnesses from my medical training to know that there's no cure except descent and that, left untreated, HACE can progress quickly and even become fatal inside of twenty-four hours. Damian weighed thirty pounds more than I did, and even if I could carry him down the mountain, I wouldn't be able to get him through the technical section without our rope, which we'd left up on the Polish Glacier. And with no other climbers camped nearby, there was no one to help us.

I began to pack quietly because he needed to rest. I separated out high mountain gear such as down mittens and goggles that I wouldn't need again until our next summit attempt and put it in tidy stuff sacks that I stashed in the mesh side pockets of the tent. I put some food and water and my sleeping bag into my backpack, and I'd begun to do the same for Damian's gear when he woke up.

"What are you doing, Keet?"

"I'm packing up to go down. We have to leave as soon as possible. I can't carry you if you get worse, and it's already early evening."

"OK."

On the descent, we moved slowly, but I felt like we were racing the devil.

"JUST SAY WHAT YOU DID"

'D BEEN ANXIOUSLY KEEPING an eye out for Damian around base camp since our return from Plaza Don Benegas the evening before, but I didn't want to interrupt his rest. Eliana was caring for him in their shared tent, and I'd have to wait to see him when he was ready to be seen.

I passed the time by hanging out at the small table in the kitchen tent listening to Lily and Santiago speak in their native Spanish as they prepared food and managed the Fernando Grajales headquarters. I understood only part of the conversation, but it still felt better to me to be around people than to sit alone in my tent. And I began to feel more accepted when Lily and Santiago offered me the shared silver *bombilla*, or straw, of their hollowed gourd filled with mate tea.

My first sip of the traditional brew concocted from a wild Argentinian shrub made the hair all over my body stand up. By the time Damian came into the kitchen tent late in the afternoon, I'd shared several gourds with Lily and Santiago and my central nervous system was wide awake.

"Damian! How are you feeling? Did you go see the doctor?" I asked.

"I'm OK, not great, Keet. The doc said no solid food today, only Jell-O and chicken broth. He doesn't know what got me sick, but now I have gastritis from throwing up." He turned to Lily. "I don't care what the doctor said, all I want to eat is buttered pasta."

She made him some and he retreated to his tent for the rest of the day while I rode out my caffeine buzz.

The second morning back at base camp, starting to feel a little panicky at not having a plan, I crossed the glacier to the pay phone at the Refugio. I got through to Rob, who was expecting to hear that we'd summited on our original schedule.

"Kit! Did you make it?"

"No. Damian got sick on our summit day and we came down. It could have been altitude sickness, but I think it was carbon-monoxide poisoning from the stove, which wasn't working right. I left my skis up at our high point because I really want to go back, but now I'm doubting myself. What's it like at home? Is the skiing good?" By the middle of December, the snow is usually deep in western Wyoming.

"Oh, that's a bummer. I hope he's OK. It's off to a horrible start here, actually. There's hardly any snow, and we're still just skiing groomers on man-made." A week and a half later, I would learn that Jackson had actually been in the middle of an epic storm cycle, and Rob had been skiing so much deep powder that he didn't have the time or the energy to snowblow the driveway. He told me what I needed to hear at the moment, though, and that's all that mattered. "That sucks that you guys had to turn around. How did you feel?"

"I felt pretty good, not great, but yeah, it was scary because Damian got worse even after we got back to high camp, so I decided we had to come all the way down. I wasn't sure if I was making the right decision or if Damian would be mad at me. I really have no idea what I should do next. He's in his tent now and he might get better enough to give it another try, but he might not. Should I just go back up there and bring my stuff down and go home? It's beginning to feel like I'm not meant to be successful this time. Besides, I can't just expect that I can change my airline tickets."

"Kit, you're there and you're super-acclimatized. Maybe Damian can help you find someone else to support your ski descent. I don't think you should give up. This is a chance for you to stay focused and be clear on your goal. Are you kidding? You know that. Otherwise you wouldn't have left your skis up there."

He had one more piece of advice. "Call Sally. She's a travel whiz. She'll take care of changing your flights for you."

After hanging up, I found a spot to sit down to cry. My tears were as much about relief that my paralyzing confusion had lifted as they were about the dangerous situation Damian and I had been in and I was now committed to heading back into. When the flood of emotion had passed, I went back to the phone booth and dialed our friend Sally, who works for Alaska Travel Source.

"Heyyyyy, what's up?" she said. She'd moved to Anchorage from North Carolina thirty-five years ago but never lost her Southern accent.

"Do you think you can change my ticket to come home a few days later? I'm sticking around to try for the summit again, since we got skunked the first time."

"I just got off the phone with Rob and he told me all about it. Good girl that you turned around. Now, tell me how I can help you. What day do you want me to change your ticket to?"

Sally's big-sisterly support helped me to pull myself out of the puddle of emotion I'd been stuck in for the last ten minutes. "Well, it's the twentieth now," I said as my resolve returned, "so best case is we go back up to high camp on the twenty-third, summit the twenty-fourth or twenty-fifth, then a few days to get back out to Mendoza. How about the twenty-ninth? I really want to be home for New Year's with Rob."

"You got it, girl."

"Seriously, Sally? Just like that you can get me a seat flying into Jackson Hole in the busiest week of the year?"

"Well, it won't be easy, but I'll find a way. You just go back up that mountain and don't worry 'bout a thing. When you get down, give me a call and I'll let you know what flights you're rebooked on. Love ya big!"

Now I just had to figure out who I'd climb with next and when.

THAT EVENING, I WAS in the kitchen tent when Damian came in for his buttered pasta. "Keet, I want to go back up with you," he said, "but in case I'm not better in a couple of days, I'm asking around for someone else who can go with you. Don't worry, it would only be someone that I know can safely climb the Polaco."

It was encouraging to hear Damian being so positive and supportive of my goal. His words lifted my spirits. "Thanks, Damian. I wish I could help ask around, but that's pretty hard since I don't speak Spanish. You know I'd still rather go with you. I can wait a couple more days to see if you feel better."

When Damian came back into the kitchen tent at eleven the next morning, I was sitting reading my book and drinking my mate. By then

I'd bought my own gourd at the gift shop in the Refugio, and Lily was kind enough to share her herbal yerba blend and keep me supplied with a thermos of hot water for topping it off.

"Good news, Keet. I found a guy named Nestor who can come with us. He's not been to the summit yet this season, so tomorrow he'll go up to Nido and spend the night with the rangers to acclimatize. We'll leave the next morning, pick him up at Nido, and go up to high camp."

"Awesome! Thanks, Damian. Are you feeling better?"

"Yes, somewhat. I think I'll at least be able to go to high camp with you and see from there."

Wow. After one day of intention-setting, I had a doable new plan. I grabbed a twenty-dollar bill and headed back to the neighbors' Internet tent. Now, instead of talking behind my back, the people there openly asked me questions as I waited in line for one of the two computers. Damian and I were among the first climbers of the season on the Polish Glacier route, and while we hadn't summited, I realized that others now saw that we had experience with mountain conditions that couldn't be gained from base camp.

"What's the snow like on the Polaco?" asked the woman who took my money and handed me the sign-in sheet.

"There's a lot of it, and what I saw was pretty wind-affected but looked like decent skiing."

The forecast I found online was similar to the one I'd seen before, and now I understood what Damian had meant when he said, "That's as good as it gets. It's always windy up there." I spent the next fifteen minutes taking that into account as I put together the plan I'd suggest to Damian. We could climb to Plaza don Benegas on the twenty-third and be in position to summit on either the twenty-fourth or the twenty-fifth. The winds were supposed to be high on the twenty-third and the twenty-fourth, so it was more likely that we'd rest on the twenty-fourth and climb on the twenty-fifth.

Damian liked the plan, so midmorning on the twenty-third, we began our hike to Nido and covered the 4,000 feet in just over four hours. Nestor and a couple of rangers were waiting in the trailer drinking tea when we arrived. We joined them for a quick cup before continuing the remaining 1,500 feet to high camp. My nagging fear that the wind had ripped our tent off the hillside during our five-day absence was relieved when I saw that it was still holding its ground, albeit straining against the powerful gusts.

The three of us wouldn't be able to fit into the two-person tent, so Damian had brought a smaller one and began to set it up as his own. Nestor and I crawled into our shelter and were spared awkward conversation because neither of us spoke each other's language, and besides, we couldn't have been heard over the whipping wind that made any loose spots in the tent fabric sound like a poorly trimmed sail on a boat in a gale.

In the tent's front vestibule, I discovered that the problem with the stove was exacerbated by the wind, which made it even harder to keep a flame alive. When Damian crawled in with us to make a group dinner, he saw the same situation unfolding that had played out the night before our summit attempt: I'd try to light the stove and the fumes from the sputtering stove would send me sticking my head out the back door for fresh air. Then I'd return to the stove and Nestor would be taking a shot at it, and I'd go right back to sticking my head out the other side of the tent.

"Keet, you should move to the small tent and I'll move into this tent," Damian said. "I'll let you know when dinner is ready."

Excellent! I'd been excused from having to use a pee bottle in the middle of the night next to a man whose last name I didn't even know and spared the distasteful job of melting snow on that stove with that fuel. I gathered my belongings, stuffed what I could into my backpack, and carried the rest in my arms to the other tent.

After dinner together in the "big" tent, we agreed that we'd wake up at 3:00 a.m. and, if the winds weren't too bad, prepare to leave for the summit at dawn. As it turned out, when three o'clock rolled around, I didn't need the alarm to wake me up. The wind had kept me up most of the night.

The decision seemed obvious, but I nonetheless unzipped the front door of my tent, crawled on my belly to unzip the vestibule, and shouted in the general direction of the other tent. "Whaddya think?!"

Damian responded as I'd expected: "Too windy!"

Nestled in my small yellow nylon cocoon, I passed the day feeling more relaxed than I'd thought was possible at almost 20,000 feet. I literally had nothing to do, not even melt snow for water, since Damian and Nestor were still taking care of that in the duplex next door.

Christmas Day promised to be a different story. My 3:00 a.m. weather check revealed that the tent wasn't threatening to sail away to Chile, and better than yesterday meant good enough. So the three of us retraced our route up to the cache of gear, which lay exactly as Damian and I had left it. Another nagging fear was put to rest.

A new fear had been developing, though, and as Damian and I collected our stashed equipment and lashed it to our backpacks, I dug into my first-aid kit for the aspirin. My head had begun pounding early in the climb, and from the intensity of it, I was afraid I hadn't caught it quickly enough for two aspirin to touch it.

The angle of the slope continued to steepen. Forty-five degrees became fifty as we kicked steps through the first bottleneck. Above 21,000 feet, the slope opened up but continued to gain in steepness without any good rest spots, and apparently fully recovered, Damian was in his element. He sailed upward with no visible effort, putting in a boot track for Nestor and me to follow. Meanwhile, my headache had me leaning on my ice axe for an extra breath every dozen steps. Nestor stayed behind me but didn't look like he wanted to go any faster, either.

A few hundred feet below the bottom of the crux, which Damian called the second bottleneck even though this one was only the width of a pair of skis, with rock walls on both sides, the slope steepened to fifty-five degrees and Damian stopped to get our rope out.

"So, Keet, are you OK climbing this without a rope?" he said as he fed the rope onto the snow.

"Yes."

"Good. We'll use it anyway because we'll want it for the section up above where the second bottleneck goes through the rocks. That's the steepest and hardest part. Now we'll use a simple running belay, but up there we'll climb one at a time."

I remembered a story I'd heard about the late Doug Coombs, extreme-skiing pioneer and Alaska heli-ski guide. When vetting his ski clients, he would ask, "How steep a slope do you like to ski? Forty-five degrees? Fifty degrees? Fifty-five degrees? Sixty?" When clients answered fifty-five or sixty, he knew he should watch out for them. Here I was, just beyond fifty-five degrees, and thinking the same thing of myself as I looked up at the gaping slash in the rock called the second bottleneck.

It was sixty degrees steep, and while there was snow in it, the snow was broken up by very large rocks protruding at varying angles. I studied it as if I were in a freeskiing competition and it was a feature I wanted to hit on my run down. A feature at 22,000 feet above sea level.

I watched as Damian began to climb the final pitch up to the bottleneck crux. Using a gloved hand, he easily pulled away the two to three feet of surface snow to reach the hard blue ice of the glacier underneath, where he placed an ice screw. Oh my God. This best-in-twenty-years snow cycle means there's only a few feet of snow sitting on top of a sheer sliding layer of millenniums-old blue ice up here. The sun is warming it up and I'm going to ski down this later? Avalanche red flag. Deep breath. OK, don't get ahead of yourself. You can't get mentally stuck on the way up. It's still a long way to the summit. Who knows what else we'll find or if we'll even make it? Stay focused, Kit. This is getting serious.

Damian glided up through the technical crux and built an anchor on the rock wall to the left as soon as he topped out, and I followed his lead on belay. I'd been climbing with one ice axe and one ski pole until this point but decided I wanted my hands to be free for the rock moves, so I tucked my ski pole into that special spot between my back and my pack and holstered my axe in my climbing harness. The hand-hand-foot-foot movements were welcome after kicking steps up thousands of feet of snow, and in no time I arrived at the anchor to clip myself in next to Damian.

"Man, this is gonna be a tricky ski," I said as we watched Nestor start up the crux.

Damian laughed. "Yeah, you'll have to point it for sure."

"I know I could do it for a comp, or on a lower mountain, or someplace with less consequence of falling and getting hurt, but here I'm not sure that straight-lining into a thirty-five-foot air and landing on steep, poorly bonded snow is the best choice." I was serious even though I was laughing from nerves. Skiing the Polish Glacier direct had never been done—of course it wasn't the best choice.

I filed away the options in my head: ski it, down-climb it, or rappel it with my skis on. I'd decide when I had to, but for now I switched my focus to the rest of the 1,000-foot climb ahead. I scoped the line above while Damian pulled the rope in and Nestor climbed.

"Nestor is too tired to go higher," Damian said in a hushed voice. "He'd slow us down too much, and that could be dangerous, so I'm going to ask him to stay here and wait for us."

Wow. If Damian could have seen into my head, which now felt like it was clamped in a steel press, he might have said the same thing about me.

When he clipped Nestor into the anchor made from pieces of rock-protection gear and let him know he'd be sitting there for the next few hours, Nestor just nodded his head without argument. Either he knew it wasn't worth trying to change Damian's mind or he really felt pretty bad. Or both.

I tried to figure out how long we'd be leaving Nestor by himself at 22,000 feet. "How long will it take us to get to the top from here?" I asked Damian.

"Two hours, probably."

Nestor hung his head. Maybe going to the upper bottleneck on the Polaco with Damian was already an egg in his basket. Or maybe Damian was paying him well enough to be his backup that Nestor didn't want to rock the boat regarding his guiding future. But as I faced the sixty-degree slope above the bottleneck, I marveled at Nestor's determination to accept the situation and realized I'd need similar determination to make it to the top and ski back down.

As Damian finished packing up, I started kicking steps up the slope, which was so steep I had to crane my neck to the side to see the fan-shaped open slope above the bottleneck. The snow was deep here where it had accumulated in the protection of the hourglass rock walls, and each step of my ski boot went in up to my knee.

Damian quickly caught up and cheered me on. "Nice, Keet. Strong."

When we got to the apron, the last part of the Polish Glacier before the summit ridge, the snow turned from powder to a wind-rippled sea of waves whose crust collapsed under the weight of our steps.

Ahh, Aconcagua's ever-present wind. Wind is the greatest shaper of snow conditions on such high-elevation mountains, and if I thought the slab avalanche danger had been notable just below the crux, the danger on this apron above the crux was extreme. We stayed out of the riskiest middle section and crossed the scariest part one at a time. As we climbed, I couldn't help thinking about how averting an avalanche would only be harder while slicing through the snow-slab layer with skis on the way down.

After tiptoeing through the sleeping dragon's lair, we sat on the ridge for a quick break.

"I think we'll have to belay this section on the way down," Damian said through the thin scarf over his mouth. The combination of cold air and wind had forced us both to keep our mouths covered for days.

I swallowed the last of my aspirin—my eighth of the day—along with a GU energy gel. "It looks pretty dangerous. If one little pocket of snow breaks loose, I'd be pushed right through the rocky crux, and it might even take out Nestor."

"That's why I wanted him to stay anchored to the wall out of the way." He stood again. "Come on, we have to keep going, Keet. It's still at least an hour and a half to the top along this ridge, maybe two. It's not steep, but it's a long way."

The undulating ridge crested several false summits, and by the third one I felt like I was going to cave under the pain of the most intense headache of my life. Like a spirit hovering just above me, a piece of my consciousness had been observing my headache since I first noticed the pain developing six hours earlier, and it let me know that it knew this was becoming more than standard pain from exposure to elevation. A headache of this magnitude had to be the beginning of HACE, so now we were facing the same potential end result we'd run away from when Damian and I had abandoned our high camp a week before. But we were so close to the summit and I didn't have any other symptoms. What would one more hour of headache be on top of the weeks it's taken me to get here? I can ski with a headache if I have to, and it's actually the fastest way down.

The angel watching over me didn't argue.

Getting to the top and skiing back down is the best choice for me right now. And turning around now would mess with my confidence on the descent. I promise that if things get worse, I'll stop and go down, but until then I need to keep going up.

Again, the angel didn't argue, but I received this message: "You should do whatever you can to ease your pain now."

Reluctantly, I gave in.

"Damian," I said without looking back at him, "do you remember how you said you'd carry my skis if I really needed help? Well, I really need help right now. I have the worst headache of my life."

Damian shocked me back to reality, reminding me of how tough I needed to be in the moment. "Keeeeet, if your headache is that bad, we should turn around now."

"No, I'm fine," I responded as I plodded along in front of him. *I can't believe I asked for help when I wasn't even dragging behind. Pull it together, Kit.*

Since I'd already decided I wouldn't turn around, there was no need for any more words until we got to the aluminum cross that marked the 22,841-foot summit. Speaking made my headache worse anyway, so even when we finally reached the top, I kept the banter to a minimum and squinted through the pain behind my eyes in order to smile for the camera. The snow had been blown twenty feet clear of the summit, and the natural circle of exposed rock beckoned me to turn 360 degrees and take in the sweeping views. To the west I could see all eighty miles to the blue of the Pacific Ocean, and when I focused on the closer distances, on the mountains and valleys of the Andes, I felt as if I were airborne.

The voice above my right shoulder reminded me that our deal was to get down ASAP, so after only five minutes at the top, I walked to the edge of the snow, set my skis on the rocks, and stepped into them.

Meanwhile, a lone climber had arrived on the summit from the normal route, and he followed Damian toward me.

Damian turned to him. "No! Not this way!"

The man looked like he was lost.

"You can't go this way! Turn around and go back the way you came. This is too dangerous."

Appearing surprised, the man didn't move until Damian physically turned him back in the direction of the normal route and then rejoined me.

"OK, Keet, rolling!" Damian had agreed to run my video camera for as much of the descent as possible, and we leapfrogged down the firm windblown snow of the summit ridge. I'd ski until I heard him yell, "STOOOP!" and then with amazing agility he'd hustle on his cramponed feet down the gentle ridge to get slightly ahead of me before yelling, "OK, Keet, go!"

The headache that had made it difficult for my eyes to focus on anything began to loosen its grip. Maybe it was because of the contentment I felt skiing Cerro Aconcagua's beautiful eastern ridge with the South American continent spread out below me. This much is clear: I was in the middle of doing my favorite thing in the world, skiing down a mountain that I'd just climbed. And while I knew that my angel—my conscience, whatever—was still watching over me, she had nothing to say. She just smiled and let me enjoy the moment.

As we arrived at the spot on the ridge where we'd climbed up from the Polish Glacier, it was clear that this was the "business section." The hard part. The area where consequences lay in wait.

"Keet, I really think we should belay this if you're going to ski it," Damian said, sitting in the snow.

I surveyed the choices. The least steep section, still at least fifty degrees, was on the left side of the snow apron, and I figured that if a pocket of wind slab were to break loose there, it would flush over the cliff bands below and I stood a chance of escaping to the middle.

In my mind, I did a quick visual scan of the dangers I faced. Skiing on belay is very difficult, since the person managing the rope has to pay out enough rope at just the right time to not trip up the skier, and the skier has to make sure the tails of her skis don't get caught in the rope. The only ski belay I'd ever taken was that tiny bit on the icefall of Vinson Massif, so I wasn't confident about doing it again. At least I trusted Damian's rope skills, though.

"OK, but I'm concerned about getting enough slack in the rope when I need it, like if I have to move fast," I said. "Just do a hip belay—don't put the rope through your belay device. And let's communicate clearly. I'll say, 'Turning,' really loudly to let you know when I plan to turn, OK?"

"Got it." Damian flaked the rope onto the snow, handed me one end to tie in to, and dug himself a deeper seat near the ridge so that if an avalanche occurred, ideally he'd be safely above the crown. "Ready when you are, girl."

"On belay?"

"Belay on."

As planned, I yelled, "Turning!" with each move. The snow was so variable that I could sometimes ride the sastrugi ripples on top, but as soon as I'd turn, my skis would punch under the crust and threaten to become stuck, and I was afraid of falling over and starting a snowslide.

After fifteen frightening ski turns, dropping as much vertical as possible on each one in order to minimize my impact on the slab, I'd worked my way down the worst of it and into the narrower area of soft snow a hundred feet above Nestor.

"Off belay," I yelled up to Damian.

I untied from the rope and made controlled but linked hop turns into the waist of the hourglass while Damian coiled the rope and prepared to climb down in the tracks we'd made on our way up. Considering that Nestor and I were below him, that was the safest option, but still I took my skis off, climbed up to Nestor's perch, and clipped into the anchor beside him.

As I watched Damian, it became clear that he has a built-in slope gauge because fifty-five degrees is the point where he turns and faces into the mountain to kick his steps coming down. Anything less than fifty-five degrees and he's comfortable facing outward. In this case, he faced into the mountain from the ridge down to the crux.

"Nice job, Keet," he said when he arrived. He began threading the rope into the anchor for Nestor.

"Thanks. And thanks for the belay. That was scary."

After Nestor clipped in and began to rappel the forty-foot section through the rocky crux, Damian turned to me. "Soooo, what do you theenk? Are you going to ski it or rappel it?"

With so many more immediate questions to deal with, I'd been keeping that one on the back burner all day, but now it demanded an answer. "I wish the sharks'-teeth rocks below lined up better, but they're at all different angles, and to get through them I'd have to straight-line from way above. It's a wicked steep landing at 22,000 feet, with huge consequences that are kind of likely, going as fast as I'd be going on that landing. Plus, there's only two or three feet of snow that isn't bonded to the ice below. I'm just not seeing it."

"No problem. Just rappel then."

"Actually, I'm going to rappel it with my skis on." I bent over to step back into my bindings.

"What?" Damian clearly hadn't imagined this possibility

"Well, it's still a ski descent if I keep my skis on. It's not a complete ski descent if I use a rope, but I already used a belay up above anyway, so

I don't know where that line is drawn and right now I don't really care. I'm comfortable rappelling with my skis on, and then when I get down there I'm ready to unclip and go."

Many years of rock climbing on desert cliffs had given me the rappelling experience I needed to maintain control with my gloved right hand on the rope behind the belay device. Every hand-hand-foot-foot move I'd made climbing up this section now translated into a tip-tail-tip-tail maneuver as I wiggled my body and my 172-centimeter skis through passages in the rocks that were less than forty inches wide. The moment my skis touched down on the snow below the crux, I unclipped the rope from my belay device and yelled, "Off belay!" I had to get clear of the bottom of the crux so that Damian could come through, so without waiting for anyone else to make the next move, I grabbed my ski poles from their stash between my back and pack and prepared to ski.

I could see that Nestor had his eyes on me from his spot tucked under the cliff and safely away from the crux. I'd been concerned about the snow, but the surface didn't seem to be as warmed by the early-afternoon sun as I'd expected. The slope was an honest sixty degrees, but it quickly relaxed in angle, and I wanted to ski, not sidestep down with the rope until it became an easier pitch. To get my skis around on the first turn, I engaged the muscles of my core, faced my shoulders down the mountain, and bent my knees in a one-two-three motion until I had the momentum and the power to retract my feet and make the skis turn. It worked. The first three turns were easily the steepest of my life, and with each one I dropped many vertical feet.

By the fourth and fifth turns, the angle had eased just the few degrees I needed to make the more fluid turns I'm used to. I skied out of the fall line from the crux and pulled to a stop to catch my breath and watch Damian come down.

"Nice turns, girl," he said as he approached the bottom.

Now, with 2,500 feet of the Polish Glacier open below us, Damian and I quickly moved into the same rhythm we'd used on the summit ridge, with Nestor following at a distance. Damian would run ahead, facing down the mountain as soon as it eased to less than fifty-five degrees, and let me know when he had the video camera ready. "OK, Keet, go!" I'd ski until well after I'd passed him and stop only when I heard him tell me to. This technique meant that my ski pitches were probably longer than they normally would have been at that altitude, and my lungs burned from the lack of oxygen. The snow had become sticky and wet by the time I skied through the lower bottleneck, but a small change in aspect would reveal still-cold, carveable snow or wind-rippled sastrugi. Even though the skiing was almost over, I still had to read the surface conditions carefully.

Near the bottom of the glacier, I waited for Damian again, but this time he detoured just above me to a house-size rock outcrop and began walking around on the melted-out ledge fifty feet above my head.

"What are you doing?" I asked.

"You don't want to know."

Which, of course, made me want to know. Even though my legs felt like lead weights from the exertion of the day, I sidestepped uphill enough to see what Damian was looking at.

It was a body.

"An avalanche," Damian said. "He was from Poland and his family couldn't afford to pay to have his body removed from the mountain, so he stays here."

I knew that the Polish Glacier had been named for the 1930s Polish team who had been the first to climb the mountain by this route, and while the corpse was partially buried in small rubble, I could clearly make out the nineties-era climbing clothing through the years' worth of decomposition. So the route hadn't been named after this dead climber, a slightly comforting thought after having just descended it on skis, but I was still disturbed by the way the climber was lying there alone on a ledge of rock, with one climbing boot missing and exposed mottled blue-gray skin that had been pecked at by birds.

"I'm glad you didn't show me this on the way up," I said.

A dozen more ski turns brought us to the bottom of the Polish Glacier, where it was time to take my skis off and retrace our traverse back to high camp.

"First ski descent of the Polish Glacier," Damian said. "How are you feeling, Keet?"

Now that I'd made it to the bottom and was taking my skis off, I was again aware of how badly my head hurt, but I wasn't going to mention that. Instead, I drew on my feeling of accomplishment. "Good. Feliz Navidad!"

Entirely out of water, the three of us stopped in the middle of the penitente field and slurped from a trickle of melting ice. By the time we arrived at camp, I'd decided there was no way I was going to spend another night at this elevation with this headache and without easy water if I didn't absolutely have to. "Please, guys, I know it's six o'clock, but if we're efficient we can be back at base camp by nine."

Damian looked pained. "Really, Keet?"

"OK, how about this? I'll pay for one porter to come here tomorrow and bring a load down of whatever we can't carry. I'm thirsty and tired, too, but if we rally, we'll be down in time for dinner." Dinner South American-style, of course—late.

Their resigned expressions said it all: *Man, this has been a long day, but what's a few more hours?*

The stove gave us one more pot of water while we worked to break camp, and it was well after dark when we arrived back at base camp. Lily and Santiago were in the kitchen with the lights on and offered me a beer and the satellite phone that belonged to Fernando Grajales Expeditions. I took a long drink and called Rob.

"We made it!"

"Did you ski it?"

"I rappelled thirty feet or so down the crux because there wasn't continuous snow—it was too dangerous not to—but I skied the rest of it."

"If you left your skis on, that still counts, Kit. Congrats to both of you. Now Merry Christmas and please come home. I miss you."

I went to bed knowing that I'd done the best I could, that I'd skied from the summit of Aconcagua and I'd skied the Polaco, but I felt a little heavy in my heart. I wondered about what Rob had said: "It still counts." *Did it? I couldn't have safely skied the whole thing, but now that I rappelled a short section, is my whole project tainted?* I'd never thought of these details before I started the Seven Summits project. I just wanted to ski the summits. *Will you please stop being so hard on yourself?! Those were the steepest turns of your life, the worst headache of your life, and some of the most dangerous snowpack of your life—you skied the Polish Glacier!*

But by the next morning, I still hadn't made peace with myself.

"What route did you climb?" asked the clerk at the Refugio reception desk, where I was paying for some postcards.

"The Polaco. I skied it."

"Really? Nice work. Years ago I heard that a man snowboarded it. I never met him, but no one has ever skied it before. You did the first!"

As he talked, I thought of Davo Karničar, the Slovenian man who was trying to ski the Seven Summits, too. He claimed to have skied Aconcagua, but he didn't give details about the route he'd taken, and since there's reportedly so little snow on the regular route, I was starting to wonder. Where exactly had he skied? And would others have doubts about me? After all was said and done, would they say I hadn't really skied the Seven Summits because I'd rappelled through the bottleneck on Aconcagua or because Kosciuszko isn't really one of them?

I recalled a conversation I once had with some friends who were professional mountain guides. One was questioning the details of another climber's recent expedition, and the other said, "It's mountain-climbing—all you can do is just say what you did."

And that was exactly right. There will always be naysayers, and all I can do is just say what I did and let others interpret it as they will. Realizing that, I felt the burden of proof lift, and in its place was a sense of liberation that could only help me reach the tops of the peaks that loomed ahead.

CALLED OUT ON A TECHNICALITY

D URING MY INITIAL PLANNING binge in April 2005, I Google-searched "skiing on Kilimanjaro" and thought I'd find helpful information about seasons and such, but instead I got something I'd never have expected. The first web post I landed on was from the year 2000 and written by a British man who had paid a guide extra money to help him hide his skis on the climb. Early in the morning, on a slope below the summit and well away from the climbing route, the Brit apparently made sunrise ski turns. Neither he nor his guide was caught.

What in the world? So it's illegal? Why?

Next I read Stephen Koch's post about his 1997 first snowboard descent of the mountain. He'd twice tried to get permission from the National Parks director to snowboard but was denied because of a rule barring "pleasure devices" on the mountain. In February 1997, he sneaked his snowboard onto the mountain under cover of darkness and summited, but to avoid being seen with a "pleasure device," he left his snowboard at the top of the glacier. After returning on foot to his snowboard, he made icy turns for over 2,000 feet, retracing his line of ascent on the Kerstan and Heim glaciers.

Knowing that Karničar was gunning to be the first person to ski the Seven Summits, I checked out his website next and saw a photo of him making a few jump turns on rocks in front of the famous Kilimanjaro summit sign—there was no snow in sight.

OK, so it's been snowboarded and skied, but not from the summit, and those guys all went under the radar. Davo tried from the summit, but is it still skiing to make a few jump turns on rock and sandy scree? It's crazy that skiing is illegal—they must have changed that rule by now.

All I could do was try to get permission and hope that since the rainy season lasts from March into June, there would still be snow on the summit in mid-June after we were off Elbrus. And maybe the money I had left over from my competition season would cover the costs of Elbrus and Kilimanjaro. Wouldn't it be cheaper to get to Africa from Europe than from the States? I wanted to get the most possible done in my Seven Summits project before having to ask my angel sponsor for more money.

As I read on, I learned that in addition to skiing being illegal, it seemed that it was illegal to climb the mountain without a local guide. I'd traveled and climbed in India, Siberia, and New Zealand, and I'd seen enough foreign culture to understand and even appreciate rules like the one that required the hiring of local people to climb Kilimanjaro—it's good for the economy to keep tourism revenue as close to home as possible. I didn't need a guide to hike to the nontechnical 19,340-foot summit, but I also didn't object to the rule even though it created a conundrum. If I sneaked my skis onto the mountain without telling the guides and I got caught, they might lose their permits and their livelihoods. I was willing to risk the consequences of a fine, but I wasn't going to put anyone else in that position.

I decided that with only six weeks until the climb, I should hire one of the best tour operators I could find to give myself the best chance of getting my ski plan approved. I gravitated toward a company called Deeper Africa that uses a less-traveled route on Kilimanjaro and makes a serious commitment to treating the mountain and those who work on it with respect. I called its US office and told the representative of my plan.

"Send us your resume and intended ski route and we'll send our best employees to file the application at park headquarters in Arusha, Tanzania," he said.

"What do you think the chance of getting approval will be?"

"I don't see any reason why we wouldn't get it. It may take until just before the trip, though, because the National Parks bureaucracy isn't fast. We'll do our best."

With still no news by the first of June when we left Jackson Hole en route to Mount Elbrus, I was getting nervous. The next day, while I was at the airport in Munich about to fly to Russia, I emailed Deeper Africa.

"We'll be in the Caucasus Mountains without access to the Internet until June 17th," I wrote. "On June 18th we'll be able to check email in

Munich before flying to Tanzania on the 19th. I hope to have word by the 17th. Thanks."

As planned, on June 18, Rob and I were back at the Munich airport, and my heart sank as I read the response from Deeper Africa: "We are very sorry to report that KINAPA (Kilimanjaro National Park) has denied permission to ski on Kilimanjaro. We are very surprised and continue to look forward to hosting your climb."

"Now what?" I said to Rob, who was reading over my shoulder. "Do you think there was ever any hope?"

"It doesn't matter, Kit. We have to go. The flights and the mountain costs have been paid for. We'll look at it like recon for next time."

As it turned out, Deeper Africa organized a great experience for us, without skis, and our climb up the scenic and remote Lemosho Route brought us to the Western Breach wall, Grade 3+ (classified as involving scrambling on rock with exposure but rarely requiring a rope), and then into the almost-two-mile-wide crater of Kilimanjaro for a night before the final 500 feet to the summit. There was no snow on the summit, just the rocks I'd seen in Karničar's photo, so I was glad I hadn't been tempted enough to sneak the three-foot Salomon snowblades Rob and I had bought in a panic in Munich. I could have hidden them in my backpack, but I would have ended up jump-turning on rocks. Besides not aligning with my ideal of skiing from the summit on snow, I didn't want to risk our guides' livelihoods by doing something illegal and concealing it.

We made a traverse of the mountain and descended from the summit via the Stella-Barafu Route. Just beyond the summit we passed within sight of the head of the Kerstan and Heim Glaciers, which were now melted back a full quarter-mile from the summit. If I wanted to ski that route the next time, I'd first have to climb 250 feet of vertical ice to gain access to the glacier.

I looked at Rob. "That doesn't look like something I want to do and it doesn't come close to the summit. Let's come back next May, in the middle of the rainy months, and hopefully there'll be seasonal snow on the summit." I pointed to the gentle ridge we were trekking on. "And we can just ski this route."

"This isn't steep but it's logical. We'll be lucky if this is the only mountain we have to do twice."

Immediately after getting back home, I began to plan the next trip to Kilimanjaro. This time I looked up the official Kilimanjaro National Park regulations on its website. Among the rules were:

> 4. Guide(s) and or an armed park ranger shall guide every climbing group.

> 18. "Parachuting, cycling, skiing, and hang gliding activities inside the park are strictly prohibited." — The United Republic of Tanzania National Parks Ordinance Government Notice No. 191 published on 25/7/2003

Maybe you should have looked that up the first time around, huh, Kit?

When I was done chastising myself, I turned my mental efforts to the task of finding a different guide service with a better chance of getting permission for my ski plan and one that was also willing to let me be a rebel and ski it under the radar if permission were denied. It was on a biweekly Everest-planning phone call with Wally Berg of Berg Adventures International that the answer came to me.

"Berg Adventures guides on Kilimanjaro, right?" I asked Wally. Why hadn't it come to me back when I'd asked Wally to put me on his Everest permit?

"Yes," he said from his office in Canmore, Alberta. "We like to think we have the best staff."

"Well, we didn't get permission to ski this year, so we just climbed it, but I want to try again for sometime before Everest. Do you think BAI could help me even if it's illegal?"

"Kit, we'd love to. The truth is that in a country like Tanzania, there are always 'rules' that someone will use to put up barriers. If anyone can get permission, we will."

We worked together to submit a new application to KINAPA, and over the next few months Wally updated the park service on the new additions to my resume as they happened: first ski descent of the Polish Glacier and first female ski descent of Vinson Massif. It seemed like overkill, since all I wanted to do on Kilimanjaro was to ski from the summit via the gentle rim of the Kibo Crater to Stella Point and then down as low as I could get away with on the Barafu Route. It would be like skiing an intermediate blue run at most North American ski resorts. Why wouldn't they grant permission?

In February, I got the call from Wally.

"It's unbelievable but we've been denied," he said.

"What? Did they give a reason why?"

"It sounded to me like the reason they won't allow skiing is because they are fearful of having to conduct a rescue when they don't have snow skills, but they didn't exactly say that."

"So, are you still game to help me?" I cringed, praying he'd stick to his word of six months ago.

"Absolutely. I know you can do this, Kit, and we'll do our part to make sure you're successful. As we always do, Berg Adventures will take responsibility for our own rescue support, but we know you won't need it."

"How do you want to do it?" In my impatience, I didn't give him a chance to answer before firing the next question. "When should we go?"

He laughed. "April and May are the rainiest months, so they hold the best chance for decent snow cover." Then his tone became serious. "I'll work on it with our head guide in Arusha. You'll have to trust us, Kit, but once we work out the details, I can't let you know too much. Not everyone will be in the loop, since I'm only going to give some of our top staff the option of helping out. Don't worry, we'll make it happen."

SENDING IN SPECIAL OPS

I N THE MIDDLE OF May, we arrived in Arusha for the second time in a year. I was jet-lagged and trying not to worry about the next logistical hurdle: How I'd actually be able to ski from the top of the highest peak in Africa. After breakfast at the hotel, Rob and I and three friends who had come with us from Jackson relaxed on couches in the lobby and waited to meet our guides. We'd invited PJ, Mikey, and Laura to accompany us on our Kilimanjaro journey on the condition that they promised not to say or do anything to let on about my skiing plan. It also came with an asterisk: The weather will be rainy—at least that's our hope!

A tall, lanky Tanzanian entered the lobby and introduced himself and his much shorter companion in perfect English. "Welcome. My name is Saramo, and this is Kwere. We will be your lead guides for your climb."

We introduced ourselves.

"It's a pleasure to meet you all," Saramo said. "We'll begin hiking after lunch, so let's start sorting our gear. Kwere, it'll be the first time on this mountain for these three, so why don't you help them with their packing."

Kwere led PJ, Mikey, and Laura to some couches on the other side of a dividing wall in the large lobby, and Saramo sat with Rob and me at a long wooden coffee table.

"So, you climbed Kilimanjaro last year, right?"

"Yes, we went via the Lemosho Route to the Shira Plateau and up the Western Breach."

"Good, so you know what it's like. We'll take a different route this year, because as you've probably heard, the Breach is closed from a massive rockfall. Do you have any gear questions at the moment?"

I laughed. "Only about how to get my skis up there!"

"Yes, I thought so." He smiled. "What do you have to put your skis in? A simple bag?"

"They're in a black ski bag right now that has some other stuff packed in it, but yes, it's a simple bag without wheels." Whenever I head into the mountains, I try to pack like I'll be carrying my bags, not rolling them. You never know what transportation will be like, and it's easier to strap a minimal ski bag to the top of a taxi or the back of a mule.

"Good. Listen carefully. I'm happy to help, but no one must know you are going to ski on Kilimanjaro, so this is all that I can tell you. Just like the others will be doing, both of you will now go to your room and bring back the duffel bag of gear that you'll each be taking on the mountain. Kit, put your skis only in your ski bag, make it as small as possible and carry it in your arms with your duffel bag, then put the whole load against the wall right here." He pointed to our side of the partition that separated us from Kwere and the others. "I'll make sure that Kwere is busy with your friends so he doesn't see, and there will be another man here to take the ski bag away."

"What about my ski boots? I'll hike in regular shoes, but should I carry my ski boots in my pack?" It was hard enough to give up control of my skis.

"Yes, you can carry those in your backpack as long as no one sees."

"OK. So Kwere doesn't know?"

"No. It's very important that neither you nor your friends speak about your plan to ski. No one can suspect anything. In order to help you and protect the people who are willing to help you, you can't know where your skis are, how it will happen, or who knows. You must act as if you are simply here to climb the mountain, and you will not see your skis again until the summit. I'm sorry, but it must be this way."

I felt like one of my favorite heroines, Annette Kellerman, who as a young woman in the early 1900s made waves with her illegal baring of her legs in a racing swimsuit. She was also the first woman to attempt to swim the English Channel. *Is doing something illegal really that bad if the law is ridiculous and no one gets hurt?* I told myself it wasn't and went with Rob to our room to grab the gear.

In the lobby, my nerves flared and I began to sweat, but I dropped my ski bag where Saramo had instructed. Then I froze as an African man even taller and lankier than Saramo calmly picked them up, smiled at me and walked away. Whoever he was, the fate of my mission to ski Kilimanjaro was literally in his hands.

That afternoon, we began our hike at the quiet Umbwe trailhead. It wasn't one of the most-used starting points, but maybe Berg Adventures had chosen it because it had fewer park-ranger checkpoints than the usual Machame gateway. In any case, I didn't ask questions. Wally had made it clear that I shouldn't expect many answers.

For the next six days, the rain came down incessantly as we hiked our way up the mountain on muddy trails. Even though we'd all expected a lot of precipitation, I felt badly for our friends. The constant downpour eventually became uncomfortable, no matter how prepared we were, and I was the reason we were enduring it. At the same time, I'd never been so happy to walk and camp in the rain for a week straight—it meant that snow was probably falling on the summit 6,000 feet above and that one of the variables of my ski project was taking care of itself.

If we were to remain inconspicuous to the park service and all the staff members who weren't in on the plan, we had to do nothing too far out of the ordinary, and that included the choosing of our climbing route. Berg Adventures had guided hundreds of Kilimanjaro climbs, and we gave them complete autonomy with our route choice as well as our porters, our camps, our meals, how my skis got up the mountain—everything. BAI had also planned an acclimatization schedule that had us wrapping around and up the mountain slowly enough that everyone could be successful and no red flags would be raised. Once we reached the Barranco Camp, we traversed for a day on the southern trail circuit to the Karanga Camp. On day seven, we joined up with the Mweka Route to get into position for a summit bid on day eight from above the Barafu Camp at 15,500 feet.

Parts of East Africa had been German and British protectorates in the late nineteenth and early twentieth centuries, and the tradition of local workers' offering the *mzungu*—Swahili for white man—a high level of service still endures. When combined with another tradition—packing out waste, including human waste, in observance of the "leave no trace" system on Kilimanjaro—the result is the practice of providing portable toilet tents on mountain expeditions, one for the *mzungu* and one for the mabawabu (porters). Outfitters like BAI pay their Kilimanjaro staff well, and even the job of carrying a toilet on your back for a week is a prized one in Tanzania's tough economy.

As we *mzungus* hiked into high camp, the rain paused and the expansive views from 6,000 feet above tree line revealed the lush green African forest canopy far below and the cultivated grasslands beyond. The BAI porters arrived just after us, singing and dancing under their loads without missing a beat of the Kenyan pop song "Jambo Bwana." There was no background music, just ten guys doing their jobs with smiles on their faces and carrying the tune along with their porter loads. They'd been teaching us the song all week, and we dropped our packs on the ground and joined in for a reggae round robin that lasted ten joyful minutes.

> *Jambo, jambo bwana, habari gani? Mzuri sana!*
> *Wageni mwakaribishwa, Kili yetu hakuna matata.*

Translation:

> *Hi, hi sir. How are you? Very fine.*
> *Visitors are welcome, in our Kilimanjaro, there are no worries.*

The truth was, these guys would break into song and dance regularly, so this wasn't unusual. It's not like getting to high camp is what inspired them to sing—they live inspired. They live *hakuna matata*.

Too bad I couldn't channel the *hakuna matata* spirit that night as I worried about how the summit and the ski would go the next day. This was it, the last night before it would either happen or not, and I still didn't know where my skis were or who on the BAI staff knew about my plan or how it would happen. After an early dinner, Babu, the head organizer, had given us a briefing that didn't even acknowledge that I'd handed my skis over seven days before.

"PJ, Mikey, and Laura, you'll start for the summit at one a.m. with Kwere so that you'll have plenty of time to go slowly," he said. "Kit and Rob, you'll leave at four a.m. with Saramo and you'll climb to the top then make a loop down through the crater for lunch. Everyone should be back here by two or three p.m. Sound good?"

PJ, Mikey, and Laura were happy to go with the flow. I was confused, though, because I'd clearly told Wally I wasn't interested in going back into the crater. My most vivid memory of spending the night there the year before was having to wear my ski goggles to keep the fine ash dust out of my eyes. My job was to not question anything, though, so I silenced my inner voice and said that it all sounded good, as did Rob. We wished our teammates a good climb, hugged good night, and retreated to our tent.

At midnight, my nerves were still keeping me awake when I heard Rob stir, and I decided to share my thoughts with him. "Why are they leaving so far ahead of us? We can't catch up if they have a three-hour head start. We're more fit, but still, that's a lot. And what the hell's with the crater lunch? Did you ask for that?"

"Kit, relax. You have to be OK with not being in control. This is all about trust, and it will only work out if you trust them. It's not about the ski descent, this mountain. What you have to learn right now is way harder than that. And this isn't just about you."

How can he cut right through the money and the time and the effort and see things so clearly? He's right again, but way easier said than done. I lay there until I heard our friends leave at 1:00 a.m. and then I finally fell asleep.

Two hours later, Saramo had hot water waiting for us in the dining tent, and Rob and I each made a cup of Milo, a mix of chocolate and malt powder that's a common breakfast drink in many countries. As we sat, Ali, the head cook, came in and picked up a big bundle. He slung it over his shoulder and started up the mountain in the dark. We hadn't seen Ali much on the trip—he always seemed to be busy with food preparation—but there was something familiar about the quiet way he came in to pick up the bundle against the wall. And why was the cook up at three thirty in the morning? I looked at Saramo.

He smiled his usual big, white, toothy grin. "Ali is going over Stella Point into the crater to set up lunch for you and Rob."

"Really? That's way over the top." The staff seemed to be taking the concept of providing a high level of service to a ridiculous extreme. "We don't need or want a tent for our lunch, we don't even care about going into the crater!"

"We are doing as we are instructed. If you decide you don't want lunch in the crater, then you don't have to take it. Let's get going."

The three of us started up in the dark, our headlamps illuminating the lightly falling snow, and it was the first time all week that we witnessed Saramo's naturally long and beautiful stride. He'd set such an easy (boring!) pace during our acclimatization that his speed this morning caught me by surprise and I had to work hard to keep up.

After an hour at our blistering pace, there were no more sections of rock that weren't covered by a foot or more of snow that had been packing a lot of moisture when it fell and was then condensed during the warm days and cold nights that it had spent on the ground. A dusting of soft snow sat on top and made for an ideal skiing surface, similar to spring corn snow. I was elated to see how much of the white stuff there was—it meant I could ski to at least this point on the way down, 2,500 feet down from the summit. As long as my skis got up there.

Another hour into our hike we neared Stella Point. It was just after six and the first light of dawn had succeeded only in making the cloudy night a lighter shade of dark. Saramo stopped and pulled out his handheld radio to answer a call. Kwere was on the other end.

"Saramo, we made it," he said. "We're on top!"

"Awesome. Congratulations! We'll take a break at Stella Point and wait for you. See you in forty-five minutes or so." He changed the channel on the radio and called someone who spoke to him in Swahili.

I turned to Rob, who just shrugged.

"What the?" It would take us only forty-five minutes to summit from here—why wait forty-five minutes? And who was Saramo talking to in Swahili? We weren't on a military mission, but this hike was starting to feel as secretive as one.

"Babu is at Gilman's Point on the lookout for climbers coming up from the Marangu Route," Saramo told us. "He said two British climbers just came through, so we'll wait to summit until after they get down. Ali already has your skis in the crater and says no one is camped there. When we leave Stella Point, I'll be in radio contact with both of them again to make sure no one else is coming up. It'll take the same amount of time for Ali to get from the crater to the summit as it'll take us from Stella, so he'll meet us on the summit with your skis."

Oh my God. With about an hour until we would get to the top of Kilimanjaro, I finally knew the plan. My skis were rolled up in the colonial-style dining tent that Ali had on his shoulder, and it was Ali who'd taken my skis from the hotel lobby! We wouldn't even be going into the crater!

Putting a guard on Gilman's Point was a brilliant idea. It made perfect sense since it's the easiest approach to the summit. Tears welled up in my eyes when I thought of the number of people who were playing a part, and no easy part, in helping me pull off my ski descent. These guys had rewarded me a millionfold for the trust I'd put in them. They'd thought of everything. And go figure—all those days while we were circumnavigating our way up the mountain, my skis had been rolled up in a spare tent kept safe by the head cook. My heart was flooded with gratitude for everyone who was helping me, including our friends who had willingly started their climb at 1:00 a.m. to play their part.

At 18,886 feet, the wait at Stella Point was a cold one until the sun rose, but Rob, Saramo, and I were dressed in every layer we had and happily sat down to drink tea from my thermos and wait for the summit team. One of the bonuses of climbing Kilimanjaro in the rainy season of May is that there are very few other intrepid travelers doing the same, and that made for a peaceful sunrise.

By the time the Brits had passed us on their way up and our friends arrived on their way down, it was close to seven. The sun had risen, though the only sign of it was some brightness trying to burn through the misty clouds. Rob and I shared hugs and high-fives with PJ, Laura, and Mikey and then took photos and listened as they told us how their knees were feeling and how happy they were. Now knowing that all we had to do was give the British folks enough time to start heading down from the summit before we arrived, I was content to linger. In fact, I was as happy about what was ahead of me as our friends seemed to be about what was behind them.

At seven thirty, our friends started down and we began the forty-minute push to the summit along the crater rim, which was never steeper than thirty degrees. We passed the Brits as they came down, and at times we walked side by side on top of footprints left in the snow.

"*Dada*, I don't know how you are going to stop," Saramo said.

He'd never addressed me with the Swahili word for *sister* before, and I was touched that he seemed to be concerned. "*Hakuna matata*, Saramo. It's very easy. I just make ski turns, and I can stop on any one of them. Have you ever seen skiing before?"

"No, *dada*. Once I saw snowboarding on television, but only once." He turned to me with a sly smile. "*Dada*, do you know why no one else will be able to do this?"

"No. Why, Saramo?"

"Because I won't help them! Or at least not until you finish your project so you can be first!"

I really did feel like his sister at that moment, and a few minutes later I felt like Ali's sister, too. As we approached the wooden sign on the summit, he approached from the other direction and unrolled the tent to reveal my skis. Ali didn't speak English and rarely gave a full smile, probably because he was missing several teeth, but he couldn't help giving me a big grin on this occasion. Pretty happy myself, I hugged both my new brothers.

Anchored to the black lava rock by tensioned cables and looking starkly out of place, the sign was nailed to peeled logs that stood taller than us and read: "Congratulations! You are now at Uhuru Peak, Tanzania, 5,895m. Africa's Highest Point. World's Highest Free-Standing Mountain. One of World's Largest Volcanoes. Welcome."

Patches of blue shone through the clouds as I turned in a circle and took in the distant glaciers. A mile and a half away, across the volcanic ash pit of the crater where we would allegedly eat lunch, were the tall glacial walls of Kilimanjaro's northern ice fields. Green forests clung to the mountain below timber line, and agricultural fields could be seen 13,000 feet below.

After the short round of photos and high-fives, Saramo checked in with the BAI sentry at Gilman's Point by radio to make sure the coast was still clear, and it was. I sat on the rock pile under the summit sign, changed into my ski boots and put my hiking shoes into my pack.

After Rob took some more photos, I pushed off from the summit on my skis less than thirty minutes after we'd arrived. I'd carried my ski poles as trekking poles for the entire hike, which is common practice on Kilimanjaro, but now I really leaned on them. The summit of the highest mountain in Africa is decidedly close to flat—it's the rim of a volcanic crater—and I had to use my poles to push myself along until the angle steepened enough for me to simply glide. Rob had run 300 yards ahead to film me, and when I arrived by his side I kept my end of the deal. I took my skis off and handed them to Rob, who ran back to the summit and stepped into the bindings, balancing delicately with just his hiking boots on, and then skied back to me and handed my skis over. Now that Rob had "skied" Kilimanjaro, too, he kept up on foot the rest of the way down, though not as easily as long-legged Saramo and Ali, who ran alongside me giggling like children.

Just above Stella Point, the pitch increased to the point where it was natural for me to make ski turns, and I felt very fortunate. The snow conditions are rarely good when I travel halfway around the world to ski, but today was a shining exception. The creamy few inches on top melted perfectly into the consolidated base and made for dreamy turns. I was in heaven and surrounded by my tribe.

And it seemed that my tribe now numbered seven. At Stella Point, Babu, who had been guarding Gilman's Point, met us along with two other men from the BAI staff. I gave Saramo another "What the?" look.

He laughed and pointed at one of the newcomers. "*Dada*, this man, Jafari, was with Ali in the crater and stayed behind to make sure that no one else came up that way." He pointed at the other. "And this man, Penda, was hiding just beyond Stella Point to make sure no one snuck up on us from the Barafu Route below."

I couldn't believe my eyes. I'd seen these men in our team for the past week, but they didn't speak English and I wasn't sure what their roles were beyond carrying some porter loads for our team. I looked at the six people around me and felt tears well up for the second time that day. I shook their hands, hugged them, and thanked them over and over from the bottom of my heart.

Rob ran ahead to get a good vantage point for filming, and when he was ready I took off skiing down the beautifully perfect slope we'd hiked up. It varied in steepness from twenty-five to thirty-five degrees, which was just enough angle for making ski turns that flowed sublimely, and I savored each one of them. I continued down into the white mist of cloud cover, and after 1,000 vertical feet I heard Rob yell, "Stop!"

Stopping to regroup with my tribe felt like the right thing to do anyway, and the members quickly arrived, their song and dance in full swing. This tune I didn't know, but however awkwardly—and I always felt awkward dancing with these naturals—I moved to the beat with my skis still on my feet and my face locked in a permanent smile, not caring how

I looked. *How often do we mzungus stop in the middle of a ski run to sing and dance together? These guys are awesome!*

After another round of high-fives and photos with my five African teammates, Saramo got practical again. "Kit, we'll go ahead to find the place where you must stop skiing. We'll wait for you there and you can give your skis to Ali to carry down."

Oh, right. We aren't safe yet. It's so weird that I can't carry my own gear. I'm tired of feeling like a prima donna, but I'm not in charge and I have to respect their judgment. I waited until they were out of sight and Rob had repositioned for another round of video before skiing again, feeling like I was in the middle of a dream, alone on my own Kilimanjaro stage set.

After having skied from the summit of Uhuru Peak for over 2,500 vertical feet, I saw Ali gesture to me from where he was waiting with the others at the snow line, and I knew it was time. I stepped out of my bindings, handed them over, and watched him wrap them up in the tent and walk off alone toward the camp, just the way he'd left seven hours earlier. I changed out of my ski boots and stashed them in my pack, and Rob and I walked out of the mist back into camp.

Though it had been too cold to precipitate up high, there was a light drizzle of rain here at 15,500 feet as our friends came out of the dining tent to greet us.

"Did you do it?" PJ and Laura whispered.

Rob and I answered with smiles and nods as we watched our guides file in behind us, take off their packs, and resume their normal camp routines. We ducked into the dining tent for tea and trip reports, and after a few minutes someone asked the obvious question: "What are we going to do for the rest of the day?" It was only 10:00 a.m.

Mikey took the lead. "We've been wondering what you two would think about hiking down from here today. It'd suck to sit around in the rain all day."

"Wait—all the way down?" I said. "Like, back to the hotel today, with cold beers, hot showers, and real beds?"

We all looked at each other as if the tent were suddenly filled with light bulbs going on over our heads.

"Why not?!" we said as a chorus.

"Rob, you ask Babu because you're the best at this kind of thing,"

We emerged from the tent and stood unified with Rob, though physically removed from him just enough to not appear to be ganging up on Babu.

"We'd like to walk all the way out today," he said. "We know it's 9,500 vertical feet and fifteen miles, but we're tired of the rain. Do you think everyone would be into it?"

Babu raised his eyebrows and studied us closely, clearly unsure if we really meant it. "The porters will want to know if they'll be paid for the next day and a half that we were supposed to take getting back to the Mweka gate. What should I tell them?"

"Of course, and we'll give them an even bigger tip if we go all the way out today!"

Babu gathered the rest of the team and relayed the idea, which seemed to be well received. It appeared that everyone was tired of the rain.

We packed up camp by noon and started our hike downhill through the five distinct ecological zones of the highest free-standing mountain on Earth, which I'd been too anxious to fully appreciate on the way up. Our high camp was in the arctic zone, where lichen was the only vegetation to be seen, and just below camp was the alpine desert, where willful shocks of grass were scattered among the rocks. Below that was the moorland and its clusters of giant senecio plants that looked like towering saguaro cactus topped with yellow flowers. And halfway down the mountain, the heather region was a riot of protea, large ball-shaped cream and yellow flower heads that sit on stiff evergreen leaves.

At the bottom of the heather zone, at the edge of a lush forest, we stopped at the Mweka Camp to rest and eat before we continued the last 3,000 vertical feet down to the trailhead. Most of us swallowed several Advil and applied tape to our feet at this point to ward off the blisters that are so common when walking downhill in wet boots for hours on end. The foot pain and, for some, the knee pain, was eased by the carpets of mosses and colorful flowers such as pink impatiens that covered the ground beneath hundred-foot-tall endemic trees, whose canopy blocked all trace of the sky and gave shelter to monkeys swinging from their branches.

Dusk had set in when we reached the gate of the park around eight, and we said our goodbyes to the porters. In the van on the way back to the hotel, we were all thinking about hot showers and dinner, of course. After all, how many people summit Kilimanjaro and then walk down 13,000 feet in the rain in one day? But even more prominent in my mind was the disbelief that I'd done it—I'd actually skied Kilimanjaro on good snow from the summit, and no one had gotten into trouble for it. Just twenty-four hours before, I'd had no clue how I was going to pull all that off, and now it was over. As we raised our beers in the back of the van, I could only marvel at my good fortune.

The next morning, Sally, our ever-amazing Alaskan travel agent, was able to change our flights from two days ahead to that very afternoon. Ali brought the black bag to the hotel, and since we had a few hours before the flight, he joined us for some shopping in the open-air markets, where he made sure we found the most authentic souvenirs for the best possible prices. Before the trip, Rob and I had researched what the fine might be if we got caught skiing, so we'd arrived in Africa carrying a little more than that amount in US dollars in case we needed to bail out our Tanzanian guides, too. Now, with the expedition behind us, we stopped by the BAI headquarters on the way to the airport and shared that entire bundle of money with our special-agent helpers.

After all, the lesson in trust they'd given me was priceless. And it was a perfect primer for the last, biggest, and most difficult mountain on my list.

"LEAVING THE VALLEY"

BEFORE EVEREST, I'D HAD plenty of experience confronting the unknown, and I learned a lot about boundaries. The learning curve was especially swift when I lived with a wolf who depended on my guidance for his survival. And it may have been swiftest on a certain autumn day when Alta was seven years old and my close friend Yukon took us for a hike on an overgrown mining trail near Ophir that he'd just discovered during his reconnaissance for hunting season. The hard-to-follow trail led westward on a steep expanse of Yellow Mountain, crossed through several avalanche paths, and narrowed in the timber above the cliff tops at the mouth of the valley. I had purposely tried not to show Alta the trails that led out of the valley like this one did, because I had the sense that they led to danger.

Well, it's not like there's an easy exit out of here. And anyway, he's all grown up and knows the rules by now.

After an hour, we were perched above a part of the highway called the Ophir Loop and were exploring a tiny, partially collapsed log cabin whose owner had probably been able to drop his ore straight down the mountain to the train depot that had been on the Loop a hundred years before. Inside, Yukon found some turn-of-the-century hinges and latches in the debris, and while I tried to be interested, I couldn't shake my concern that it had been ten minutes since I'd seen Alta.

Just as I opened my mouth to say we needed to start back and find Alta, a blur of caramel-colored fur appeared from around a corner of the cabin before disappearing. As soon as I realized it had been an elk racing through the tightly grouped trees, I also recognized the look of panic in its eyes.

Oh, no.

On cue, Alta came peeling around the corner, following in the elk's trail. With an infinitesimal pause in his stride, he looked at me standing in the cabin doorway as if to say, "Did you see that?" and then he was gone.

"Alta! No!" I yelled as I raced after him, focusing on going as fast as I could on the rocky, overgrown trail. After rounding each corner, I lifted my eyes from my footing just long enough to desperately scan the terrain for a sign of either animal.

When I finally caught sight of the elk, I couldn't believe what I was seeing. Faced with crossing the scree-covered avalanche path that obscured the trail ahead, the elk turned sharply downhill instead and ran toward a cluster of trees that was like a finger jutting over a seventy-five-foot cliff that I knew was on the other side of them. Alta was a hundred feet behind.

I stopped in my tracks. "Nooooooo!"

The elk launched off the cliff, and Alta must have realized it was airborne, because at the last possible second he slowed down and veered to the right of the finger. His adjustment was enough to limit his own flight to fifty feet, and he landed in the rocks above the elk. Certain I'd find them both dead, I ran down to them on rubbery legs. Instead, they were both making horrible sounds of pain. Judging by the way she tried to move but couldn't stand up, the elk had probably at least broken her hind leg. Meanwhile, Alta lay crumpled in a heap and didn't try to stand until I reached him, and when he did wobble to his feet, he looked unable or unwilling to walk.

Having worked as a stonemason for seven summers by now, I was able to carry Alta when I needed to, and I scooped up all eighty-five pounds of him and stumbled on an upward diagonal back toward the trail on the other side of the rocky avalanche path.

"What the…" Yukon said when he met us on the trail.

Shaking with sadness, disbelief, and fear for Alta's life, I gently put him down and sat next to him with my arms wrapped around him. "He chased the elk off that cliff. She went farther than he did, but they're both hurt."

Yukon approached the elk, which tried to move but couldn't, so we decided to go home and come back with his hunting rifle.

I prodded Alta's hips to try to get him to stand. "Woo, can you walk?" He wouldn't take a step, so I picked him up again and started along the forested trail.

Many rest breaks later, during which I'd gently lower him to the ground to ask him to try again, he finally began to walk. After no more than fifty steps, though, he stopped and looked up at me as if to ask, "Will you please carry me again?" So I carried him again.

When we got back to Yukon's cabin, I set Alta on the old beanbag chair that was his bed and massaged his legs and hips to check whether anything was broken. He seemed to be in one piece, and I gave him two baby aspirin tucked inside some meat before Yukon and I went back to check on the elk. We found her in the same spot, but this time Yukon prodded her with a stick and she got up and limped away.

While I don't know whether the elk survived, Alta recovered slowly over the next several weeks, and the ordeal left him with a permanent bad hip. I hadn't wanted him to leave the valley for fear that he'd get a taste for wandering that far, and his run-in with the elk confirmed that my fear had been founded. As for me, the ordeal bolstered my already-healthy respect for the unknown.

Little did I know that nine years later, that respect would swell to epic proportions while I planned an Everest expedition and analyzed the potential dangers. The fact was, Everest was the biggest unknown I'd ever faced. I'd never been higher than 22,841 feet—the height of Aconcagua's summit—and if that climb had given me the headache of a lifetime, what would my body be in for on the highest mountain in the world? Meanwhile, Rob had never been higher than the 20,320-foot elevation of Denali's summit, and the hypoxia he'd experienced high on that mountain had compromised his decision-making abilities. Ultimately, though, I felt no less compelled to climb and ski Everest than I had about the other six of the Seven Summits. I was heeding my direct navigation—following my heart— and there was no question that come autumn of 2006, Mount Everest was where I belonged.

As for the skiing, I'd studied photos of Everest and believed it was skiable under the right conditions, but if anything were less than perfect on our summit day, which was highly likely at 29,000 feet, I'd want a ski belay down the forty-foot Hillary Step, which is as steep as the crux on Aconcagua's

Polish Glacier but 8,000 feet higher and with a far narrower margin of error. What would it be like to manage life-or-death rope work from behind oxygen masks with Nepali-speaking Sherpas as our sole partners? Obviously, with so many unknowns to confront, I needed to eliminate as many of them as I could. Just because I was "leaving the valley" in search of the same kind of potentially treacherous unknown that I'd tried to protect Alta from didn't mean I didn't want to control things to whatever extent possible.

Wally Berg had made his first climb to the summit of Everest in October 1992, but this time he'd be staying at base camp and manning the radios in a support role. In one of our biweekly planning phone calls, I asked him to recommend an American guide for the expedition. Having a guide would take the language barrier out of the equation.

"I'd suggest Dave Hahn," he said. "Right now he's tied with Pete Athans for the most Everest summits of any non-Sherpa, with seven, and he's a ski patroller at Taos in the winter, so he understands skiing."

"Will you call him for us to see if he's interested?" I was imagining what Dave's response would be if he heard from me first: "Who is this girl who wants to ski Everest, and in October? Fat chance." The days are shorter, colder, and less forgiving in October than in the spring—probably why no one had attempted to climb Everest during that post-monsoon season in several years.

Wally made the call, and Dave agreed to be our guide and accepted our unique conditions:

> 1. Rob and I want Dave's help with the decision-making and general guidance that will help us get to the top—things like the best time to leave Camp II to climb to Camp III.

> 2. We want Dave to be available to give us a ski belay on the Hillary Step.

> 3. Rob and I want complete autonomy once we begin our ski descent. Dave will be relieved of all standard guiding responsibility from the summit down.

Being a professional mountain guide, Dave was nervous about No. 3 and drew up a contract that spelled out our responsibilities as well as his.

Section 1.D covered the exception to his guiding obligation:

> *As it is a stated goal of the Climbers to conduct a ski descent of*
> *Mount Everest, it must be acknowledged that such activity is*
> *not within the expertise of the Guide. Hahn will not be expected*
> *to ski any portion of Mount Everest during the Expedition.*
> *While Hahn will make a reasonable effort to aid, enable, and*
> *advise Climbers with regard to decision-making and safety*
> *in the conduct of a ski descent, acknowledgment must be*
> *made that such a descent, and the consequences incurred by*
> *its undertaking, are beyond the Guide's control. Once begun,*
> *such a descent will take Climbers onto terrain which has not*
> *been adequately assessed for hazard by Hahn and which may*
> *well place Climbers in situations and locations which are not*
> *accessible to the Guide. Climbers assert that they have sufficient*
> *expertise to safely attempt such a descent. Furthermore, they*
> *acknowledge that once on skis, they have released Hahn from*
> *responsibility toward their personal safety.*

Rob and I were only too happy to sign—this wouldn't be a muddled situation like we'd had on Vinson.

As for physically preparing ourselves for the climb, we spent long days climbing favorite alpine routes in the Tetons. The North Face had signed me on as a member of the Global Athlete Team in 2005 (and matched my sponsor's contribution toward the Everest expedition so that we could afford to hire Dave), and I'd requested that the company send Jimmy Chin, its most accomplished alpine-climber photographer, to document the Everest trip. Jimmy had accompanied Stephen Koch to the north side of Everest in 2003, when Koch snowboarded the Japanese Couloir from 23,000 feet during an attempt to snowboard from the summit. And in the spring of 2004, Jimmy went back to Everest and climbed to the summit via the Southeast Ridge as a working member of a film project led by David Breashears. Beyond his obvious qualifications, Jimmy lived just on the other side of Teton Pass from us and loved to ski.

Jimmy didn't know if he could squeeze such a long trip into his schedule on such short notice, but in the meantime he joined us for a couple of fifteen-hour training days that involved technical-climbing traverses of the highest mountains in the Tetons.

High on a spicy rock-ridge training route, Jimmy would sometimes say, "Do you need a rope here?" Although I wanted one, I knew I really didn't need one, so I said no. I also knew Jimmy was testing me—he'd told us he was 80 percent sure he could make the Everest trip, which really meant he was only 80 percent sure that Rob and I could pull off the climb—but I was also testing myself. Like Jimmy, I wanted to find out what I was capable of.

"Good," Jimmy would say, "because if you did, then we wouldn't make this in one day."

We forced ourselves to move fast and light, which is an equation for safety in the mountains, but it's also one for thirst and hunger because you just can't carry enough food or water, or stop long enough to eat and drink, if you want to cover that much terrain before darkness. Jimmy had a saying that coaxed us to run down the mountains: "No double-headlamp day!" For professional climbers to need a headlamp at the beginning and the end of a day is to admit defeat or at least admit that something hadn't gone as planned. We would start our climbs at 4:00 a.m., illuminating the trail with a headlamp, and finish at 7:00 or 8:00 p.m., so we regularly ran downhill to avoid defeat. Challenging ourselves this way was exactly the kind of training in teamwork, endurance, and attitude that we needed for Everest.

By the time the three of us completed our single-day climb of the Cathedral Traverse on August 8, Jimmy had decided his schedule could accommodate an October expedition to the Himalayas.

ROB AND I LEFT Jackson Hole on August 25 and flew to Kathmandu, Nepal, where we met Wally and Dave and two Canadian climbers who had signed on to the Berg Adventures Everest permit. After two days of organizing, we flew to Lukla in an eighteen-passenger plane designed for short takeoffs and landings, which would be necessary at an airport that's little more than a small piece of asphalt glued onto a 12 percent-grade mountainside among forested peaks and valleys. Sir Edmund Hillary, the first man to climb Everest (in 1953), built the airport in 1965, and although the landing is terrifying because the mountain that's dead ahead doesn't allow for aborted attempts, the flight saves the extra weeks of trekking from Kathmandu that early expeditions had to endure.

Even when starting from Lukla, though, it's a ten-day trek up the Dudh Kosi River and through Nepal's Khumbu region to get to base camp. While it's possible to walk the forty miles in fewer than ten days, it's normally not advisable due to the extreme elevation gain—base camp is at 17,500 feet. In his planning, Wally did everything he could to set us up for success with our acclimatization, and that included adding an overnight side journey to the village of Thame and the Thame Monastery so that our trek covered more distance and lasted eleven days.

"You aren't trying to get to base camp as fast as possible so you can turn around and go home," Wally said. "Eventually you'll be climbing 12,000 feet above it, so you should feel good when you get there."

Our side journey also extended to the village of Khumjung, where Hillary built a school in 1961 and where Jimmy met us because his tight schedule hadn't allowed for trekking slowly through the lower Khumbu.

In Kathmandu we'd separated our gear so that when we landed in Lukla, we could hand our duffel bags of high mountain gear and skis to the Khumbu equivalent of a truck driver—a yak herder. In our case it was a woman, and she loaded them onto the backs of her zopkios. The hybrid offspring of a yak and a Tibetan bull cow, zopkios are excellent pack animals at high elevations, and they regularly work as cargo carriers in this land of no roads. While our bags rode the express to base camp, the single duffel bag we'd packed with our sleeping bags and other daily items for camping on the trail or sleeping at lodges traveled via a zopkio convoy that paralleled our route—and pace—through the villages of the Khumbu. All that we carried on our backs were day packs with drinking water, snacks, and several clothing layers to match the changing conditions in the region, which was experiencing the end of summer's wet monsoonal pattern.

And this was a great place to travel light and focus on the beauty surrounding us. As we passed through the humble villages of stone homes with some of the most spectacular views to be found anywhere in the world, I couldn't shake the feeling that we were crossing through someplace every bit as exotic and otherworldly as Shangri-La.

IN 1923, BRITISH CLIMBER George Mallory was attempting Everest for his third time when a reporter asked him the question, "Why do you want to climb Mount Everest?" Mallory, who would never return from that attempt, famously replied, "Because it's there."

Mallory's reason had never resonated with me, yet like many climbers, I was at a loss to answer that question as succinctly as Mallory had. I wanted to ski the Seven Summits, of which Everest was the highest, and I'd always been drawn to high places and personal challenges, but none of those explanations pulled it all together. Incredibly, within an hour of meeting the esteemed Lama Geshe, I finally had my answer.

As important as devising a plan for getting gear to base camp is, almost as much emphasis is placed on visiting a Buddhist lama along the way to receive an auspicious blessing for your climb. Wally had arranged for our team to receive its blessing from Lama Geshe in the village of Pangboche, at 13,000 feet, on the seventh day of our trek to base camp. Lama Geshe had studied Buddhism in the 1950s in Tibet, where he earned the Buddhist equivalent of a PhD before fleeing the Chinese occupation and returning to Pangboche at the end of the decade. He's one of the highest-ranking lamas in the region—*geshe* means an academic degree accorded to a master—and we were thrilled to be granted a meeting with him. Not least of all because Rob, Jimmy, and I needed all the help we could get with the ski descent we'd planned.

Along with Wally and wife Leila Silveira, the Canadian climbers, and several Sherpa climbers, we stepped into a house nestled at the top of this hilly village in the Buddhist Khumbu region. Seated in his receiving room at a table that held a bowl of rice and stacks of Tibetan scripts, the gray-haired lama greeted us. Out the window to his left was a view of the terraced farming valley below, stone walls segmenting the small plots. To his right was a wall filled from countertop to ceiling with photos of climbers holding Lama Geshe blessing cards atop Everest, also known in Tibetan as Chomolungma ("goddess mother of mountains").

In observance of ancient Tibetan Buddhist tradition, each of us approached Lama Geshe with the offer of a white *kata*, a silk scarf that symbolizes the purity of intention, while the exchange itself symbolizes the karmic principle of giving and receiving. It wouldn't have been right to arrive expecting a blessing without first bringing a gift. Smiling, Lama Geshe took the *katas* from our open palms, said something in Tibetan, and placed them delicately around our necks. Then, with hands in prayer position, he bowed his head and touched his forehead to ours. When it was my turn, I could feel his warmth radiate to my heart and already felt blessed.

After we'd all taken seats, Ang Temba—our sirdar, the manager of the Sherpas and all the details of our overland journey to base camp—made introductions for us, since he could understand Lama Geshe's Tibetan enough to translate it into Nepali for the Sherpas and into English for the Westerners. When he was done, Lama Geshe cut to the chase.

"Why do you wish to climb Chomolungma?" he asked, as translated by Ang Temba.

What? This is supposed to be a blessing ceremony. I wasn't expecting to be put on the spot with a question like that!

Draped in dark red robes with saffron accents, he leaned forward and looked carefully into the eyes of each person present as if to invoke an answer. Thoughts swirled in my head, but I refrained from putting any into words because they weren't clear enough yet.

Another climber spoke up. "I want to raise money for a children's charity in my hometown of Vancouver."

He went on to elaborate, and then Lama Geshe spoke again. "You must have kindness for all beings at the root of the reason for whatever you do if you wish to have continued success." Then, as if to be sure that we grasped what he was saying, he said it again.

"If someone is climbing for himself," he added, "he may have good luck for a couple of years before his life falls over and the good fortune stops. But if someone is climbing and in general acting for the betterment of others and always keeping others in mind, then this person will continue to be lifted up and will continue to find success."

We all smiled as we contemplated his words.

"I am here to continue in all ways," Wally said reverently. "To continue to lead trips and continue to work toward the goal that we all return home successful and as friends."

Lama Geshe nodded. "The eyes and the ears are the sun and the moon of the rest of our body, which is the Earth. The top of our head"—

he made a circle above his head with his hand—"is the junction of heaven and Earth. We all want to be up that high, and this is why we touch foreheads with lamas, with each other, to recognize that higher place. It is also important to remember the heart, in the realm of the Earth body, and to act from there."

The truth he'd captured pierced my heart, and I suddenly understood why I wanted to climb Everest.

I want to go to the top of the highest mountain in the world so that I can experience my own junction of heaven and Earth at the junction of heaven and Earth. And if I'm able to have the kindness of other beings at the root of the reason for whatever I do, then my climb and ski become less about me and more about what I may be able to do for other people.

I was so moved by this revelation that I couldn't begin to comprehend wanting to climb Chomolungma simply "because it's there."

Lama Geshe went on to explain meditation techniques and the concept of mental control.

"Have you noticed the prayer flags that flutter in the wind?" he asked.

It was impossible not to notice them. We'd seen the small colorful flags hung from every bridge, pole, and spiritually significant place in Khumbu. The prayers printed on them are thought to be spread by the wind.

"The prayer flags in our minds are moving too fast, and we have to slow them down. Similar to sitting next to a body of moving water and stopping it from flowing downstream. Quiet the mind. Slow the prayer flags down."

After his lessons, Lama Geshe gave each of us a small cloth square tied delicately with crimson- and saffron-colored blessing strings. He chanted over each pendant, tossed rice over his shoulder during his pauses, and placed the gifts around the *katas* we were still wearing.

"Never take them off while you are climbing Chomolungma," he said. "And after you are finished, wear them whenever you are someplace dangerous, like in an airplane."

He concluded the three-hour blessing by writing personalized notes to the Mother Goddess Chomolungma, whom Tibetans believe inhabits the high reaches of the mountain. In the notes, he used our first names and asked Chomolungma to grant us permission to safely climb to her summit and give us help when we needed it.

"Make sure that at all times this card is on the top of your backpack so that Chomolungma can see it easily." He handed Rob, Jimmy, and me our cards. "Since you will be skiing, I asked for special protection for you on the way down."

Like I said, all the help we could get.

AFTER VISITING LAMA GESHE, I had plenty of time and mental space in the next three days of trekking to contemplate what he'd said, and as I did, my reason for wanting to climb Everest crystallized further. For my entire life, I'd been called to seek the highest places, just like Alta had always been. But now I also understood that being in those places—the juncture between earth and sky—opened my heart to a heightened kind of love, a higher love for the planet, her people, and myself. And I realized that maybe the greatest limitation people experience is thinking they can't achieve something they want to achieve. By challenging myself here, perhaps I could inspire others to challenge their perceived limitations— that's why I wanted to climb and ski this mother goddess of mountains.

But first I had to do it. And live through it.

DON'T RUSH THE MOUNTAIN

O N SEPTEMBER 9, THE last day of our trek, we left behind everything that was alive and green and entered a world of rock and ice known as the Khumbu Glacier. Thankfully, a dozen Sherpa members of our team had already been setting up base camp, and it looked as much like a home away from home as we could have hoped for under the conditions. Front and center was a six-foot-tall stone *chorten*, a structure that marks a spiritually significant location, in this case the entrance to the climbing route. A wooden pole stood twenty feet high in the center of the *chorten*, which our advance team had built, and together they served as the anchor point for prayer flags hung on thin strands of rope that stretched north, south, east, and west.

A tan outfitters tent big enough to stand up in and to seat ten people at the card tables in the middle was the dining tent for us Westerners. Next to it, the Sherpas had carefully built the expedition kitchen inside a similar-sized dark green tent. Hand-stacked stone walls lined the cook tent and offered seats for the Sherpas to use while eating, as well as nooks and crannies for the supplies that would sustain us for two months if necessary. On the other side of the dining tent from the kitchen was a smaller green tent to be used as our communications headquarters, home to Wally's computer which was powered by a generator. Our yellow North Face sleeping tents had already been set up around the periphery of the common cooking, eating, and communications zones, so our bedrooms were ready to move into.

One of the joys of adventure travel is immersing yourself in the local culture and customs. I'd certainly enjoyed our visit with Lama Geshe, and from reading accounts of others' climbs on Everest, I knew that we wouldn't be going higher onto the mountain, or even into the icefall, until we conducted our *puja* blessing ceremony. The *puja* is an unwritten requirement of practicing Buddhists, who believe it's not safe to climb Everest until the proper chants, offerings, and blessings are made at the altar built into a *chorten* at the base-camp entrance to the mountain. Lama Geshe had appointed a young lama to officiate at our ceremony, and conveniently, he also happened to be the camp cook. I had to appreciate the fact that a spiritual leader would be in charge of nourishing us.

Lama Geshe had also done a meditation and divination on the question of what the best day for our *puja* ceremony would be, as Ang Temba told us that evening during our first dinner together at base camp.

"His answer was, 'September 11, but the Americans probably won't like that day, so a second choice is September 13.'"

The Americans among us looked at each other and laughed.

"If Lama Geshe says it's the best day, then let's do it that day," I said.

There was no way we'd come this far and invested this much time, effort, and money to start our climb on the second-most auspicious day. Besides, considering the fact that Wally lived in Canmore, Alberta, that made it three Canadians on the expedition, and the rest of us thought the ceremony would be a fitting homage to those killed in the 9/11 terrorist attack in 2001.

The next day, September 10, was designated a day of rest so that we could grant all due respect to our new high-elevation home. Sleeping at altitude produces more hypoxia than day trips to altitude that include a return to low elevation, and I'd be lying if I said I didn't feel the effects of sleeping at 17,500 feet. I had a slight headache, and if I walked from the sleeping tent that I shared with Rob to the kitchen tent too quickly, I became short of breath. The risk of altitude sickness isn't necessarily affected by training or physical fitness, although adequate hydration and, to a certain extent, an increased respiratory rate can help the body acclimatize. The process would just take time.

After breakfast the next morning, all twenty-two of us gathered around the *chorten* to prepare for the ceremony. An immense blue plastic tarp was folded in half lengthwise so that it stretched out a full twenty feet, with the middle in front of the three-foot-square *chorten*. The central spot in front of the *chorten* was reserved for the lama, who placed a heavy-duty black plastic storage box on the tarp. It had probably held critical kitchen tools during the approach to base camp, but for the *puja* it would serve as a table for scrolls and other ceremonial items. On each side of the lama's cushion there was room for five of us to sit cross-legged shoulder to shoulder, and the other ten expedition members stood at the corners or behind the lama. On the *chorten* in front of us were two altars of burning juniper branches, and beside it, touching the stone, were piles of our boots, ice axes, and skis, which we'd placed there to receive the *puja* blessings.

During the ceremony, there was much reading from sacred texts, chanting, drumming, and cymbal-clanging, along with offerings to the gods, or goddesses, and the mortal consumption of fruit, chocolates, tea, and even *chang*, a Nepalese/Tibetan alcoholic beverage similar to beer. The ceremony was punctuated by frequent refills of our cups of traditional butter tea that we placed on flat rocks in front of us, mostly so we could keep our hands together in front of our hearts in prayer position. My favorite part came at the closing, when bowls of *tsampa*, a fine light-gray flour made from barley, were passed around and we took turns smearing it on each other's faces to symbolize that we hoped the recipient would live long enough to have gray hair.

The cloud ceiling had been 2,000 feet above our heads at the start of the ceremony, but it gradually dropped until a mix of light snow and rain began to fall. When it became apparent that the ceremony would last a while, some of us retreated to our tents to change into warmer clothes and then returned to our positions, though the lama never left his. He used a Ziploc bag to protect his scripture pages when the precipitation started, and another Sherpa held an umbrella over the lama's head when necessary.

After the ceremony, Ang Temba passed on to us the good news that the Sherpas had deemed it successful and that we would be able to begin climbing through the icefall immediately. Instead of throwing a party to drink the alcohol left over from the *puja*—none of us were willing to ingest anything that would compromise our ability to acclimatize—we spent the afternoon organizing food to be carried to Camp I. It finally felt like we were going to go climbing.

THE NEXT DAY, A light snow fell in the morning, just as it had during the *puja*, so from a weather perspective, things seemed to be right on schedule. We'd arrived at base camp at the end of the summer monsoon season, when it rains or, at high elevations, snows every day, but now the daily precipitation appeared to be tapering off. According to the annual pattern, the weather was due to clear any day now as the winds shifted toward the south. For climbing, the post-monsoon season is less popular than the spring because of the shorter, colder days, but it suited me for two reasons: I don't like crowds, and there was a good chance that there would be more snow on the mountain than in the normal climbing season. This was perfect timing: No other Everest climbing permits had been issued during the post-monsoon season that year, and from base camp, there was no other expedition in sight.

In the dining tent, we hunkered over a calendar as Wally sketched out our ideal climbing schedule. When he was done, it looked like this:

Ideal Everest climbing schedule

Part 1: Icefall to Camp I

9/13	Base camp to CI, round trip
9/14	Rest at base camp
9/15	Rest at base camp
9/16	Climb to CI and spend the night
9/17	Rest at CI
9/18	Climb to CII then back to CI to spend a 2nd night
9/19	Return to base camp
9/20	Rest at base camp
9/21	Rest at base camp

Part 2: Nights at ABC

9/22	Camp II
9/23	Camp II
9/24	Back to base camp
9/25	Rest
9/26	Rest
9/27	Camp II
9/28	Climb to CIII for the day and back to CII for night

9/29	Back to base camp
9/30	Rest
10/1	Rest
10/2	Camp II
10/3	Camp III to sleep for the night
10/4	Back to base camp
Part 3:	**Summit Rotation**
10/5	Rest
10/6	Rest
10/7	Camp II?
10/8	Camp III?
10/9	Camp IV?
10/10	Summit?

It's important to have goals and targeted dates, but it's just as critical to be flexible, especially in the mountains. As soon as the final date had been filled in on the schedule, though, Wally laid down a ground rule that didn't sound flexible at all.

"This first round trip climb to CI shouldn't take you more than eight hours, five up and three down. If it does, then you probably shouldn't be climbing Everest. By the time you go for the summit, you'll probably be able to get to CI in three hours."

Wally had been nothing but sweet and supportive with all his communications regarding the climb, and I was a little surprised by the way he was laying down the law now. Not to mention a little nervous. But at least I knew my anxiety would be short-lived. By the same time tomorrow, I'd know whether I had what it takes to climb higher on Everest.

WE GOT UP AT 4:00 a.m., and with the help of the kitchen cook, who made us hot water and breakfast, we were ready to go an hour later. As we approached the *chorten* in the dark, we saw a juniper fire burning on the altar, and we followed the lead of the two climbing Sherpas who were with us and used a wave of our hands to waft the juniper smoke over our bodies and then took a pinch of rice from the altar and tossed it over our shoulders. This was no time to deny ourselves extra protections.

Besides the maintaining of a protective juniper fire while a climber is on the mountain, Sherpa traditions surrounding an Everest climb include always moving around the *chorten* in a clockwise manner, leaving on the left side of the *chorten* and completing the circle on the return. So we headed to the left and officially embarked on our ideal climbing itinerary.

It wasn't without trepidation, though. There have been more deaths in the icefall of the Khumbu Glacier than on any other area of Everest, and that sobering fact weighed heavily on me as we started up it. The cold of the early-morning hours keeps the glacier frozen and reduces the chance of spontaneous serac collapses, but the Khumbu moves about three feet down the mountain a day, and there's no knowing when this slow-moving mile-wide river of ice blocks will send one of the blocks tumbling. Meanwhile, the snow beneath our feet could easily have been hiding a crevasse that could snap an ankle or swallow us forever, never to be seen again. Despite the danger, though, it was a place of surreal beauty, with blue and white ice towering overhead like walls and spires.

Ahead of our arrival, "Icefall Doctor" Ang Nima, the Sherpa on our team whose responsibility it was to keep our route open through the ever-shifting icefall, and his team had forged the "easiest" path through the 2,000 vertical feet of ice, though it was just barely passable at best. And it would require the use of aluminum ladders. Lots of ladders. Both horizontal and vertical, usually with two or three tied together because most of the spans we'd need to cross were wider or higher than fifteen feet. And hundreds of feet deep.

At the first horizontal ladder, I took a few steps into the mouth of the crevasse but backed up again to gather my composure. The ten steel spikes on each crampon didn't always match up perfectly with the rungs and it felt as if I were wearing metal vampire fangs on my feet, with the object of the game being to balance on them while tiptoeing across an obstacle course that swayed and buckled with every step. The absolute trust I needed to have in myself and in Ang Nima's ladder system was more than I could muster at the moment.

I looked at Dave on the other side of the ladder. "Can I just scoot across on my butt?"

"You could, and I've seen it done, but it would take longer than just walking across, and we might not make it in five hours." Translation: Kit, if you can't do this, you can't climb Everest.

The line of demarcation had been drawn, and from that moment on I went as fast as I could across the ladders without stopping or retreating again. I focused on breathing audibly and exhaling completely, a mental training device I'd adopted for lead climbing on rock and making dicey ski moves. I also counted out loud because it helped me stay aligned with the task and in the moment.

Forty-two ladders and nearly five hours later, we topped out on our first run through the icefall. Right on target.

ON SEPTEMBER 16, THE weather threw us the first curveball. We woke up to snow falling at the rate of an inch an hour on our base-camp tents, so we called off the planned climb to CI. The next day, though, decent weather allowed us to move up to CI for the night, and in terms of our overall objective, we were still on target.

After a rest day at CI to acclimatize, we climbed up the low-angle glaciated valley called the Western Cwm (pronounced "coom") to see how our bodies felt at CII, which is at 21,000 feet. Cwm is Welsh for bowl-shaped valley, and this one is two and a half miles long and nestled beneath Everest and two other 26,000-foot-plus peaks, Nuptse and Lhotse. The several thousand feet of rock walls that surround the Cwm insulate it from the wind enough that early Everest climbers called it the Valley of Silence. When the sun rises in the morning to reflect off the snow and ice of Everest's west shoulder to the north and Nuptse to the south, the combination of still, silent air and the extreme solar radiation can cause temperatures to rise to one hundred degrees during the day before dropping back below zero when the sun sets.

As it turned out, probably as a result of the combination of the midday heat, the elevation, and the exertion, I came down with a thumping headache at CII that had me marveling at the acclimatization phenomenon. *To think that I'll really be able to sleep here for several nights and feel as normal as I do at base camp right now—that's almost unreal.*

I've heard that if an unacclimatized person were just dropped off at the summit of Everest or even at Camp IV, he or she would last about three minutes, and I was getting a taste of what that was all about. As for Rob, his main problem was that his back was out of whack, probably a delayed result of carrying his fairly large video camera and tripod on his shoulder for the climb through the icefall two days before. And Jimmy—well, he's so gifted at high elevations and adverse conditions that if he was feeling any adverse effects, I couldn't tell.

The three days of sleeping at Camp I were the first time on the expedition that Rob, Jimmy, Dave, and I cooked for ourselves on camp stoves. At Camp II, there would be a cook to prepare the food for everyone, but at Camp I there were no Sherpas with us and we ate the meals we'd carefully chosen and brought from North America. When Dave reheated some of his no-cook bacon for himself, the rest of us began to salivate.

"That smells delicious!" I said. "I could use some fat in my diet."

"Yeah, we really haven't had any meat since we started this expedition," Rob said, "and now we're up here eating bowls of instant mashed potatoes with butter. It's good, but it'd be better with some steak in it!"

"This is cruel, but do you want to know what I'm thinking of right now?" Jimmy said. "Tuscan steak. I had it at a restaurant in DC this year and got the recipe. You take a bunch of arugula, toss it with lemon, and mound it on a plate, then sauté thick slices of portobello mushroom while you grill a juicy rib-eye steak. Slice the steak and layer it on the bed of arugula, drizzle with some truffle oil, top it with the portobellos, and finish it with shavings of really good Parmesan cheese. The heat just lightly cooks the arugula and it's insane."

"Stop! You're killing me!" I said. "My body is so hungry for that!"

Jimmy laughed. "Mine, too. You know, when I was here last year with David Breashears, we were on the mountain for so long with the film project that he had meat flown in from a butcher in Kathmandu. Maybe we could do the same."

"Ooooh, I bet Ang Temba could arrange for that when we get back to base camp."

"I'll pay my part for sure," Rob said. "We can't climb this mountain without protein. I feel like my muscles are wasting away."

When we got back to base camp midmorning on September 20, the first thing we did was ask Ang Temba to order some meat for four carnivores in need.

SEPTEMBER 21 WAS A rest day at base camp, but a new storm came in at noon that dropped more than an inch of snow an hour and didn't show any sign of letting up. By the twenty-second, we were shoveling out our tents and the paths between them as the snow continued to fall. During a tea break in the dining tent, Ang Temba came in.

"Did you order the steaks?" Jimmy asked.

Ang Temba laughed. "I didn't think you were serious."

"Oh yes we are!" the three of us said in unison.

"OK, I'll go do it right now and we'll send Nima to pick them up in Lukla. It will probably take a week or more to get here, though."

The promise of fat, juicy steaks to fuel our muscles, which were atrophying from exertion and the drain of high elevation, gave us something to look forward to during the storm.

In the meantime, we read and practiced yoga together in the two-meter North Face dome tent that we'd set up for storing and sorting through climbing gear. When we'd arrived at base camp two weeks earlier, none of us could make it through all the standing poses in the Ashtanga Yoga primary series without becoming lightheaded and out of breath, but by the fourth day of the storm, we could do an entire ninety-minute yoga practice with almost no heavy breathing.

The gear tent also became the movie tent when Jimmy invited all the members of the expedition to watch a movie on his computer at four o'clock every day of the storm. About fifteen of us would show up, and the cook provided tea and popcorn. One day we watched the Academy Award-winning documentary *The Man Who Skied Down Everest*, which features Yuichiro Miura's spectacular ski descent from 26,000 feet on the South Col in 1970. At the time, Miura's specialty was daredevil speed skiing, and he'd developed a system in which he strapped a parachute to his back and deployed it to control his speed. During his descent of Everest, his plan backfired when the parachute did little to tame his excessive speed and he lost control and slid thousands of feet down the Lhotse Face—an uninterrupted fifty-degree pitch of hard snow and ice—covering a vertical mile in two minutes. Jimmy, Rob, and I had carefully studied those two minutes of film because the line that Miura tumbled down was the one we hoped to ski. Nobody had done it since Miura's attempt, and after watching the film, the climbing Sherpas in the audience became very uneasy.

"We're *not* using parachutes," I said. "We're going to make ski turns to slow down, so you don't need to worry about us."

Though they were as baffled by the idea as Saramo had been on Kilimanjaro, they trusted us and seemed to feel reassured.

By late afternoon of the fifth day, the storm finally came to a stop and clear skies returned. When the sun came out the next morning, the thunderclap of avalanches was almost as regular as the sound of waves would have been if we'd been lying on a beach. A perfect storm had laid down the perfect sliding conditions—thick slabs of snow that didn't bond well to the surface of the already-existing snow—and the daytime temperature change exacerbated the situation. Some of the releases were particularly large, and if I was in our tent when they happened, I could hear the hissing spindrift of snow hit its nylon walls. Even though we were more than 8,000 feet below and two miles away, the feeling that I might be buried alive in my tent without seeing my opponent was too much for me, and I'd rush to put my boots on and stand up outside just in time to see almost everyone else in camp doing the same thing: staring at a cloud of snow bearing down on us.

Even though we knew we were too far from these gigantic releases of new snow to be in grave danger, when the avalanches finally stopped at the end of the day, a certain weight was lifted. The storm was over. And we weren't the only ones who were relieved. Over the radio in the communications tent, Ang Temba and Wally heard that the storm had been a major event throughout India and Nepal, where it dumped as much as eight inches of rain in places. And all the expeditions that had been trying to climb the nearby 26,000-foot peak of Cho Oyu had packed up and left.

We hoped this was the last storm of the monsoon season, but even if it was, our schedule had been delayed by over a week now. The team held a meeting in the dining tent to discuss the situation.

"Some Sherpas will go into the icefall tomorrow to work on the route," Ang Temba said. "Three feet of snow fell, so we don't know how long that will take."

"There's not much we can do but sit tight until the Sherpas get the icefall open," Wally added, "so we'll probably be in base camp for another two days."

During the storm, I'd experienced plenty of moments filled with anxiety about the additional adversity we were being dealt. All this time and money and effort and we hadn't even spent a night at Camp II yet, much less climbed to Camp III like we would have by now on our ideal schedule.

In my yoga training, I'd learned the concept of "detachment from the outcome," an approach to life that acknowledges how stress develops when we're attached to a particular outcome; whether looking at success or failure, detaching yourself from that outcome is the only way to cultivate security in yourself. In this case, unless I stopped worrying about whether I could and would actually ski from the summit of Everest, I'd never get up there to try. The storm we'd just endured was forcing me to own the stress I was hiding from.

Before we'd left home in Jackson, Rob, Jimmy, and I had agreed on several books we could share on Everest, and one of them was the I Ching. Also known as the Book of Changes, the I Ching contains a divination system in which coins or sticks are tossed to create six lines that are either broken or solid and together form a hexagram, and the book itself is an oracle that describes the sixty-four possible hexagram combinations. Before Everest, all three of us had sporadically enjoyed using the I Ching as a tool to help answer difficult questions in our lives. My experience was that it usually helped steer me toward truths that on some level I already knew but were hard to accept. And on some level, I knew that this situation called for the I Ching. I called Rob and Jimmy to our tent.

"I can't stop thinking about when we should go back up the mountain," I said. "This sitting around is driving me crazy. Let's throw the I Ching coins."

They were game, agreeing that it would be a good way to gain some clarity on the issue. I went first, and as I shook the coins in my clasped hands, I silently asked my question.

When should we start pushing back up?

I threw the coins onto the sleeping bag and got hexagram No. 16, titled "Enthusiasm": "The path of least resistance is nonresistance."

Even though I didn't tell them my exact question, Rob and Jimmy laughed because they knew enough about what was on my mind. I had to laugh, too. I could finally hear myself. *Pushing back up? Kit, didn't you learn this lesson on Denali when you were trapped by weather? Or on Vinson Massif with that three-day storm? You thought you did, but obviously you didn't.*

Rob and Jimmy took turns with their own questions and got answers that corroborated mine. The message was clear: We would take it as it came but continue to be enthusiastic and ready to work hard. Personally, I would try to learn to add the path of least resistance to my mental repertoire. Not rushing the mountain was now as important as visualization, clarity, commitment, trust…*whew.*

While I worked to control my mind, the elite Sherpas on our team worked hard in the deep snow that the strong sun had crusted over. After just two days, they reported that they'd dug out the fixed lines and reset the ladders through the icefall. On September 29, they reached Camp I, where the top of only one of our four tents showed through the snow. They dug the tents out and discovered that, amazingly, only one pole was broken. We could climb back up to Camp I tomorrow, pack up our gear, and move on to Camp II the next day.

Actual Everest climbing schedule—Part 1
Icefall to Camp I

9/13	Base camp to CI, round trip
9/14	Rest day at base camp
9/15	Rest day at base camp
9/16	Woke to inch-an-hour snowfall and called day off at 4:00 a.m., stayed at base camp
9/17	Climbed to CI and spent the night
9/18	Rested at CI
9/19	Climbed to CII then back to CI
9/20	Returned to base camp

9/21	Rested at base camp—snowstorm began midmorning, heavy snowfall
9/22	Base camp—snowstorm
9/23	Base camp—snowstorm
9/24	Base camp—snowstorm
9/25	Base camp—snowstorm
9/26	Base camp—snowstorm stopped in the afternoon
9/27	Base camp—while the avalanches settled, clear weather
9/28	Base camp—Sherpa team worked to reestablish route through icefall
9/29	Base camp—Sherpa team reached CI to dig it out —tents buried

HAPPY ANNIVERSARY!

A N HOUR INTO OUR climb through the icefall on September 30, I was struggling to keep up with Rob, Jimmy, and Dave in the predawn.

"I don't feel well," I said. "I think I have too much weight in my pack."

"It's probably from ten days of inactivity," Dave said. "Give us all a little something to carry."

My mind raced through the reasons that it might be hurting so much to keep a normal pace. I did have a lot in my pack because we were going to be up high for the next week and I wanted Rob to have a lighter load so he could take it easy on his back—it was still bothering him from our last rotation to Camp I, when we carried our skis and he carried the heavy camera. Or it could have been the lack of fat and protein in my diet, since our steaks hadn't arrived.

Whatever it is, Kit, you don't need to be so strong all the time. Just take a little help.

So I gave a few pounds away, which did feel better, and it must have helped because this time it took us only four hours to get to Camp I, ahead of the Canadians.

See, you didn't have to be so hard on yourself, Kit. At least you made it in good time carrying a decent load.

Because the storm had taken so many days away from us, we readjusted our schedule with the aim of getting a lot done during this rotation. The plan was to acclimatize well to Camp II and even spend a night at Camp III before heading back to base camp. The next day, we broke down the tents at Camp I and carried everything that we could to Camp II. What we couldn't manage we left for the Sherpas to pick up on their way through. Rob's back acted up en route, so once we passed the last ladders in the lower cwm and could take our crampons off for the deep-snow trek to Camp II, he let me carry his crampons. It felt good to be able to return the favor he'd done me the day before, and I was reminded that there's a strength in receiving help, especially if it's the safest and most efficient choice for your teammates.

By the time we rolled into Camp II at 10:45 a.m., we were sweating profusely from the heat of the sun, which had been nearly unbearable for the past hour, and we settled in for some acclimatizing. From our position looking up toward the Lhotse Face, parts of the rope that our Sherpa team had fixed on the climbing route above Camp II weren't visible, even with binoculars. Avalanches had either buried them or ripped them off the mountain.

The next morning, the four of us and Mingma Ongell Sherpa, one of the hot-shot climbing Sherpas who'd done the most work putting the route in before the storm, left Camp II at seven thirty to check out the situation for ourselves.

"How long should it take us to get to the bergschrund at the bottom of the Lhotse Face?" I asked Dave. I found that I always wanted to know what the norm and the ideal were so I could make sure I stayed within that range. I was constantly concerned with whether I was going fast enough, whether I was keeping up a summit pace. I hadn't felt that pressure on any other mountain.

"An hour and a half at most. But we're not acclimatized yet, and we'll have to break trail."

That elevation gain of just under 1,000 feet ended up taking us two hours to cover, and from the bergschrund we could see that there was rope almost up to where we would establish Camp III at 23,000 feet. When we returned to Camp II, Mingma radioed Ang Temba to let him know we needed more rope even if it had to come from Kathmandu.

The short outing had been strenuous enough that we spent the rest of the day, and all of the next, in a mode that we began to call "aggressive resting." On the second day, when the sun hit the tent at 8:15 a.m. I could hardly get out of the tent to have coffee in the group dome tent where we sat on foam pads for meals and meetings. And after breakfast, I had no problem going back to our tent and sleeping for a couple of more hours.

It was 12:30 p.m. when I woke up, and a warm yellow glow was lighting the tent.

"I don't know who could be bored up here," I said to Rob. "There's so much quality chillin' to do. Resting is a full-time job."

He laughed.

"I'm really grateful we aren't moving today. I feel I really needed this."

Incidentally, sex wasn't an option during such downtime or any other time. During the trek a month before, Wally had given us the lecture: "There is no sauce-making on Everest, not even at base camp. It's considered an insult to Chomolungma. So if you want or need to do that during your climb, then hike down to Gorak Shep or someplace else for a night or two." Afterward, I said to Rob, "You know, once we get to base camp I'm not leaving the mountain. If we can't honor the mother goddess by waiting, then we shouldn't be here. I'd rather keep our focus than miss a climbing window or, worse, get sick from being inside a lodge with other people's colds just so we can have sex."

If there was any doubt, the benefits of taking rest days seriously became perfectly clear the next day, October 4, which started with Dave and me climbing the fixed lines toward where the climbing Sherpas were beginning to stockpile the equipment that would become Camp III. Rob and Jimmy decided to test the snow and see what it was like to climb up the lower part of the Lhotse Face ski line directly under the South Col and then ski down it. They were a horizontal mile away from us, and when blowing snow wasn't obscuring our view, we could see them as dark specks moving upward across the immense white slope. At times, the spindrift coming off the Lhotse Face above us would mix with a blast of wind that felt like sandpaper on the exposed skin of my face.

Halfway into our climb, Dave pulled out the radio and called Jimmy and Rob. "Don't hang it too far out there if the wind is ripping as hard as it is here."

They were climbing without the security of a fixed rope, and while Dave was doing his best to temper his guiding approach to match our independent focus, his concern was palpable and justified. The wind tried to knock me over several times, and I dropped to a knee so that it didn't get the upper hand. There were no useful breaks on the forty- to forty-five-degree snow and ice, so to keep my fingers moving and ward off frostbite, I had to constantly shift my hands into slightly different positions on my ice axe and jumar, which is the name climbers use for the clamp that automatically tightens onto a fixed rope when it's weighted and slides forward when no weight is applied. I worried that the temperatures and the wind chill were getting the best of the toes on my right foot, which I couldn't feel. The discomfort reminded me of the familiar saying, "Mountaineering is the art of suffering. The sooner you decide you like it, the better you'll be at it." Though I'd always liked suffering and even though I was pretty good at it, today was testing my limits. That silly saying seemed about as lousy an answer for how to deal with my pain as "Because it's there" is for why I climb mountains.

I searched for a better way to wrap my head around the grueling climb up the Lhotse Face, during which the two front points of my crampons were the only part of my footwear that made contact with the steep, icy slope. Many times I couldn't even see my boots thanks to the raging spindrifts. Halfway up, I remembered Lama Geshe's prayer-flag teaching and tried to apply it to this climb. In my mind, the prayer flags that had been moving so fast became the wind and the blowing snow, which sometimes pulled a piece of my long hair free from under my hat and pinned the strands down my throat, creating a feeling of choking on myself. When I was successful at applying Lama Geshe's lesson, I felt like I was on a Hollywood set and none of the actual painful circumstances had any real bearing on me. Not the elevation, the wind, the snow, the cold, the fatigue, the lightheadedness—nothing could alter the wonderful peaceful sensation that I was climbing nearly effortlessly in perfect conditions. When I let the elevation and the wind and the cold and the blowing snow into my head, I lost the ability to slow the prayer flags down and wanted to cry out in desperation and go home. Instead, I fought with everything I had to get back to the feeling of slowing the flags down.

By the time we turned around at Camp III four hours later, I'd made it to a new personal elevation record—higher than Aconcagua. And on our way down, I watched Rob and Jimmy ski the lower South Pillar route and was filled with hope at seeing that it was technically possible. Now, if I could just get better at slowing down the flags, I stood a chance of climbing and skiing this mountain.

When we got back to camp, the skies had completely clouded over and a roaring freight train of wind was whipping around the massif above us. During dinner, the sound of the train was momentarily replaced by a loud explosion, and we scrambled out from the dome tent in time to see a massive slide come off Nuptse. Its plume crossed the Western Cwm before stopping a few hundred feet from our Camp II. I took a deep bracing breath. Being at this particular spot on the globe was like standing on the ledge of a skyscraper, with danger above, below, and in front of us.

After our fourth night at Camp II, we needed a day of rest to recover from the sleepless night we'd all spent with headaches caused by so much exertion in the thin air. There was plenty to do, though, and in the afternoon we packed to move up to Camp III the next day, October 6, to spend the night. Sleeping at Camp III, at almost 24,000 feet, was a grim prospect given my experience on the Lhotse Face the day before, but it had to be done. If it didn't happen on this rotation, we wouldn't be finished with our acclimatization, and we'd originally hoped to be going for the summit by October 10.

Enthusiasm. The path of least resistance is nonresistance.

AFTER MAKING THE FIVE-HOUR climb to Camp III, a part of me wished I had made that ski run with Rob and Jimmy two days earlier, but on that day it had felt more important to accompany Dave to Camp III to make sure I could get there and remove that unknown from the map I was making in my head. As tired as I was, today was my last chance to do a practice ski run, because early tomorrow morning we'd leave our skis at Camp III and retreat all the way to base camp until it was time for our summit bid. I'd practiced skiing with an oxygen mask in the Tetons in June, but that was four months ago and I hadn't been on skis since. Even though I was nervous about overextending myself after the climb and before a long night at high elevation, if I were going to make practice turns on Everest, this was it.

It was just after four, with the afternoon light waning, when I strapped my crampons back on and prepared to climb out of the tent to follow the Sherpa's boot track above. Rob looked concerned.

"Are you sure you want to do this? You don't have to, you know."

"Actually, I do. I have to know that I can do this before I try from the summit." I struggled to figure out the best way to put my oxygen mask on and then my goggles and the hood of my down suit all while connected by an oxygen hose to the cylinder of gas in my backpack, which was waiting outside the tent. "I'm really nervous and feel a little shaky. I probably won't go far." *Go now, Kit, or you'll change your mind.*

As Rob watched from the tent, Jimmy followed me just far enough to take photos. Alone a few hundred feet above camp, I tried to take my pack off so that I could get to my skis and start my run, but the oxygen hose was tangled in my ski bindings and I felt trapped. My frustration mounted until I felt as if I were pinned under heavy surf. I realized I wasn't breathing well because I was trying so hard to extricate myself, and for a flash I desperately wished someone were with me to help. Then, just as quickly, I accepted that that wasn't the case and slowed the prayer flags down and figured out how to disentangle myself.

Once I got my skis on, I was faced with a very wind-rippled snow surface, like frozen waves in an ocean. I began to ski but didn't like the way I had to hold on to the bottom of each turn with an intense grasp, as if I'd be bucked off my feet by the hardened ridges of snow if I didn't. Eventually, I moved to the skier's right, where the surface looked smoother, but it also put me farther from the security of the tents and left me far more alone and exposed.

"Take it easy out there," Jimmy shouted.

By the time I'd descended to the elevation of Camp III, I had a good sense of the ski conditions, and they were horrible. It didn't matter, though, because in just that short descent, I'd learned to tailor my ski technique to match the mountain. As I faced 2,500 vertical feet of serious potential consequences below me, I felt humbled but confident, both of which were good because when it came time to descend the Lhotse Face for real, we'd be skiing an even steeper pitch of more than 5,000 vertical feet with the tents a horizontal mile away.

THE NEXT MORNING, OCTOBER 7, it was finally time to leave the high mountain for a rest at base camp. Rob and Dave got ready first and began their descent, but I was delayed because my hands were so cold from the winter temperatures that had ridden in on the days-long windstorm. The sun hadn't hit our Lhotse Face camp yet, but we had to get going quickly so we'd be through the icefall by noon, and even that was a stretch. With Jimmy watching, waiting to accompany me down the fixed lines, I repeatedly tried to get my harness buckled before finally crying out in fear and frustration. I didn't want to take the time to crawl back into the tent to warm myself, because Jimmy might get cold while he waited, and worse, I'd jeopardize the entire team's safety if we arrived too late at the icefall.

"I'm scared," I said. "My hands are so cold. Can you do this for me?" I held my mitten-covered hands out of the way so Jimmy could see that my harness was still unbuckled. Exposing my vulnerability like that, I felt as close to Jimmy as I ever had.

"Sure," he said. As he deftly threaded the webbing, I was filled with gratitude and relief. And he stayed right with me for the entire descent, which I made as fast as I could with an arm wrapped around the fixed line because my hands were useless. After our team regrouped at Camp II and the cook fed us breakfast, my hands finally began to thaw in the warmth of the sun, but the heat brought its own problems. We walked as fast as we could through the cwm to the icefall, but it was after ten and the snow surface had heated up to the point where water was dripping from the crevasse overhangs. As we crossed the first narrow snow bridge, a collapse occurred far beneath it and felt like an earthquake. I jumped back, and Dave and Jimmy and Rob, who had been in front, jumped ahead.

"At least it already went," Jimmy said.

I gathered my composure and speedily crossed the new dip in the snow bridge, and without any more big events, we exited the bottom of the icefall—with the help of the forty-two ladders again—two hours later.

There's a great degree of luck whenever somebody goes through the icefall, no matter what time of day. We certainly had our share, and I was grateful for the *puja* rituals we'd honored.

"Welcome back!" Ang Temba greeted us back at base camp. "I bet you're hungry. There's a cooler waiting for you in the dining tent."

Expecting to see rib-eye steaks marbled with dreamy fat, Jimmy and I opened the lid of the plastic white cooler to find it filled with filet mignon. We couldn't mask our disappointment.

"Is there something wrong?" Ang Temba asked.

"Not really," Jimmy said diplomatically. "It's wonderful and we can't wait to eat some. It's just that we thought we ordered rib eyes, because we wanted the extra fat, and these are filet mignon."

"I'm sorry. Maybe the butcher was surprised by the order and wanted to send only the best to you, so he chose filet mignon. That's probably why it took so long, too. Nima carried it on his shoulders from Lukla in three days and just arrived."

As we looked dejectedly at the packages of filet mignon that most people would have welcomed with open arms and open mouths, Jimmy noticed that some bacon had been tossed into the mix, and he came up with the perfect solution: bacon-wrapped steaks! We'd get our "marbled" beef after all.

The cook would go on to prepare the steaks for us several times over the next few days, during which our biggest obligation was to eat and rest. And Rob and I would celebrate our sixth wedding anniversary over a breakfast of filet mignon, bacon, eggs, and rice.

"Happy anniversary," Jimmy said, raising a mug of tea. "And please don't invite me to another one!" We all laughed and were grateful to have three more rest days ahead of us. Aside from resting, I would be welcoming my mother to base camp if she arrived as planned that afternoon. In July of that year, her friend Wendy had guessed that I was doing the Seven Summits, and when Mom surprised me by asking if it was true, there was no denying it. Even though Rob and I had just wanted to focus on our climb and not be distracted by visits from supporters, I'd felt compelled to offer her the option of joining Leila Silveira on a ten-day trek to base camp that she'd be leading while we were on the mountain. It didn't seem likely that she'd accept, though. At age sixty-three, she'd never left America and had lost interest in hiking more than a decade earlier when my parents moved from Colorado back to Massachusetts. And we didn't have the kind of relationship where we talked on the phone once a week or visited more than once a year. My dad still liked to ski, so he spent a week in Jackson Hole with Rob and me every winter, but not liking the cold, my mom preferred not to.

So it was a surprise when she called a week later to say that she and Wendy and Wendy's coworker Linda wanted to go. I connected her with Sally, my travel agent friend in Alaska, and Sally and her husband, Chuck, decided to make the trip, too.

Sally, Chuck, and Wendy all trained for the trek and arrived at base camp around noon on the first day of our four-day rest, but my mom was conspicuously absent. "Kit, you really should go check on her," Sally said after hugs. "She's tough as nails, but she's been having a hard time these last few days. Chuck and I didn't think she'd make it, but she's coming. She's just slower."

I took off at a trot down the rocky moraine toward the village of Gorak Shep, and along the way I was surprised at how effortless it felt to hike at this elevation, so different from how I'd felt when I came through here over a month ago. When I finally saw my mom, she was much farther from base camp than I'd expected. Linda and Ang Temba were with her, and another Sherpa was carrying both women's day packs. As I approached, he handed their water to them. *They aren't even carrying their own water bottles?* When I leaned over to hug her while she rested on a boulder, I was shocked by her pallor.

I hadn't noticed that Ang Temba had left base camp ahead of me to meet her group and escort them for the last few hours from Gorak Shep, and I was glad to see him. If anyone could summon help at a moment's notice, it was him.

"Is she OK?" I whispered to him.

He smiled knowingly. "Yes, she is OK," he said loudly enough for Mom to hear. "We are watching her carefully. Mom is tough."

Mom smiled. "Oh, I'm fine. I'm just slow."

I walked with her at a snail's pace the rest of the way to base camp, where I helped her settle into the tent she would share with Wendy. When it was time for our pre-dinner ritual of popcorn and tea about an hour later, I stopped by and took her to the dining tent. Once there, Mom didn't eat, drink, or join the conversation, though, and her discomfort was visible. Before dinner was served, she leaned toward Wendy and whispered something that prompted Wendy to stand and offer my mom an arm to lean on. They left the tent, and when Wendy came back, she was alone.

"Catharine isn't feeling well, but she says she's fine," she said with a nervous smile. "She's resting."

I excused myself and went to their tent, where she was lying in her sleeping bag in the near darkness. "Mom, have you had any water since you got here?"

"A little. I'm OK. Don't worry about me."

"Mom, please, this is serious. You have to drink lots of fluids at altitude. Just try."

She refused to take a drink. "Wendy had to help me to the toilet just now," she said. "My stomach has been sour for the past few days. Will you wash some of my clothes for me?"

The possibility of this kind of nightmare had never occurred to me. "Of course I will." I knew how hard it was for her to ask for help, a trait we had in common. "But you need to listen to me. Did you see the remains of that crashed helicopter just before we got into base camp? You either walk out of here on your own two feet or that's the other option. You need to tell me the truth about how you're feeling. None of this 'I'm fine' stuff, OK?"

To make sure that she got the message, I went to get the satellite phone from our tent so I could call my father. It was the middle of the morning in Massachusetts, and out of my mom's earshot I explained her condition to him and how I was afraid she wasn't taking the situation as seriously as she should. I handed the phone to her and watched her come close to tears as she listened, and then she assured him that she was OK before hanging up.

"Don't worry, Kit, I get it," she said, "and I'll let you know if I need anything. Go have dinner. I'm OK."

I didn't sleep much that night because I couldn't stop worrying about her. At midnight I heard someone throw up and was convinced it was her.

"Please go check on her," I said to Rob. "She hides it from me, but she'll be honest with you."

Rob went out with his headlamp, and when he came back he said that it was actually Linda who'd been sick and that there was no sound coming from Mom's tent.

When he was back in his sleeping bag, I explained myself. "I just couldn't go check because as much as I'm worried about her, I'm also actually mad that she's here in this condition. I don't need this kind of stress—I'm supposed to be resting. If she'd actually taken this trek seriously and respected what I'm trying to do, then she would have trained for it. She talked about it, but I don't think she went hiking more than twice all summer. And now she's on the verge of dying while we're getting ready to climb Everest!"

"Kit, stop it. You should be grateful for her effort to be here. No matter the question, love is the answer."

Actually, I *was* grateful, and I immediately felt guilty about my response to her illness. It shouldn't have been about me. I'd let ego get in the way. But in the past day, I'd developed a sore throat that I convinced myself was a result of the stress and fear and feelings of helplessness my mother had caused me. The situation was far from black-and-white.

The next day, I voiced my fears to Sally and Chuck. "She's stumbling around, which is a sign of ataxia. Mom definitely has altitude sickness, but she might even be developing HACE, and that could be deadly. I don't think she should be here and I'm so bummed that I'm in this position. I can't take the constant worry that she's here because of me and she might die because of it."

"You're doing a good job, Kit," Sally said. "And Rob is right. No matter the question, love is the answer. Let Wendy and Ang Temba worry about her. They've been taking good care of her. We're all leaving tomorrow morning, and hopefully she'll be OK until then."

On October 10, I said goodbye to our visitors. I was proud of how my mom had toughed it out, and as she walked away I *was* grateful that she'd come all this way in support of Rob and me. I spent our remaining rest time alternately lamenting the way I'd acted and celebrating the arrival of my menstrual cycle with the full moon just as I'd expected. It's rare that a woman gets excited about menstruation, but during my time in the mountains over the years, I'd learned that I'm physically at my strongest and have the most mental reserve in the ten days after my moon time. It would take a theoretical physicist to explain how the gravitational and electromagnetic fields of the Earth work together to influence the changes in my energy levels—I just know it's my truth. And I felt incredibly fortunate that the timing was in alignment with our mid-October summit window, even though it wasn't the original "ideal" summit window.

Now all I had to do was keep trying to live the lessons that Lama Geshe and Chomolungma had taught me.

Actual Everest climbing schedule—Part 2
Nights at ABC

9/30	Climbed to CI—had to reestablish acclimatization above base camp
10/1	Took CI down and moved to CII
10/2	Climbed to bottom of Lhotse Face, no sign of our fixed rope
10/3	Rested at CII (although a Sherpa team reset fixed ropes to CIII)
10/4	Climbed to CIII for the day and back to CII to sleep
10/5	Rested at CII and spent 4th straight night here after 1 night at CI
10/6	Climbed to III and spent the night
10/7	Descended all the way to base camp
10/8	Rest day at base camp. Mom arrived with her trekking group
10/9	Rest day at base camp. Mom's one full day here
10/10	Rest day at base camp. Mom's trekking group left. Sherpas stocked CIV
10/11	Rest day at base camp. Sherpas came down from CII to rest at BC

AN INNER JOURNEY

MY LEG MUSCLES TWITCHED, throbbed, and felt trapped in my down mummy-design sleeping bag stuffed full with all the extras I needed to stay warm and dry at night—ski-boot liners, gloves, socks, water bottle. My legs cramped and burned. They felt like they were itching to move. *Is this restless leg syndrome?* Especially in my right leg, the sensation was much more intense than anything I'd experienced after a day's exertion. Yes, we'd climbed from base camp to Camp II today in well under six hours, but that was nothing extreme given that this was the beginning of our summit rotation and we should be acclimatized by now.

I'd woken up to this feeling after being asleep for only an hour. Rob was still lying awake next to me, reading by headlamp and looking perfectly calm. Writhing in discomfort, I turned so many circles in my cocoon that a twist in the fabric, like a towel being wrung, separated the gear stashed at the foot of my bag from my body.

I rubbed my quadriceps, but the sensation refused to go away. And now a growing unease seemed to be spreading through me. *I'm supposed to be resting. How come I can't rest like Rob is? Why am I suffering when I should be feeling good? Tomorrow is a day to chill out and wait at Camp II for the Sherpas to come up before we go for the summit, so there isn't even any performance anxiety about the day. What's up with me?*

The more I thought about how poorly I was adapting to Camp II on this final summit bid and how at ease Rob seemed to be, the less I could control my breathing. I felt like I couldn't exhale completely or I might stop breathing. I began to take shallow breaths and wish for a fully oxygenated inhalation, but my body wouldn't comply and my respiration rate increased.

The muscle tension, the tremors, the headache, the fatigue, the shortness of breath—was I having a nervous breakdown? But that concept seemed too bizarre to actually be happening to me, especially at 21,000 feet on my way to the summit of Everest. I'd never experienced anything like that before and it just didn't seem logical. What did seem logical was that I was suffering from something entirely different: altitude sickness.

What medications do I have that might rule out some of the symptoms so I can make sure this is all mental and I can get it under control?

I settled on acetazolamide, aka Diamox. Climbers often take a small dose—125 milligrams—prophylactically at high elevations, and although I'd never used it, I had some in my medical kit. The most common side effect is numbness or tingling in the toes and fingers, but since we weren't climbing tomorrow, I wouldn't confuse that with frostbite, so I rummaged around my first-aid kit in search of the pill that might be my salvation.

"What's up with you?" Rob asked as I broke a 250-milligram pill in half. "What are you taking?"

"Diamox. I don't know what's wrong with me, but I can't breathe, I have a horrible headache, and my legs are twitching. I don't know if it'll help, but it can't hurt." I swallowed it with some water. "This is so weird. I've never felt like this before... I don't know if I can climb this mountain."

Then Rob threw a curveball right into my spiraling thoughts. "Do you want to go home right now and make babies?"

What?! For our entire six years together, Rob had let me know he'd be happy to start a family whenever I wanted to, but he knew perfectly well I still wasn't ready.

"No," I said so vehemently that it helped snap me into the reality of the moment, and suddenly I was able to laugh at my situation. I was poised to summit the world's highest mountain in the next few days, and if I didn't get my shit together, for the first time in my life making babies seemed like a very sensible option.

"All right then. Just checking." Rob laughed. "Try yogic breathing."

I lay back down in my sleeping bag and tried to focus on breathing from my belly, but after a couple of breaths my body began to twitch again and I couldn't resist the urge to move. I flipped over onto my hands and knees and buried my head in the down jacket I used as a pillow. But I couldn't get to the peaceful place I wanted to get to. A place where I was in control again.

"Put your iPod on and listen to the guided meditation," Rob said.

Good idea. All I'd have to do was listen. The musical meditation was designed to lead the brain into a state of deep relaxation without the listener having to work on breathing or taming her mind. I could just be. I put earbuds in, found the file on my iPod, and, after entertaining a last few anxious thoughts while my body screamed not to be ignored, I drifted into a state of consciousness where I lost track of time and my problems. When I came to several hours later, Rob was sleeping and I was safely beyond the one and only anxiety attack of my life.

At nine the next morning, I woke up exhausted, but I also felt a strange sense of calm. I'd been someplace that I never wanted to go again, and although I didn't know exactly how to avoid it, I did know that simply staying calm would go a long way toward keeping me safe.

In fact, the value of calm and patience was confirmed only a few hours later when we all gathered in the cook tent after lunch to listen to the weather report. Wally had arranged for a meteorologist in Seattle to send us forecasts during our summit window, but they cost a hundred dollars each, so we'd waited until now to order our first one. Wally's voice crackled over the radio as he read the news.

"Winds at 8,000 meters will be forty-five to fifty miles per hour on the sixteenth and seventeenth. Guys, I don't think you should hurry to Camp III tomorrow. If I were you, I'd stall for a day."

Yesterday, a few of the Sherpas on our team had made a final carry to the South Col and reported much the same story. "It was not possible to even speak up there," Lakpa Gelu Sherpa said. "We had to hold on to each other at times." They'd hoped to set up a couple of tents to make moving in easier whenever we arrived, but the wind didn't allow it.

In light of the information we had, it was unanimously decided among the Sherpas and the Westerners that we'd wait.

Making it to the summit was beginning to look like a stretch, since our best case would be to get a new and improved forecast tomorrow, climb to Camp III on the fifteenth, Camp IV on the sixteenth, and the summit on the seventeenth. But I was happy to wait and, ideally, avoid climbing into winds that would force me to hold on to my partners just to stay on my feet 3,000 feet below the summit.

We retreated to our tents for the afternoon, and I wrote in my journal about the previous night's anxiety attack and the book I'd finished reading two days before at base camp, *The Places That Scare You: A Guide to Fearlessness in Difficult Times*, by an American Buddhist nun named Pema Chödrön. Not all my reading choices were so heavy, but as I'd watched my mom's struggles with the elevation at base camp, I was glad I'd brought this one. I wrote down the message I remembered most vividly: "No matter how much planning and goal setting and ups and downs of life, real life is made up of those moments in between. Enlightenment is only attained in daily life. It is important to learn how to live in this manner more than any other. I am trying and last night was a journey in self-knowledge."

The heat of the Western Cwm was fully upon us by now and we kept the front and back doors of our tent open so that fresh air could blow through. This also allowed us to watch the white clouds swirling like ocean waves against the deep blue sky above the massifs of Everest and Lhotse. When the waves met to form the shape of two conjoined hearts, I knew the image belonged in my journal and I set to sketching.

When I was done, I turned to the only book I'd brought for this summit bid, the slim modern classic *The Alchemist*, by Paulo Coelho. I'd read it fifteen years before when I was a young traveler falling in love in the Swiss Alps and hitchhiking to climbing destinations, but reading it this time was an entirely new experience. It seemed to have been written for me, with lessons about improving my ability to ward off the horrible trapped feeling I'd experienced the night before, as well as messages about approaching the great unknown that, for the moment, loomed unattainable above us due to high winds. I devoured the story and made myriad notes in my journal as Rob cuddled against me in his sleeping bag. Among them:

> Pg. 104—*Every day was there to be lived or to mark one's departure from the world.*

> Pg. 108—*The secret is here in the present. Pay attention to the present...you can improve on it. Also, if you improve on the present, what comes later will be better.*

> Pg. 120—*When a person really desires something, all the universe conspires to help her to realize her dream.*

Pg. 122—*Remember that wherever your heart is, there you will find your treasure.*

Pg. 132—*There is only one way to learn…it's through action.*

Pg. 136—*The fear of suffering is worse than the suffering itself.*

Before I knew it, the sun was setting over Nuptse, and Arita Sherpa, the only person on our team who spoke no English, finally halted his daylong prayer, which could be heard throughout camp. The temperature had dropped enough to rouse Rob from his aggressive resting mode and force him into his down suit.

"Time for tea and popcorn," Ang said as he walked among the tents.

As we walked across camp to celebrate Jimmy's thirty-third birthday, I gave thanks for being another day closer to finding my treasure. Although the weather had stalled us, I'd started down a path toward greater clarity, toward a better, more secure personal place from which to start my climb. Toward higher love.

THE MORNING OF THE fourteenth, we woke to hear the wind roaring around Lhotse and slamming into Everest six, seven, even eight thousand feet above our heads. When we gathered around the radio in the kitchen tent for another weather report, Wally told us what Michael Fagin in Seattle had deciphered from his forecasting software.

"Winds are still high through the sixteenth at fifty to sixty knots but diminishing on the seventeenth, eighteenth, and nineteenth, with ribbons of air more calm than otherwise, thirty-five to forty knots. Fagin says that something interesting and unusual may be happening during those days, although they don't look like an obvious summit window above eight thousand meters."

In the green glow of the kitchen tent's walls, there was nervous laughter among the Westerners and the Sherpas as we huddled shoulder to shoulder like we had during the *puja* ceremony.

"What does he mean by 'interesting and unusual'?" Dave said. "Does he mean less wind?"

"I know, Dave, it sounds confusing and it is," Wally said. "I asked Fagin and he said it's not obvious one way or the other, but there are a few different patterns showing up and they could point to a short window, and then again it might not work that way. Sorry, but interesting and unusual it is."

"OK. We'll discuss it and let you know what we decide."

Back in the dome tent, I offered my two cents first. "If Fagin is saying that the winds look like they'll diminish on the seventeenth, I think we should climb to Camp III on the sixteenth, Camp IV on the seventeenth and go for the summit on the eighteenth."

Just then the door unzipped and the lead climbing Sherpa, Dasona, stepped into the tent.

"Sit, please," Dave said, gesturing toward a pile of gear just like the rest of us were sitting on. "We were just discussing what might be our summit day and everyone was thinking that the eighteenth would be as good a day as any. What do you think?"

Resting his forearms on his knees and clasping his hands in front of him, Dasona smiled uneasily. "Sherpa are discussing, too. Yanje (Ang Temba's wife) went to ask Lama Geshe, and he said a snowstorm is coming on or before October 20. We believe Lama Geshe and want to be off the mountain by the nineteenth, so we think summit day should be the seventeenth."

We looked at each other in surprise. None of us had thought of asking Lama Geshe's opinion about a summit day, but it made sense. We'd asked for his blessing regarding our climb and for his help in choosing the right day for the *puja* ceremony, and we'd already survived an immense storm. Considering that we were on the verge of winter, though, it was likely that we'd get only one shot at the summit—should we base our decision entirely on what Lama Geshe said? Or should we go with our Western forecaster's suggestion? Was there a way to blend the two?

"How about we call the meteorologist and ask if he sees that storm," Dave said, "and then we'll get back together to discuss it?"

Dasona nodded and followed Dave out of the tent, and when Dave came back he told us Fagin said that he didn't see any moisture riding in on a monsoonal pattern from the Bay of Bengal but that an increase in clouds was very possible on the twentieth.

Hmmmm.

"Well, if we go up tomorrow to Camp III," Rob said, "then on the sixteenth to Camp IV and start for the summit early on the seventeenth, we might be too early for the window where the winds will be lessened. I still think we should wait another day and go for the summit on the eighteenth. Then we should all be down by the nineteenth."

"*We* will be—we're skiing," Jimmy said. "But it might take everyone else another day. If we summit on the eighteenth, everyone can get back to Camp II on the nineteenth but might not get back to base camp until the twentieth. I'm getting the feeling the Sherpas want to go up sooner because they want to be done with this expedition. If we promise them that we won't ask for a second chance if we all go for it on the eighteenth and it doesn't work out, maybe they'll agree."

"I'm OK with that if you all are," Dave said. "Besides, we don't have enough oxygen stashed up there to make more than one attempt."

"Sounds good to me," I said, and Rob signed off on the plan, too.

Dave left to talk with Dasona and came back a few minutes later with the verdict: "The Sherpas are in for the summit to be on the eighteenth unless tomorrow morning's forecast is for the wind to be favorable sooner. I think they were relieved to hear we're willing to give it only one try. I'll get up with Dasona at five to assess the winds and we'll call Wally for an update. We should know by six if we're moving up or staying put for just one more day. Either way, we'll go for the summit on the seventeenth or the eighteenth and we'll only try once."

It was our second full day of aggressive resting and we retreated to our tents, but I wasn't tired enough to nap. Maybe I was finally as acclimatized as I could be to 21,000 feet. Maybe I'd finally reached the point that had seemed so unlikely back on September 19. As I wondered what I should do with myself for the next few hours, my thoughts wandered back to Lama Geshe. *How interesting that Yanje asked Lama Geshe for his opinion on when we should climb. Maybe I should tap into his energy, too.* Meditation had worked so well on our Lhotse Face day, and if I'd stuck with it, I probably could have headed off the anxiety I'd had a few nights before.

The temperature in the Western Cwm that afternoon was high enough that Rob and I could keep the front door to our tent tied open, and I had the summit of Lhotse 6,000 feet above me to stare at in the unfocused gaze of meditation. My mind wasn't totally without focus, though, as I noticed thoughts appearing.

What if the winds are too strong? The physical therapist who helped rehab my knee was right—I'm too selfish to have kids. What if one of us dies up there? Will we be able to ski?

Each time a thought came, I imagined it was a story printed on a prayer flag and it was flying in front of me trying to get my attention. I smiled gently and, without actually focusing on Lhotse, held the mountain in my gaze and denied the thought any more of my energy. If, after a thought dissipated, another would creep in in its place, I just repeated the process. When ignoring my internal voice was especially difficult, I focused on my wish that Chomolungma would grant us safe passage. Eventually, quality time occupied the spaces between the fluttering prayer flags and my mind was quiet.

When the sun dipped over the ridge on Nuptse, I became aware that I was cold and that I'd passed nearly two hours sitting in meditation. Rob was dressing for popcorn-and-tea time.

"That was amazing!" I said as I did the same.

Rob smiled knowingly, having been practicing meditation regularly for several years. I wanted to share everything I'd just experienced—all the moments of clarity I'd just experienced, all the ups and downs and ins and outs I'd moved through—but it was too much to convey, so I settled on just one revelation I thought Rob would be interested to hear.

"If I make it off this mountain alive, I want to become a mother. I want to have kids with you."

"Are you sure? Where did that come from?"

"I just had the most amazing experience. I get it. I *have* been too selfish to have kids, and I used to hate hearing that, but it's actually OK. It's the way it had to be to do what I wanted to do. But now I need a change. I'm ready to change, and that's what I want to experience next. If I make it off this mountain alive."

"Do you want to go home now and start?"

"No! Let's climb first!"

With a newly light heart, I emerged from our tent and walked to the kitchen. On the way, I felt an interesting sensation when passing by fellow members of our team—I found myself looking them straight in the eye with a deep and loving acknowledgment of all the effort they and their loved ones had made for them to be here in this moment. I felt as if, in a way, the summit had already been achieved and now the team just needed to go through the final motions of the expedition and it didn't matter what happened—we'd already been successful.

When I arrived at the group tent, I encountered an entirely different kind of energy. I watched as the Sherpas shuffled out of the kitchen tent with distress on their faces. When Dave came out, he explained what had happened.

"There's been an avalanche on Pumori, just across the valley. The report is that two Sherpas and two Italians were on the fixed lines approaching Camp III when a big avalanche apparently broke loose above them. It ripped out all the ropes and carried them two hundred meters. They all died."

If I'd needed a reminder, here it was: Regardless of the sense of peace my meditation had brought me, I'd need to remember everything I'd learned in the past two days if I wanted to make it up and down this mountain and then go home and have kids. We may already have been successful, but the summit *hadn't* already been achieved.

"WHO CALLS THIS THE EASY WAY?"

KIT, WALLY HAS SOME news to share with you," Dave called from his tent at Camp III on the morning of October 16.

What?! Did something happen with Mom's trekking group on their way down the Khumbu? My stomach churned as I unzipped my tent door to take the radio from Dave.

"How's it going, Kit?" Wally asked. "Are you ready?"

"Yeah, I'm feeling pretty good and as ready as I'll ever be. I hear the footsteps of the first Sherpas reaching us from Camp II, so it's time to pack up and head up."

"Great, glad to hear it. So last night I received a phone call from Megan Carney in Canada and she asked me to pass a message along to you."

At least this wasn't about my mom, but I braced myself anyway. During critical moments at the top of my competitive skiing career on the world tour, I'd seen more posturing attitudes of superiority between women than supportive well wishes, and even though I'd never met Megan, I felt a protective wall rise inside me as Wally spoke—I just didn't have any mental room for negativity at this moment. I took a deep breath. "Really? What did she say?"

"She said, 'Please tell Kit that I wish her a great climb and ski. Tell her to get it done, for all of us.'"

A chill raced across my skin and made the hair on my arms stand up even under several layers of clothing. I stared at the yellow nylon tent wall. It was as if I were perched on a cloud suspended high above the Earth yet hoping to float up another 5,000 feet into the atmosphere. As I digested Megan's message, I became acutely aware that I was the only woman on this team and that there were other women out there who had the same dream I had. With no negative undertones, the only other woman to have attempted to ski Everest had encouraged me to go for it on this morning when I was about to enter the Death Zone, an elevation at which human beings can't acclimatize, which means they're in a state of slowly dying until they get down.

"Thanks, Wally. Please thank Megan for me and tell her that her message means a lot to me, especially right now."

With a boost of greater resolve and awareness that I might even be serving others, I hurried to pack my stuff and get out of the tent to jump into line behind the Sherpas heading for Camp IV. Though sleeping at Camp III's 24,000-foot elevation hadn't been as brutal as it had been ten days before, everyone was groggy and we climbed slowly into the Death Zone, moving our carabiners along the fixed line and using the long straight shafts of our ice axes as walking sticks.

A few hours later, we crested the rock formation of the Yellow Band, and during the last steps of the uphill traverse, I began to feel the effects of the elevation despite the oxygen mask I'd started wearing since leaving Camp III. And it wasn't just the elevation that took my breath away—the wind was blowing so hard that it sneaked inside every zipper of my suit regardless of the baffles designed to keep it out.

As soon as we arrived at the South Col, we dropped our packs and helped the Sherpas set up camp. The wind had thwarted these highly skilled, handpicked high-elevation workers, sending the tents billowing like parasails. The oxygen masks everyone wore made the scene even more chaotic, obscuring faces and making it hard to tell who was who. Rob, Jimmy, Dave, and I joined the effort and, by sheer virtue of having eight extra hands to hold the tents, helped bring the situation under control.

Once camp had been established and we'd all settled into our respective tents, Jimmy came over for a visit, during which each of us fortified a wall of the tent against the wind gusts by leaning against it.

"Jimmy, you've been up here before," I said. "If it's still blowing like this at midnight, do you think we'll climb?"

Jimmy smirked, much like he had when he'd asked me if I wanted a rope on the Cathedral Traverse of the Tetons. "Yes."

I gulped and returned his smirk, knowing I was up to the challenge. "Well, let's just *hope* that Fagin's forecast of 'interesting and unusual' turns into a little break from these winds, 'cause they're as bad as he said they'd be."

Jimmy nodded, looking more contemplative than he usually did in the mountains. "How's everyone doing? You guys psyched?"

Rob smiled nervously. "Yeah, I'm psyched."

"Me, too," I said. "I'm not going to lie, though—I'm scared of this wind."

Just then Dave's footsteps squeaked in the cold hard snow outside our tent. "You guys in there? Can I come in?"

"Sure," I said.

Rob and I were eager to hear what Dave had to say. Spending the night at 26,000 feet was entirely new territory for us, and although we'd absolved Dave of any guiding obligation during our ski descent, on this eve of our first climb above the Death Zone we were willing to accept our role as mentees, or even clients. The term assigned to our relationship didn't matter at the moment, but being with someone who knew what to expect did.

Dave's tall, lean body barely fit inside our already-cramped tent, so he cut to the chase. "We should wake up at eleven and aim to leave here at 1:30 a.m. Mingma Ongell and Passang Sherpa are leaving at midnight so that they can set some fixed lines up high and hopefully get the Hillary Step in before we get there. Plan on a liter of water per person and a few energy gels plus maybe a Snickers bar. You won't want to stop and eat or drink much, so try to eat tonight. And the water has to stay in your down suit or it'll freeze. Oh, and try to rest. I know it's hard, but it's critical."

With nothing left to do but aggressively rest, Jimmy and Dave went back to their tent while Rob and I lay down for some Pringles-eating. I'd polled several accomplished alpinists before the expedition about what to eat at high altitude, and they'd all said, "Whatever you can. It's all about calories." At home I ate only whole foods, preferably the elk that I hunted every autumn and vegetables from my garden, but at Camp III I'd eaten noodle soup supplemented by a dark chocolate bar with peanut butter squeezed on top, and now I dug into the Pringles—a whole sleeve, 960 calories—and some instant miso soup. It worked—I was able to eat it all without feeling nauseated, and my stomach was satisfied enough to let me fall asleep easily.

When the alarm on our watch went off at eleven, we were surprised by the silence—the wind had stopped. But the cold was as apparent as ever. When I rolled over to start the small backpacking stove I'd brought, I felt the same sensation I'd felt when we waited out the storm at high camp on Vinson Massif: The slightest movement inside my sleeping bag exposed me to fabric not pre-warmed by my body and sent shocking shivers to my core. *Oh, well. It's not like anything's going to be easy from here.*

Being on time for departure at an elevation of 26,000 feet is one of the best ways to show your concern for your teammates, since no one can stand around for long at 1:30 a.m. in the middle of October in the Death Zone without becoming dangerously cold. I'd thought I'd be able to be on the early side of on-time, but the tediousness of working in the dark, combined with breaks to suck a breath of oxygen from the one mask we had set up on a low flow, slowed things down. As did the need to go number two, which set in for both Rob and me before we were dressed enough to brave the world outside the tent. We'd unwittingly practiced for this moment during the horrendous storm at high camp on Vinson Massif when, one at a time, we used the back vestibule for privacy and a large Ziploc bag as a toilet. Since the cold instantly froze even human waste, the smell lingered for only a few seconds, and it was a better alternative than making a mistake in my down suit. Just like in a hospital, nothing is sacred on a cold, high mountain except staying alive.

When we emerged from the tent to join the rest of the team, it was actually just a few minutes after one thirty. Unfortunately, at that point I had to pee so badly that I had no choice but to step outside the glow of the headlamps, unbuckle my harness, and unzip the drop seat on my down suit. In the minute that the whole process took, my fingers became so frozen inside my glove liners that I simply couldn't grab the webbing of my harness to thread it back through the buckle once I'd finished. I was swinging my arms wildly to get some blood flowing when a Sherpa—whom I could only see in silhouette against the glare of the headlamps now focused on me— came over and proceeded to zip and buckle me up as I stood there with my arms held out like a toddler being dressed to go outside and play. I had to laugh at the absurd beauty of this generous gesture.

Once we were all standing together again, with oxygen flowing to the masks on our faces and ice axes in hand, Dave led off in the direction of the

Triangular Face. After several steps, though, he stopped and shared a few words with Jimmy before resuming the initially flat walk across the South Col.

That's curious.

A minute later, Dave stopped again and spoke to Rob for a moment before resuming the march. And then it was my turn. Dave pulled his oxygen mask to the side and looked into my eyes.

"Are you ready?"

"Yes," I said.

"Good, because you're mostly on your own above here. Don't go too hard. Watch your eyeballs—they might freeze. And remember the mask." With that he gave the thumbs-up sign, put his mask back in place, and continued on.

As I followed closely behind him, I wondered if eyeballs could really freeze. On my Siberian expedition seventeen years before, my eyelashes had frozen shut and a teammate had joked about frozen eyeballs, but I hadn't taken it seriously. *Anything's possible up here, though. There's fluid in your eyes, so I guess they could freeze. Keep an eye on them, so to speak... And remember the mask.*

The masks we'd bought were a new type called Top Out. They were an improvement on the previously used oxygen-demand systems which supplied a continuous flow of oxygen even during the exhalation cycle, which meant that a portion of the precious gas carried so high on the mountain was lost. The Top Out mask stores that portion of the oxygen flow safely in a reservoir bag contained inside a plastic cylinder. At the beginning of the inhalation cycle, the highly concentrated oxygen from the reservoir is the first gas to reach the lungs, and the final part of the inhalation is composed mostly of ambient air that comes in through a valve in the side of the mask. Although the masks are made of a silicon compound that doesn't harden when the temperature drops, the valves are prone to icing up when the moist air of an exhalation meets cold air, but all masks are prone to icing up in those conditions. More important, Top Out had reported that its masks were showing an improvement in climbing performance as well as an overall decrease in oxygen consumption, which meant a tank could last longer.

On a moderate oxygen flow of two liters a minute, we climbed up the thirty-five- to forty-five-degree snow and ice and through some short sections of steeper rock, all of which required great care in the placement of each step we took with our crampon- and neoprene-covered ski boots. The rhythm of my breath coming through the mask valves as they popped open and closed reminded me of the forced calm needed to breathe through a scuba apparatus, though I felt more comfortable climbing the Triangular Face on Everest than I had during my only scuba diving experience.

The stars were so bright that they stood out against the inky dark sky as distinctly as words on a page. As I climbed, I noticed a change appearing on the eastern horizon at nearly the same elevation as we were at, a glimmer of light unlike anything I'd seen before. At first I assumed it was the beginning of the sunrise, but when it didn't look any different after an hour, I second-guessed myself. *It's not quite three in the morning. Isn't it too early for the sun to be rising? Maybe it's a reflection of the sun from the other side of the planet, just like the moon reflects sunlight from the other side of the planet. Anything's possible up here.*

Before long, I turned my scientific musings to the abnormal sensation I felt in my left eye. It was slow to focus, and I paid attention to what exacerbated or ameliorated the sensation. I eventually realized that when our climbing team was moving up and to the west, the right sides of our bodies were closer to the mountain, and that's when I felt discomfort in my eye. When the boot pack aimed us in the other direction, my eye readjusted and recovered.

When a faint breeze came from the west, to my left, I shielded my left eye to see if that would change anything. Sure enough, this held the discomfort at bay.

"My left eyeball is freezing, Dave," I calmly said. "I need to put my goggles on." There was no obvious or easy place to stop on the Triangular Face, and I didn't want to make anyone stand still for longer than absolutely necessary, but with my oxygen mask attached by a hose to the tank in my backpack, I thought it would take me longer to get my pack off and rummage around in it for my goggles than it would take Dave to do it for me with the pack still on my back. Without my having to say another word, Dave opened my pack and found my goggles. Yes, we were mostly on our own, but we still had each other's backs.

With my dark-lensed goggles on, I missed out on the rest of the light show, and my attention turned to making sure they didn't fog. I alternated between moving the goggles away from my head to clear the moisture and get a better view of the slope and switching the battery-powered fan off and on to create air-positive flow inside the lens. *Man, I knew attention to detail would be important up here, but this is crazy.*

Within a half hour of putting the goggles on, I became a little more lightheaded than I thought I should be. Worried that I might be one of the many who don't get past the small plateau at the top of the Triangular Face known as the Balcony, I focused my compromised cognitive skills on the possible causes. The most likely seemed to be that hypoxia had sneaked up on me while I was preoccupied with the fundamentals—making proper foot placements, staying the proper distance behind Dave, adjusting my goggles. And then I remembered the mask, just as Dave had advised. I exhaled forcefully and found that my suspicion was correct: The valve on my mask was iced shut and I wasn't getting enough ambient air to make a complete inhalation. It may have started when I took my mask off to talk with Dave about my eye, giving the condensation a chance to freeze, or it may have been just one of those things that happen. After all, we'd been climbing for two hours—plenty of time for things to happen.

"Dave, my oxygen mask is iced up." Again, I hated to be the one to make the team stop, and again, I didn't have to say anything else before Dave came to the rescue. I felt about as tall as a toddler for the second time that day, and about as capable of making this climb. Then I caught myself. *Be careful what you think, Kit.* It's been my observation that when you devote mental and emotional energy to things that could go wrong, they often do. So I shifted my energy to being thankful that we'd hired Dave to help us with the unforeseen mishaps we couldn't avoid.

It was hard to focus on being thankful, though, when Dave put his mouth over the air intake on my mask and blew his heavy, warm, wet breath into the valve. The valve released its icy grip after his second breath, but by then I knew exactly what he'd eaten last: freeze-dried Mexican beans and rice. I fought back the urge to vomit and was rewarded with a relatively deep breath for what must have been the first time in a half hour. My cognitive powers returned slowly but surely, as did my belief in my ability to climb the mountain. Even though I'd been reduced to asking for help twice before it was even light out, now I felt amazingly strong.

When we arrived at the Balcony, we took a short break to change out oxygen cylinders and share tea as planned, and with apparent pride, Dave told us we were climbing faster than he'd thought we would. By the time we moved on to the lower-angled Southeast Ridge, the sky was blooming with color, and Jimmy moved ahead of us to capture a sunrise photo with Lhotse in the background. But just as our elation was dawning with the day, a complication surfaced in the landscape ahead of us: Mingma Ongell and Passang Tenzing Sherpa were descending the steep pitch below the South Summit.

They left almost two hours before us! What are they doing here?

Dasona huddled with the Sherpas he'd chosen for the summit team, and then he called over Kami Sherpa and Lakpa Gelu Sherpa, who were assigned to assist Rob and Jimmy with their photography and videography needs. After a moment, Kami and Lakpa made their way to us and delivered the news.

"Mingma and Passang made it to the South Summit but they ran out of rope and need more to fix lines up the Hillary Step," Lakpa said. "Do you feel comfortable enough climbing up and down this ridge without a fixed line?"

The ridge between the Balcony and the fairly steep start to the rocky blocks of the South Summit was benign stuff as far as climbing Everest goes. There was several thousand feet of exposure on each side, but crossing the ridge itself would be more like walking along an elephant's back than a racehorse's. If any of us lost our balance, which there really was no reason for, in theory we could self-arrest with our ice axes. Besides, there was no doubt in my mind that we would want the rope for the Hillary Step ahead, even if mostly for the ski descent. In the name of efficiency, and for a chance to summit, we decided to cross the ridge without the rope.

"Let's go ahead and clean it all the way back to the Balcony," Dave said.

We took our carabiners off the rope and, along with Kami and Lakpa, unclipped the rope from the snow-picket anchors that held it to the mountain and then coiled the sections of rope and carried them up to the waiting lead climbers. The delay of over an hour lessened our chances of reaching the summit ahead of schedule, but doing it on schedule certainly remained a possibility, and we optimistically followed the Sherpas up the ice bulges and rock outcrops on the way to the South Summit.

Conditions are everything when skiing or climbing, and the recent storms had certainly factored into the snow condition on the Southeast Ridge. As Rob, Jimmy, and I wove our way along the eastern edge of the exposed rocky ridge, I was immersed in a vision of what it might be like to ski down the Triangular Face, the section we'd climbed so quickly about a thousand feet below. It had an obvious, if circuitous, line through the rock sections, so it was certainly doable. But then my thoughts turned to this upper part of the Southeast Ridge, which had been scoured of the fresh white stuff. To have enough snow to ski, we'd be forced to the right, to the east of the ridge crest, and it looked ominously wind-loaded with snow.

Without talking about it, we took turns venturing a body's length into the skiable zone, which was actually the top of the Kangshung Face, the 10,000-vertical-foot East Face of Everest. Whenever I poked my ice axe below the snow slab surface or penetrated it with my ski boot, I couldn't shake the feeling that the three inches of cohesive slab, bridging the kind of snow you'd never make snowballs from, wanted to break loose and slide to the bottom of the Kangshung Face. It was like walking on a drum. No one would stand much chance of riding that kind of avalanche alive.

"That snow didn't feel good to me," Jimmy said as we neared the top of the pitch on our way to traversing the west side of the ridge and gaining the top of the South Summit. "And it's the same aspect of the avalanche that just happened on Pumori."

He was right to draw that parallel. I'd missed it because I'd been so caught up in imagining how I might be able to make my ski turns straddle the very edge of the snowpack and the rocky ridge crest. I'd been wondering if it was possible to ski in that tiny zone without getting tripped up by the rocks and without triggering a sensitive-enough spot in the snow to take a fatal ride down the Kangshung Face.

"It's punchy and breakable for sure," Rob said. "And super dangerous. I'd vote for skiing the rocks."

"The slab doesn't support my weight," Jimmy said. "I just collapse right through to the sugary snow underneath, so it won't hold you guys either."

I certainly felt better hearing that we'd all reached the same conclusion. "Well, let's talk about it again when we get back here," I said. "There's still a lot of mountain above us."

Minutes later, we topped out on the South Summit and stared across the knife-edge ridge toward the formidable, nearly vertical forty-foot Hillary Step. A mini-traffic jam had formed at its base, and it was made up entirely of our team—the only people on the mountain. *Seriously? This is just what we wanted to avoid by being the only ones up here!* Mingma and Passang had just crossed the 200-yard ridge from the South Summit to the Hillary Step and had just now begun climbing and setting a fixed line for the rest of us. There was no reason for us to go over and wait on a ridge the width of a sidewalk, so we huddled on the South Summit, turned our oxygen flow down to a liter per minute, and watched.

"I hope they go up and right, since it looks like a better line to ski," Rob said.

"Yeah, and our ropes would be straighter for a ski belay," I said. "I'd rather sideslip the right side on skis than go all the way around that huge boulder on the left. But I wouldn't want to lead up it—it's totally loaded."

"I bet they go left," Jimmy said. "It's the normal way and it looks easier. Plus there are ten of us waiting for them."

Whichever way they went, we were lucky to be poised an hour's climb from the summit even if we had to wait another hour before we could start moving again. I turned my thoughts to what I could do to improve our chances of success.

"Dave, what do you think about trading out our oxygen bottles now instead of at this spot on the way down?" I said. I was concerned that with the two hours of delays we'd experienced since leaving the Balcony, our oxygen might run low before we could get to the summit and back to the full bottle we'd cached at the South Summit.

"Seems like that'd be a safer option," Rob said in agreement.

"If we change out too soon, we risk running out of that bottle before we get back to the Balcony," Dave said. "Especially because you're skiing and might need a higher flow. Let's stick with the plan."

The part of the equation that Dave didn't mention, and the one that kept me from defending my instinct to swap out bottles, was that the old Russian regulators we were using to connect to the oxygen tanks were like the guns in a game of Russian roulette. During our oxygen-training session at base camp, both Wally and Dave had let us know that the regulators were the weak link in the oxygen-delivery system, with an unknown life expectancy and a tendency to blow the gasket and the gauge when they were being attached to an oxygen bottle. Our team had been sent up the mountain with several extra regulators, but by now they'd all been used.

Instead of dwelling on the decision, we shared a Snickers bar I'd been keeping in an inside pocket of my down suit. We also tried to free each other's suit zippers where the condensation from our masks had frozen them in place. Since we were standing still, we needed to close every opening against the cold temperatures.

When it was time to approach the Hillary Step an hour later, I found that it was even steeper and more intimidating up close than it had looked from the South Summit. I looked at the others and only half-jokingly wondered why Dick Bass had called himself a "high-altitude trekker" if he'd climbed up this.

"Who calls this the easy way?" I asked no one in particular as I tried to laugh off my nerves.

"The guys in *Alpinist* magazine," Jimmy said with a perfect deadpan.

While I love to push my skiing right to the edge of my ability, standing on the thin snowpack under the Hillary Step and imagining skiing it made my stomach drop to my knees. As I leaned on my ice axe waiting my turn to climb, I considered what would happen if it turned out that I wasn't able to ski it and had to take my skis off. At sixty degrees, it looked like a really bad investment in risk-management terms. It would have been kind of like changing out of skis while hanging off a big rock wall like the cable route on Half Dome's east face in Yosemite.

"I don't know how we're going to ski that," Rob said.

"I think I'm going to down-climb it," I said, again to no one in particular, and as soon as I'd uttered the words, it was as if I'd released a weight from my shoulders. I'd acknowledged that I might not ski it, and now I felt free to accept all versions of getting down alive, including a ski descent on belay, which would be a notch above simply down-climbing it.

Rob gave me the easy out. "Let's ski it on belay, then."

I recognized the opportunity to set the intention record straight. "OK, I'm game for that," I said with my gaze fixed on the southwest face's 8,000 vertical feet of relief below us. We were standing a mile and half above Camp II on the most exposed section of the climb, and the other side held 10,000 feet of relief down the Kangshung Face. With the cloud cover rising up from the east, I was thankful I couldn't see all the way.

With a deep breath, I began a rhythmic placement of the front points on my crampons into the Hillary Step and then swung the ice axe in my right hand so that it got a good purchase in the ice and used my left hand to slide my jumar up the rope that Mingma and Passang had placed for us. This part of the climbing was very real, but I actually enjoyed every move on the near-vertical forty-foot pitch. Within minutes, I was taking a big step to the left to exit the vertical section and begin the traverse under the cabin-size rock outcrop that slightly overhung our heads. The wind had whipped around any available snow up here at 28,750 feet, and what remained beneath the outcrop was so unconsolidated that it had taken on the consistency of refined granulated sugar under the weight of those ahead of me. With no handholds for my left hand on the smooth rock, my feet threatening to skid off their perch, and my belly being pushed away from the mountain by the bulge of snow in front of it, I felt stuck and didn't know how to proceed. I desperately wanted another ice axe so that my left hand could also plunge a shaft deep into the sugary snow, but I only had one. Forward, back, high, low I went until I resorted to asking for advice.

"How should I do this?" I asked Jimmy, who was patiently waiting behind me.

"Stick your left arm in up to your elbow and pretend it's an ice axe."

Now I knew firsthand why the Sherpas had gone around instead of straight up the unconsolidated snow. I just hoped getting back down wouldn't be harder than getting up.

THE SUMMIT

"**G**UESS WHAT'S RIGHT OVER *here*," Jimmy said teasingly at 10:48 a.m. and pointed with his mitten toward the summit just several steps away. We'd climbed to the top in close to nine hours, and given that there had been no well-trodden boot path to follow and it was October 18, this was a respectable accomplishment.

Sure, there are hardcore high-altitude alpinists who can do it in far less time, and even without oxygen, but they're also the ones who think the Southeast Ridge is "the easy way," and at any given point in history, their numbers can be counted on just two hands. The truth is that Everest will always be the highest mountain in the world, and no matter the style or the amount of time it takes, getting to the top is *not* easy.

We were all smiling, but the excitement was more felt than seen, since we were still wearing the Darth Vader-style black oxygen masks. As we clasped hands with one another in acknowledgment of our achievement, which had taken more than six weeks of effort, our energy was palpable.

A fog-like air mass had crept up beneath the northern and eastern sides of the mountain as we climbed and now obscured the panorama that we knew was below us, but there was nothing that could interfere with what we could see *around* us from the summit: a sea of black and white mountains set against the deep blue sky and extending all the way to the round horizon.

Dave called Wally on the radio to tell him the good news.

"Wow, you guys made great time," Wally said. "Congratulations on number eight, Dave."

"Seven and a half. Thanks!"

The true summit is only big enough for two, maybe three people to share, and just as it became my turn to stand on top, a visibly fatigued Dasona handed me my skis. At Wally's urging, we'd made the tough decision to allow our trusted Sherpa friends to carry our skis up on summit day so that we might be able to save some extra energy for the descent.

"Kami will carry them down for you," Dasona said, handing me the skis and sounding as tired as he looked.

These guys don't believe we're really going to do this.

"Thank you very much, Dasona, but I'll wear them down," I said, truly appreciating the huge effort he'd made so far and his concern about what was next.

His face contorted in surprise, and with a shrug of his shoulders and a shake of his head, he turned away. Lakpa and Kami handed over Rob's and Jimmy's skis along with a new set of prayer flags Lama Geshe had blessed, which we wrapped around our skis for a symbolic moment.

We *were* going to do this, and the reality of that hit me in a wave. My heart opened with gratitude for everyone's efforts, and I experienced an upwelling of joy and incredulity at the fact that we were about to make the ski descent I'd been dreaming about for a year and a half.

"I think I'm gonna cry."

Rob leaned over and we shared a quick church kiss, but as soon as our lips parted I pulled myself together.

Don't delay. Now is the time to be fully focused.

I began the process. I took a deep breath, bent over, and wrapped the leash of one ski around the ankle of my boot. The last thing I wanted to do on a high, remote mountain was lose a piece of critical gear, so I was in the practice of using ski leashes on my bindings instead of brakes. As I fastened the leash buckle, my brain moved on to the next step: digging out the ice from the binding-receiving holes on the toes of my ski boots to make sure I had a positive connection—more insurance against *losing* a ski.

Oh, no!

I realized that when I was dressing the night before, I'd forgotten to put my multitool in the front thigh pocket of my down suit even though I'd been rehearsing this in my head for weeks.

Dave saw immediately that I was upset. "What's wrong? Can I help you?"

"I forgot my awl!"

"You gave it your *all.* I'll give you my *awl!*"

In a flash he had his tool open to the perfect point for reaming out the tiny holes, and I continued the process through my laughter.

No sooner had I handed Dave's tool back and finished stepping into my skis than he took off on foot down the ridge to set up the rope belay we'd talked about using to get around the Hillary Step. Now it was my turn. I planted my poles as if pushing out of the starting gate at a ski race and made my first turn off the summit.

I was aware that the Sherpas didn't quite understand skiing, so I wasn't surprised that some of them were standing right in front of where I would make my next turn. We'd overlooked planning the part of the day where I'd ski off the summit with twelve other people standing around. Given the language barrier, the tight quarters on the summit, and how difficult it is to speak through oxygen masks, I sideslipped slowly toward them, which sent them scurrying away from my line until I had enough room to make a few more turns.

Immediately below the summit, the Southeast Ridge of Everest has an off-camber fall line, so it's not at all like skiing a familiar run or mountain face. My movements were more like a ski turn to the right that was just enough to lose some elevation, followed immediately by a turn to the left and a good old-fashioned traverse along the ridge, most of which wasn't wide enough to make any turns at all. The snow conditions didn't make for fast going, either. Beneath my skis, the surface felt extraordinarily firm, and eons of intense winds had created patterns of frozen six-inch snow waves eager to trip anyone attempting to ride them. When we'd climbed up, the steel points of our crampons had left tiny marks in the snow, but now with my weight distributed over 164-centimeter-long skis, I detected barely a hint that we'd passed this way.

After skiing down 250 vertical feet to the top of the Hillary Step, I came upon Dave, who was setting up an anchor in the very circumspect, loose-grained snow. A safe ski belay is almost an oxymoron, since little is safe about trying to ski with a rope attached to you, and while I'd worried that the Sherpas might not have the technical skill to create one, Dave was a different story. Besides working as a guide on international mountains and as a ski patroller at Taos Ski Valley in New Mexico, he's a regular guide on Mount Rainier in Washington, and has some astounding rescues to his credit. While I waited for Rob and Jimmy to ski down to me, I watched Dave chop himself a seat in the steep, snowy ridge next to his anchor and, with his weight placed firmly on the earth, thread a rope through both the belay device on his harness and the anchor. My biggest concern was that the anchor would be no better than the snow in which it was built.

I wished I could tie in to the end of the rope right away to begin my ski down the Hillary Step, but I'd promised Rob he could go first because he wanted to film me making the improbable moves I'd need to make.

I only had to wait a few minutes before Rob skied up to me. He tied in to the rope, exchanged ready signals with Dave, and started down around the corner of the Step. When he was out of sight and out of earshot, I watched Dave pay out sections of rope in accordance with the gentle pull he felt from Rob's downward progress. But then the rope stopped moving. None of us expected to be able to hear Rob shout the standard "Off belay!" but we did expect him to untie from his end when he reached the bottom of the Hillary Step so that Dave could pull the rope up and I could take my turn.

When too much time had passed without any signals from Rob, we tried to call him on the radio, but the only response we got sounded like a cross between the first man-on-the-moon transmissions and Charlie Brown's teacher. Jimmy, Dave, and I traded frustrated looks. Meanwhile, the Sherpas and Bryce Brown—the other remaining Westerner in our group after Michael Boni had turned back before the Lhotse Face due to illness—appeared from the summit and waited patiently above us. Still no word from Rob.

At the end of an eternity, the rope went loose and we pulled it in. I wasted no time tying in and starting around the corner of the Step on my skis. When I got to the place where I'd stuck my arm in up to my elbow for purchase on the climb, my heart stopped—Rob was dangling by the fixed rope from the top of the vertical section of the Step, his skis still on his feet. I pulled my mask to the side and yelled his name, but he showed no sign of having heard me even though he was only twenty-five feet away. His left arm was hanging limp by his side, and with his right arm bent over his jumar—which was still attached to the rope at eye level—he looked like he'd rested his head in the crook of his elbow to take a nap. I surmised that he'd lost consciousness in this of all spots, on a sixty-degree slope forty feet above the knife-edge ridge with over 8,000 vertical feet of space beneath him.

My mind started to race. *Rob's a better skier than me, so if he lost it, then I could lose it. Should I go to him? If I run into trouble, there are twelve people behind me that will be trapped above the Hillary Step. And what can I do to help him by myself anyway?* The only responsible choice was to go back up to where I could take my skis off and tell everyone what I'd seen and *then* go to help Rob. I had to switch to rescue mode, and this was no time for me to be thinking about trying to ski.

Do what you have to do, fast.

I sidestepped back around the Step while fighting to keep the tails of my skis from getting caught in the snow. After several strenuous uphill steps with my skis still on, I could see the others. I pulled my oxygen mask to the side, but before I could speak, they made their own impassioned pleas.

"We are running out of oxygen."

"Go, go."

"We have to go down."

Everyone but Mingma was still wearing a mask, so it was impossible to tell who else was shouting. *Where's Mingma's mask?* Mingma's principle job high on the mountain was to serve as Bryce's climbing partner, and when I saw that Bryce was wearing Mingma's mask, I began to put two and two together.

Rob must have run out of oxygen on the traverse!

Everyone's eyes were fixed on me, blocking the way off the mountain.

"Rob needs help," I shouted and pointed in his direction. "Please step over me and start down."

I clipped a carabiner from my harness into the fixed line beside the rock outcrop and untied the knot that led to the rope Dave had used to belay me. "Off belay," I said loudly so Dave would know he could pull the rope toward him. Then I took my backpack off, clipped it into the fixed line as well and inspected the regulator on my oxygen tank: next to empty.

Maybe if I turn my flow way down I'll be able to adjust to the lack of oxygen instead of running out as fast as it looks like Rob did. I turned the dial so that less than half a liter per minute flowed into my mask and then tried to find a way to sit down and take my skis off in the one place in the world I'd hoped not to have to do it.

When the first Sherpas arrived, they asked for consent before stepping over me.

"Yes, yes, please go, please go," I implored them as I struggled to attach my crampons to my ski boots. The slope was so steep that only a small piece of my left side sat on the snow, which meant that my right side was hanging 8,000 feet above Camp II. I couldn't get my right crampon strap as tight as I wanted to, and the struggle to breathe at 28,750 feet with almost no supplemental oxygen became even more of a struggle in my crouching position.

When I was finally back in walking mode after the hardest transition out of skis I'd ever made, I shouldered my pack and jumped into the line around the Step for a second time. Several of the climbing Sherpas were ahead of me, and the rest were waiting their turn behind. Given that neither Jimmy nor Dave rushed to the front of the line, I obviously hadn't clearly communicated the danger Rob appeared to be in.

When I got to the vertical part of the Step, I figured that Rob must be OK since he wasn't hanging on the rope anymore. In fact, he was nowhere to be seen. I tried to make the reverse crux move, but the snow was so loose and sugary and had been stamped so much that it was hard to get enough purchase to step up and over it. *If only my legs were a little longer! This must have been where Rob got into trouble.* On my third try, I felt a little extra lift from somewhere and I sailed through the motion. Looking over my shoulder, I saw Kami Sherpa standing there grinning. He'd given my butt a little push, and we shared a laugh at the most bizarre possible time.

I could now see down the trajectory of the vertical section and I searched for Rob between my careful foot placements down the Step. When I approached the bottom, a Sherpa was still hanging on the fixed line below, preventing me from descending farther. Three Sherpas were huddled on the narrow ridge at the base of the Step, and the terrain was so steep that I still couldn't see Rob. I felt trapped.

"Get off the rope!" I shouted after pulling my mask aside again.

The Sherpa in front of me joined the other three on the tiny ridge, and then I could finally see Rob. Inexplicably, he was twenty feet downhill from the ridge on the Nepal side, lying facedown in the snow.

An eerie sense of confusion surrounded the scene. Rob was in a place where no one would voluntarily go. How had he gotten there? The only thing that was clear in this landscape that was otherwise suddenly devoid of logic was that Rob was in grave need of assistance.

"Help him!" I screamed.

No one moved. Everyone was as still as Rob.

As I down-climbed the remaining feet to the bottom of the Step, I quickly ran through my options. *Kit, you're out of oxygen or close to it. You don't have anything to physically offer anyone, least of all someone who needs to breathe oxygen and maybe be carried. You have to get new bottles from the South Summit if you're going to help him.*

And then an entirely different kind of thought pierced my consciousness. *If he dies, how am I going to explain this to his mother?*

Here I was desperately trying to make all the right judgment calls about how to handle this absolute-worst-case scenario, and out of the blue I had this logical, objective vision, as if the rational part of me had already accepted that Rob's death was inevitable. I was unnerved for a moment until I reminded myself that the rational part of me was doing exactly what it was supposed to do. We'd entered into this climb knowing that the ski descent was risky. This was the life we'd both chosen, and we'd agreed not to regret living it.

But that wouldn't make it any easier to explain the circumstances of a climbing death to someone who didn't have the intimate relationship with the mountains that we did, someone like Rob's mother. Many non-climbers don't comprehend the level of safety we practice in the mountains and seem to believe we're comfortable with the potential for death. To Rob's mom and many others, the risks we take could only be perceived as foolish.

So what was I going to tell her? That I went to get more oxygen for Rob and left him with four men who didn't appear to be willing or able to help him?

Before heading for the South Summit, I had to make a final, definitive attempt to propel the others into action so that I wouldn't have to tell her anything.

Just before stepping off the bottom of the Step, I used my elevated height to command the attention of the four Sherpas standing below me.

They were all family men, and I hoped to appeal to their sense of familial duty when I yelled one last time at the top of my lungs.

"Save my husband!"

It worked. They began to scurry with obvious purpose. And that was the last thing I saw before my world went white.

"DO NOT SIT DOWN AND DIE"

N THE MOUNTAINS, DANGER begets danger. When someone gets into trouble and someone else sets out to find help, the element of the unknown takes on a much bigger role in an already-unknowable situation. Especially on Everest, where *everything* is bigger. But at least when it's two human beings doing the problem-solving, their powers of higher reasoning just might prevail. Imagine the heightened danger of exploring the mountains with a wolf, or any animal, that doesn't understand the plan quite as clearly as you do. I confronted that danger during a day of backcountry skiing in our home valley of Ophir with Alta when he was three years old.

Protocol in avalanche terrain dictates that skiers go one at a time in order to not trigger a snowslide onto partners and to keep a watchful eye on each other from a safe perch, and I worked hard to teach Alta to stay at the top of a ski line until he heard me howl, which was his sign to start running down in my tracks. Eventually, he became so good at following the rule of waiting at the top that I was shocked when one day I watched him take off ahead of me down a slope loaded with fresh snow while I was still stepping into my ski bindings.

"Alta! No!" I screamed, terrified of the risk he'd taken by departing from the plan.

The storm that had dumped the new snow was still creating whiteout conditions and quickly covered his tracks. The accumulation was deeper than his thirty-two inch height, and an avalanche would put him in grave danger.

After a few minutes of calling and getting no response, my ski partner and I began our leapfrog descent on the timbered left edge of the open bowl. On nearly every ski turn, I howled for Alta and called his name but saw no sign of him, not even his wake in the snow, which had disappeared into the far side of the ski run. When we reached the bottom, 1,500 feet below, I stopped in a safe spot and saw Alta plowing toward me like a submarine, his muzzle poking above the trench he made with his powerful stride. Moving at a side-slope angle is always hard work in deep snow, but even taking that into account, he wasn't moving as fast as I knew he was capable of, and I wondered why.

When he came to within fifty feet of me, I saw the reason. A six-month-old malamute puppy was following him—Alta was leading it to safety! Alta must have heard him while I was putting my skis on and he took off to rescue him. The puppy was a quarter of Alta's size and had snow stuck to the fur of his belly that made it hard for him to move his short legs even in the track that Alta had plowed. I gave him some water from my pack and a granola bar, which he devoured, and we descended to town and returned him to his owner.

The dog went on to grow into an animal that outweighed Alta by thirty pounds, but whenever they would meet in town, the malamute bowed down, ever the grateful puppy who'd been saved by a wolf.

Now, as I tried to do for Rob what Alta had done for that puppy, my fortitude was falling far short of Alta's. I felt and saw literally nothing but a comfortable soft white space that not even the cold could permeate. I did *hear* something, though. "Do not sit down and die," the voice said.

During the oxygen training session back at base camp a month earlier, Dave had concluded with some powerful advice: "If you find yourself out of oxygen up there, remember—this is not scuba diving. You can still breathe, you will just have to work harder and go slower. Do *not* sit down and die."

After the effort of each step, the white light again beckoned me to relax in that easy, peaceful place, but before I could allow myself to be enveloped, the voice spoke again.

"Do not sit down and die."

I shook my head like someone trying to stay awake behind the wheel. "Do not sit down and die," I told myself and took a step. The warm bath of white light approached again as I rested and considered the easy option, and then the voice spoke again. I shook my head, clearing it of enough of the whiteness that I could see in front of my feet, and I took another step.

With no concept of time or space beyond the footprints I was following over the narrow ridge of cornice minefields ready to explode and carry me down the Kangshung Face, I somehow eventually arrived at the oxygen cache beneath the South Summit. Two Sherpas, including Mingma, who had left the bottom of the Step ahead of me, were taking turns power-breathing into an oxygen mask that was connected to a cylinder lying on the ground with a dozen others. We looked at each other, but in my survival state I couldn't tell who the second person was, and since they didn't immediately offer me their mask, I took off my pack, picked a tank up from the pile, and went about the methodical process of unscrewing my regulator and installing it on the new one. I silently prayed that I'd picked a tank that would let me backtrack to Rob *and* get down the mountain.

My regulator sealed, but to my horror, it showed that the tank was nearly empty. Now I was in a different kind of survival mode. I'd made it across the ridge without succumbing to the white light, but that danger had been replaced by the game of Russian roulette that I'd feared enough to not change out to a fresh tank during our initial wait at the South Summit. My future flashed in front of me, and I saw myself failing to get to Rob's aid because my regulator broke while I attached it to a second tank. My instincts were tied in knots as I weighed the options.

You have no choice but to try again. Pay better attention to the weight of the tank so you get a full one this time.

Harnessing all my powers of intention, I unscrewed the regulator from the first tank and began to put it on one that appeared to be full. But then everything came to a terrifying halt. In a matter of seconds—before I could finish screwing my regulator onto the second tank—my hands literally became useless to me. They'd frozen into claw-like positions as if rigor mortis were setting in.

But I'm so close!

I tried to beat my hands open with my forearms. I didn't even care if a few of the bones broke as long as they opened. But the level of oxygen in my blood was obviously too low for them to unclench. I looked up at the Sherpas, and by the detached way they met my gaze, I could tell how close to the edge these guys were, too.

"Help," I pleaded with a quiet, desperate calm.

The Sherpas handed me their mask, and after just a few inhalations my fingers miraculously began to uncurl. It wasn't over, after all. I was being given another chance to get out of this maze I found myself in at the top of the world.

Enormously relieved and immediately rejuvenated, I screwed my regulator on the rest of the way, put an extra tank in my backpack, and started back toward Rob.

As I finished the short climb up from the cache spot and raised my head from the focus of putting one step in front of the other, I was met with what I thought had to be a visual trick of the mind. Rob was holding the arm of Sonam Sherpa, who helped him to sit down in the snow about ten feet below the ridge and just in front of the South Summit. *Someone did help him! This is really happening! He's conscious! We both have another chance!*

I was still staring at Rob and processing the idea that he wasn't an apparition when Sonam walked past me toward the cache. I approached Rob, who was breathing from Sonam's low-tech military-green Poisk mask. "Are you OK? Can I help?"

His eyes were vacant. "Sonam gave me his oxygen. I'm all right."

I could tell he wasn't. He didn't have sunglasses or goggles on, and he had only one crampon on. His skis were propped in the snow next to him, where Sonam had probably put them. Up at my changeover spot on the Hillary Step, I'd been unable to efficiently attach my own skis to my pack, so I'd tucked them out of the way under the rock and tied them in to the fixed line. If Dave didn't pick them up for me on the way down, I'd probably never see them again, but my sole mission had been to go to Rob's aide. Now, as I saw Rob's skis in the snow, I wondered what had become of mine. "Where are Dave and Jimmy?"

"I don't know."

"You aren't going to ski anymore, are you?"

"I don't know. Maybe."

Dammit! You almost died and you still look close to it. You're not in your right mind. What do I do now? I wanted to get down—running out of oxygen had been terrifying—but we still hadn't discussed the section of dangerous snow beneath the South Summit, and now both of us had had close calls. It wasn't a good time to be taking on another unknown.

I remembered the way I'd led the last few hundred feet to the summit of Denali and then down for 2,500 feet before Rob recovered from his bizarre bout of altitude-induced euphoria. I decided that the most effective way I could help him now while also seeing to my own survival was to start down ahead of him and carry his skis. I knew he and Sonam would follow me, and Dave and Jimmy were close behind. We'd be like an accordion on the mountain with Rob in the middle. He was in good hands.

The grim reality that two highly accomplished Himalayan climbers still rested in their decade-old deathbeds just around the corner from our oxygen cache clinched it. "I'm taking your skis," I said as I attached Rob's skis to my pack. "You almost just died, and I don't think you should ski down. I can't stand still any longer, so I'm starting down slowly. Hopefully you guys will catch up and I'll see you on the way."

When he didn't respond, even with his eyes, I stood and struggled my way up the soft, body-length holes of sugary snow to get from the ridge back to the top of the South Summit and started downhill for Camp IV. Every few minutes, I paused to look up toward the South Summit, but I couldn't see anyone coming down. *They should be on their way by now. Where are they?* My crampons were so loose that I tripped several times. And to exacerbate the situation, when I'd put Rob's skis on my pack, the side compression straps had been difficult to tighten because the frigid temperatures made the nylon webbing stiff, and the whole carrying system had become so loose that the tails of Rob's skis hit me in the back of the calf when my stride was too long. Between the dangling skis and the loose crampons, I wanted to stop, but I was afraid to. *Just move slowly, Kit.*

When I reached the top of the rock outcrops about halfway down to the Balcony, I saw some climbers coming down the ridge. Slowing my pace and sometimes pausing so they'd catch up, I continued down the first rocky slab by wrapping my arm around the fixed line and facing into the mountain to down-climb because of the steep pitch and the way Rob's ski tails had been catching on the rock. Despite my caution, though, when I turned sideways the skis still caught and I stumbled a body length down on rock and ice until the rope that was wrapped around my arm spun me around and I came to a stop. With tears of fear beginning to well up, I decided to wait and see if the approaching climbers were Rob, Dave, and Jimmy. I sat on the slabs, tightened my crampons, and contemplated giving Rob's skis back to him.

When the climbers arrived, I was disappointed to see the faces of Bryce and Mingma.

"Are you OK?" they both asked.

"Yes, but I'm waiting for Rob and Dave and Jimmy. Have you seen them?"

"They were getting ready to start up the South Summit when we passed them."

I borrowed Mingma's radio. "Dave, this is Kit. Are you guys all together and all right?"

"Yes, Kit. We're on our way down now. How are you?"

"I'm fine. I'm halfway down the slabs, but I've been carrying Rob's skis and they're tripping me up. Can I leave them here for you to pick up?"

"No problem. I'll get them. Be careful."

"OK, I'm going to continue down. See you soon."

"Copy that."

I'd surprised even myself. I *wanted* the accordion that was our team to come back together, I *wanted* to wait, but I just couldn't. The loose crampon and the stumble had given me a scare, but now that problem was solved and I just wanted to keep going. Besides, I actually enjoyed being alone up there now that everyone was accounted for and heading for the South Col.

As Mingma and Bryce continued ahead of me down toward the gentler snow section that led to the Balcony, I repeated the motions I'd performed on the Hillary Step: I clipped my pack in to the fixed rope, took Rob's skis off my pack, and clipped the skis in to an anchor. When I resumed the descent, unencumbered by the ski tails, I could trust my foot placements to stay in place, and my pace increased.

When I reached the Balcony less than an hour later, Mingma and Bryce were laying down resting with their oxygen cylinders out of their packs.

"Are you OK?" I asked. "Do you need anything?"

"We're OK," Mingma said, "just tired and thirsty."

My head was pounding with dehydration and exertion, but I didn't feel like I needed to lie down, so I pulled out the water I'd planned on finishing then anyway and shared it with them. "Can I call Dave again?"

Mingma handed me the radio.

"Dave, this is Kit. I'm at the Balcony. Is Rob OK?"

"He is, Kit. I've got him on a short rope. He's walking down and Jimmy's with us. How are you?"

"I'm OK, but I'm tired and I want to keep going down."

"Go ahead, Kit. Just be careful."

As I started down the Triangular Face, the sun beat down and a new layer of bone-tired fatigue set in, which I tried to ignore. Occasionally I'd catch a crampon as I plunge-stepped straight down the fall line and Dave's words echoed in my head: "Just be careful."

No one was between me and Camp IV, and although the Triangular Face beneath me looked like a ski run that I could normally be down in two minutes, I was so tired that I had to stop every ten steps to rest and it took me close to an hour to descend.

When I arrived at Camp IV, I got into my tent and stared up at the Triangular Face, feeling tired, alone, anxious, and concerned that not waiting for Rob and Jimmy had been the wrong decision. With the lack of exertion, I quickly began to chill down, so I stripped my harness and boots off and climbed into my sleeping bag. It was three thirty—about the time that Rob, Jimmy, and I had hoped to be skiing down the Lhotse Face below Camp IV as the next step in our descent. Instead, it was obvious we'd be spending a second night at 26,000 feet.

Racking my brain for some way to help Rob, I remembered a trick I'd learned as a nineteen-year-old during my National Outdoor Leadership School course in Alaska. We were taught to use only one of the two pairs of socks allowed for each person on our twenty-day backpacking expeditions, and now I dug around in the bottom of Rob's sleeping bag and pulled out the extra pair of socks he'd left there—frozen with moisture just like everything else in the tent. Although it sent shivers throughout my body, I lifted all my layers and put his cold, stiff socks against the skin of my stomach. As for my own extra pair, they went on my shoulders, held in place by the straps of my bra, and I lay on my back, stared up at the Triangular Face, and thought about what I'd seen up above.

Over an hour passed before I saw our team walking down the Triangular Face. As I watched them near the bottom, though, two of the members broke away from the third in smooth, sweeping movements that looked decidedly like ski turns, and my joy turned to angry disbelief.

Really, Rob? After all that up there?

I caught myself.

Kit, he's with Dave and he's in his element. You knew he'd ski if he had his skis. You're just jealous that you didn't ski that section yourself and you're wishing you'd stuck with them instead of having your tail between your legs.

When they got to camp, I helped Rob into the tent, and he took his boots off and curled up in his sleeping bag just like I had an hour and a half before.

"Here you go," I said, handing him his socks. "I dried them... Do you want to talk?"

"I'm cold and tired," he said as he put them on. "Not right now. That was pretty intense."

"LIKE YOUR LIFE DEPENDS ON IT"

THE ALARM WENT OFF on the watch I'd strapped to the inside of my sleeping-bag hood the night before. Several years ago, I'd adopted the practice of keeping my watch close by my head during nights spent in a tent because it's too easy to sleep through wake-up calls when layers of clothes are muffling the alarm. In warm weather, it works to fasten the watch strap to an overhead loop in the tent ceiling, but while winter camping at 26,000 feet, the battery would never survive.

Too bad I didn't give as much thought to the radio. We were supposed to call Jimmy at 6:30 a.m. and make a decision on skiing the Lhotse Face, and I'd hung the radio above my head to make sure I could find it easily. Now it was coated with the same rime that was coating everything else in the tent.

Really, Kit?

After what I'd witnessed yesterday, I didn't expect Rob to rally and make plans anyway—actually, I didn't expect *anything* today beyond some sort of descent from 8,000 meters—but still I untied the radio and put it inside my down suit to warm it up. It felt like I was cuddling a rock from the bottom of a frozen lake, but we *had* to discuss our day as a team, and doing it by radio was preferable to getting dressed to go to Jimmy's tent. The way the wind had picked up, there was no way we could talk through the tent walls. That "interesting and unusual ribbon of potentially calm air" had come and gone.

"How are you doing?" I asked Rob while I waited for the thaw.

He rolled over. "I have a headache, but I'm OK. You?"

"Me, too. What do you think about skiing down today?" I held my breath with a nervous flutter in my gut.

"I'm totally in. It's the best way out of here."

The night before when Rob had said he still wanted to ski the Lhotse Face direct from Camp IV along the South Pillar line, the same one that the Man Who Skied Down Everest had tumbled down, we'd agreed to put the discussion off until the morning. Now that morning was here, I wasn't prepared for his unequivocal determination. *Does he even realize what happened on the Hillary Step?*

My reluctance must have shown.

"Look, Kit," he said, "I only have one crampon, but I have two skis. We've always said we were going to ski it and we should. Jimmy and I talked about it on the way down yesterday. He wants to ski it, and I think we should, too. If you don't want to, then you don't have to."

Beyond fatigue, dehydration, and having spent a second night at 26,000 feet, there was nothing wrong with me, but Rob had to be hurting. He was adamant, though, and the discussion was apparently over. As soon as my body had warmed up the radio enough that the battery showed some life, I turned it on.

"Jimmy, can you hear me?"

"Yeah, go ahead, Kit," Jimmy said.

"How are you guys?"

"We're good. You?"

"We're fine. Hey, what are you thinking about skiing?"

"Let's do it!"

"OK, we're in," I said. "What time do you think we should plan on being ready?"

"How about a half hour?"

"*What?*" Everything we owned was frozen solid.

"Just kidding." I could hear him laughing. "How about nine thirty?"

When you've just decided to ski 5,000 vertical feet of steep, bulletproof ice, any grounding influence is welcome, and as it so often did, Jimmy's humor helped to keep things in perspective.

It took the whole three hours to get dressed, make enough warm water on the stove to thaw a single packet of GU energy gel to have as breakfast, and stuff what we could carry into our backpacks. At exactly 9:30 a.m., Rob, Jimmy, and I stepped out of our tents and into our ski bindings, and Dave and several Sherpas were braving the elements to see us off and looked anxious to get going themselves. There was a sense that none of us wanted to delay, and it wasn't just because of the frigid temperatures and high winds. For my part, I didn't want to think about the magnitude of the ski descent we were about to attempt—I just wanted to do it.

"There are two stuff sacks in the tent," I told the Sherpas. "One is the gear we'd really like you to bring down if you can, and the other we don't care if we ever see again, so make sure you don't try to carry too much. And thanks for everything."

"Call on the radio when you cross the bergschrund at the bottom," Dave said, "and I'll try to catch you lower on the mountain. Be careful, you guys, and have fun." That last bit cracked Dave's voice a bit, and we all knew what he meant. Everyone, Sherpa and Westerner alike, shared hugs and we skied away.

For the first few hundred feet down the fall line from Camp IV on the South Col, we made careful ski turns within a few body lengths of one another, and I was surprised by how reasonable both the snow conditions and the angle were, although I also knew it was too good to last. When the slope steepened to forty-five degrees and, just ahead, it rolled over to a pitch that I couldn't see below, I stopped. I was several turns ahead of Rob and Jimmy, so they stopped to wait behind me as I assessed the situation. Instead of a best obvious line choice, the conditions amounted to patches of snow in the shape of gigantic tongues on the square-mile sheet of shimmery blue ice known as the Lhotse Face. The icy sections were pocked with marble- to grapefruit-size black rocks, balls of white ice, and small sections of wind-redeposited snow. As I saw it, the task would be to ski down the tongue-shaped portions of firm snow, which would just barely hold an edge, and then levitate across the ice to the next patch of snow and follow it down, repeating as often as necessary—an extreme-skiing descent with enormous consequences. But who was I to tell Rob and Jimmy the best way to do it?

I've never tried to ski anything like this before, much less communicate how to do it. It all looks horrible!

I remembered how a guide in Alaska had handled a similar situation during a helicopter-skiing trip. He went ahead to assess the danger and then used his ski poles to communicate his recommendation of the best ski line to me and the other clients above. He made an *X* over his head, which meant, "Don't go straight beneath me! Danger below!" Then he pointed the poles to the right and the left to signify that either of those directions was a good option.

I turned uphill to face Rob and Jimmy and raised my poles to form the X. When I could tell that they'd seen me, I lowered my poles, shrugged my shoulders, and bent my elbows outward with palms facing up. I hoped they understood that I was trying to say, "I have no idea which is the safer, better way. Proceed with the greatest caution and choose your own route." Jimmy and Rob skied toward me, and as they approached they could see for themselves what I'd been trying to tell them. There was a bright side to the firm icy conditions, though: Since the high winds of the past few weeks had scoured most of the September snow off the Lhotse Face, we didn't have to worry much about avalanches.

Though I'd started the descent with a ski pole in each hand, the angle soon reached fifty degrees and I paused to sleeve one ski pole in the spot between my back and my pack and pull my ice axe from the harness where I'd put it for easy access. Beginning a ski descent with the equivalent of a two-foot ice pick dangling from your waist is dangerous, so I often keep the axe in that special spot between my back and my pack while I'm skiing something spicy, but after seeing the icy face with tongues of snow below, I'd done some risk-reward analysis and decided to move it within closer reach. So now, with the axe in my uphill hand and the pole in my downhill hand, I made a turn and then switched them out—I wanted to have the pole in my downhill hand to help center my upper body and I wanted to have the axe in my uphill hand in case I lost my balance. The risk in this situation was that during the brief moment while I made the switch between turns, my only contact with the Lhotse Face was through the edges of my precariously perched skis.

Skiing this steep a pitch for a vertical mile in such frightening conditions, without a single place to escape and take a genuine rest stance, was more than any of us had experienced before. Up to fifty degrees and even a few degrees beyond that, is comfortably inside our skill sets, and those kinds of slopes offer the opportunity for the complete mental focus we love to immerse ourselves in, but this was new territory for us and the unspoken consequences of a fall were clear. One real slip would mean a fall to the bottom of the Lhotse Face and certain death unless we were somehow as lucky as Yuichiro Miura had been during the face's only other descent, thirty-six years before. The statistics on climbers falling to their deaths down the usual climbing route of the Lhotse Face reinforce how unusually fortunate Miura was.

Another unspoken consequence was the lack of a chance for rescue. Should any one of us get hurt or simply lose our mental edge and be unable to continue, frozen in fear, a rescue couldn't come from inside our group—we didn't even have a rope. A rescue probably wouldn't happen at all, since the only people on the mountain were the members of our team preparing to descend on foot from Camp IV, and they'd given all they had yesterday. As we'd acknowledged in our contract with Dave, "Once begun, such a descent may well place Climbers in situations and locations which are not accessible to the Guide." The South Pillar Route on the Lhotse Face was one of those places.

So as we began our descent on the morning of October 19, we did it knowing we would have to be self-reliant, and by the middle of it, I felt like we might as well be soloing a 5.14X rock climbing route—free-climbing a line that's close to the limit of what's humanly possible and where a fall means almost certain death. I don't rock-climb anywhere near that level, but I suddenly realized I was skiing it.

And then I remembered the need to document that I was skiing it. When Jimmy got close enough to me that we could hear each other, I offered him the chance. "Do you want to take photos?"

"Sure," he said and continued slowly down the mountain. I kept expecting him to stop and set up for a shot, which would be my cue to start skiing, but after waiting several interminable minutes perched on the steel edges of my skis without seeing him give me a signal, I couldn't stand still anymore and started skiing again. After about ten minutes of sideslipping and making precise turns, I skied up to him.

"Jimmy, I thought you were going to take photos."

"I tried, but I couldn't raise the camera to my eye."

Oh my God. The impatience I'd been feeling was immediately replaced by a deepened appreciation for how much we were hanging it out there. If Jimmy Chin thought that putting the camera to his eye might cause him to lose his balance, no wonder I was scared.

And it got worse. When we resumed skiing, I became aware that fear had crept into my head like a burglar. It had happened while I waited for Jimmy to set up, and it had grown as my trembling legs tried to hold me still on the steep icy slope. The consequences of losing an edge now infiltrated all my thoughts. I knew I had to find a way to ski without that vision or that would be exactly what I got.

I was only a third of the way down the Lhotse Face when I heard another voice. This time it was my own.

"Like your life depends on it, Kit. Turn."

Without consciously searching for it, I'd found a way to spin my fear of the consequences into positive action. I was reminding myself of the importance I needed to place on each ski turn and on the need to keep going.

"Like your life depends on it," I repeated to myself. "Turn."

After making a turn, I'd switch my ice axe and my ski pole, and it was in this manner that I made it through the second third of the Lhotse Face, another 1,500 feet.

As we neared the only boulder feature on the route, the one that had sent Miura airborne as he tumbled down the face, Rob skied to within speaking range. "How are you doing?" he asked

If ever there was a moment in my life when I was completely humbled and in touch with my mortality, this was it, and I answered him truthfully. "I'm scared and I don't want to die."

"Good. Then make a plan and keep going!"

I'd been gutted to the point of admitting being scared—a big admission for me—and my hackles rose in frustration at his quintessential-male "fix it" response to my open-hearted answer. *Seriously? I've gotten to this point by looking way ahead and keeping my time on the ice between the snow tongues to a minimum, I haven't stopped once except to wait for Jimmy to take photos and I've created a mantra to get through my fear and stay attuned to every move I make. I have my plan and it's working.*

But then I caught myself and had to laugh. "Hey, no shit," I said. "Thanks." This was no place to get tweaked by everyday relationship dynamics. I needed to detach from relatively petty emotions and keep my eyes on a different plan, the one we'd made after Rob and Jimmy's October 4 ski reconnaissance of the lower portion of this South Pillar route. We'd decided that when we got to the boulder, we'd trend right so that we crossed the bergschrund where it was smallest, and that's where I redirected my focus as I continued saying my new mantra and skied ahead.

A hundred feet above the ten-foot-wide crack at the bottom of the slope, Jimmy and I stopped near each other. As I looked down at the gaping crevasse that could easily swallow all of us, I felt a strong desire to not be the one to go first. I'm the type who prefers to have a visual to follow. Everyone has particular strengths, and "air awareness"—feeling as oriented when you're airborne as you do when you're walking on the ground—isn't one of mine. But fortunately, it *is* one of Rob's, and with barely a pause to acknowledge my and Jimmy's hesitation, he pointed his skis down the mountain, and at just the right moment he lifted up and over the bergschrund as smoothly as a bird in flight.

"Really?"

Jimmy smiled and shook his head. "That's Rob D—he makes it look so easy."

Although I hadn't wanted to be first, I also didn't want to be last. I made a couple of turns to get closer to the bergschrund before forcing myself to point my skis straight down the fall line and keep my hands in front of me as if I were dropping a cliff jump. With just enough speed to clear the gap, I made it across.

A moment later Jimmy followed, and we all let loose with some whoop-whooping. We'd just skied the most difficult descent of our lives and I was feeling the most alive I'd ever felt.

After skiing another hundred feet to a spot farther removed from what would be the worst line of fire if rock or ice fell down the mountain, I pulled the radio out of my pack. "Who wants to make the call?" I asked with a smile.

Jimmy took the radio. "Base camp, this is the ski team."

"Go ahead, ski team," Wally said.

"We're down!"

"Congratulations! This is historic! For the record, it's ten forty-two a.m.! Great job!"

As Jimmy snapped photos of our ecstatic faces, it felt strange to me that he was documenting us when this moment was just as much about him. So I grabbed the camera and held it at arm's length for a shot of all of us. No matter what happened for the rest of our lives, we'd have a photo to go with our memory of being alive—in a *heightened* state of being alive—on the edge. Impermanent in the truest sense.

Everest doesn't let anyone bask in a sense of ease for long, though, and as we stood up after stowing the camera and the radio in our packs, we looked up to see black dots tumbling down the Lhotse Face.

"Oh my God!"

"What the hell—"

"Is that—"

I stared in horror as members of our expedition team fell toward the fate we'd just escaped. When they reached the bottom, they exploded above the lip of the bergschrund and scattered in dozens of pieces, some of them disappearing deep into the bergschrund itself.

It took me a second to realize I wasn't actually seeing arms, legs, and heads separate from the bodies of my teammates.

"God, I'm glad that wasn't me," Jimmy said.

"What *was* that?" I asked.

"I think I saw duffel bags." Jimmy said.

I pulled out the radio and called Wally. "What just fell down the Lhotse Face?"

"It must have been the Sherpas tossing gear. They said they might and were waiting until they heard you were down."

I laughed. "Well, I did say we don't care if we never see some of that stuff again."

With that, we pushed off and breezed down the last low-angle bit of the Western Cwm into Camp II. Though the stretch was fraught with rocks and crevasses, negotiating it was as easy as a game of hopscotch compared with what we'd just done.

Back at camp, we needed to decide whether to keep going or rest for the day and continue the ski descent in the morning. Jimmy and I wanted to stay at Camp II, where Ang Pemba could feed us and help us rehydrate until the cold morning temperatures returned and we could continue more safely, but Rob felt otherwise.

"I'm done and want to go all the way down. Today."

He wasn't being rational about the dangers of continuing down the mountain, especially in the relative heat of the afternoon, but Jimmy and I could understand his need to race for the barn.

There's an approach to moving in the mountains that I've almost always adhered to: If one person on a team feels strongly about something, be it a perceived danger or a need for action, the rest of the group should submit to his or her wishes. And that's what Jimmy and I did in this case.

The three of us packed as much gear as we could into our packs and left the rest organized in our tents so the Sherpas could carry it back to base camp, and Rob led the way out of Camp II.

During the storm several weeks ago, we'd made a plan for skiing through the icefall on the descent. After spending the night at Camp II, we'd start early the next morning in the stability of the cold and ski in a zigzag across the Western Cwm to end up under Everest's western shoulder at the elevation of Camp I. From there we'd ski an avalanche-strewn gully to the right of the icefall that we hoped would hold its relatively safe conditions in the dawn of a clear day.

The circumstances that real life had thrown our way were an entirely different story. As we headed for the icefall, it was neither dawn nor clear. The skies had clouded up and were now the same shade of white as the snow in the Western Cwm. Hmmm, what was it that Lama Geshe had predicted? "There will be a storm on or before October 20."

As Rob skied westward past the last climbing track to get underneath Nuptse like we'd planned, he was brought to a halt by an uphill slope that was indiscernible from the horizon. I watched Jimmy try to gather more speed and set the track beyond Rob, but he made it only fifty feet farther. When it was my turn, I made it only fifty feet past Jimmy.

This was ridiculous. We didn't have the time or the energy to switch out to climbing skins, and the milk-jug visibility wasn't helping in the slightest.

"Let's ski down to meet the track," I said.

Rob and Jimmy agreed, and I turned my skis down the fall line to lead the way. I didn't get far, though. After two hundred feet, my survival instinct screamed at me to stop, and I laid my skis over and dropped to my side.

I was lying on the lip of a crevasse at least twenty feet across.

Splaying my body to distribute my weight as evenly as possible, I expected the crevasse edge to collapse at any second. But I couldn't just lie there being as still as a stone—I had only seconds to save Rob and Jimmy from going over the edge. I threw my arms overhead in the "Danger!" position and looked back to see them headed right for me .

"Stop!" I screamed at the top of my lungs.

After they'd thrown on the brakes and stopped fifty feet uphill of me, I inchwormed my way uphill away from the edge. When I finally felt confident that I was out of harm's way, I lay still and cried into the snow, releasing my fear in a rush.

"I almost skied right into one of the biggest crevasses I've ever seen," I said shakily as I stood up. "Let's get out of here and go horizontally right back to the up-track. I've had enough."

Rob and Jimmy just stared at me in silence. They hadn't seen what I'd seen, but they could obviously tell how strongly I felt and deferred to me.

A few minutes later, we were back on the track we remembered from our climb through the cwm a week before. Still on skis, this time Rob led, and we soon came upon a section where the climbing path ran along a hundred-foot-long, eighteen-inch-wide ice spine flanked by yawning crevasses. Though it was at an easy downhill angle and the Sherpas had attached a fixed rope that ran down the middle of the spine, the rope was anchored too tightly to the ground to want to use it while skiing, so it held no protection against a mistake—and therefore no protection against the logical consequence of ending up in a crevasse. I watched in amazement as Rob skied down and across a two-foot gap and hockey-stopped on the other side. Like Jimmy had said, Rob makes it look easy, and I've learned to make my own judgments about what to ski.

"I don't think so," I said when it was my turn. I'd just looked into the jaws of death and was still shaking. "I'm taking my skis off."

"You can do it, Kit," Rob assured me from the other side.

"You got it, Kit," Jimmy said gently behind my back.

They're right. You know you can do this, Kit. Just erase everything else and focus on the finish line. I pushed off.

Looking ahead instead of straight down, I was already across in my mind, so what happened next shocked me to the bone. The fixed rope that lay on the ice spine became lodged under the toe piece of my right ski, stopped me short, and sent me headfirst into the crevasse to the left. But as I went over the edge, I was saved thanks to a combination of the rope stuck in my ski and the way I'd tightened my ski binding enough to prevent an easy release. While my left leg and most of my body dangled in the hole, I grabbed the rope and held on with all I had. My right ski binding had released, but the ski strap was still connected around my boot, which kept my right leg mostly on the ice fin.

"Goddamn *motherfucker!*"

It was too small and dangerous a space for Rob or Jimmy to come to my aid unless I really needed it, so they watched as I harnessed my entire body's worth of strength and pulled myself back onto the fin, sick to my stomach with fear. There was just enough room for me to sit precariously while I carefully switched from skis to crampons like I'd done on the Hillary Step, and then I was finally able to walk the rest of the way across the spine.

I looked at Rob. "I'm done. Done. Done. Done. I'm walking down from here and I think you should, too, unless you really *are* trying to kill yourself."

"Do whatever you need to. I'm skiing."

"And how do you plan to ski across the ladders?"

"I'll just walk across them with my skis on."

"What for? I mean, we didn't even make a complete descent up there. If we had, then I might get it. But this is just stupid. *Why?*"

"Because I want to. I only have one crampon and I ski better than I walk."

I shook my head and prepared to continue alone. I'd had two close calls in less than five minutes, and I wasn't about to ask for a third. I put my skis on my pack, tightened my crampons, and started walking across the Western Cwm feeling very alone but believing I didn't have a choice. My body shook with a mixture of fear, adrenaline, and anger.

Why did I do that when I didn't want to? We didn't make a complete ski descent anyway, so what does this matter? It's not like we can ski down all the ladders in the icefall. And now that the weather crapped out, we can't get across to the west shoulder. What is he thinking?

Constantly looking over my shoulder to watch Rob and Jimmy scoot across a ladder section, I'd stop whenever I got far enough ahead that they were out of sight. I stayed close enough that if one of them needed a rescue, I'd be able to hear their calls, but I refused to watch their descent. In my mind, that would have condoned it.

About fifteen minutes after I'd left them, I looked back to see Rob and Jimmy walking along the track with their skis on their backs. I was so glad they'd stopped skiing that when they caught up to me, I didn't say another word about our disagreement. We continued down past the old Camp I and into the icefall as if nothing had happened.

There was no ignoring what had happened to the icefall in the week since we'd last been there, though. It had become an entirely different beast. Entire sections were gone, collapsed, with remnants of fixed lines buried under blocks of snow. On the other hand, new fixed lines led out of the chaos and into uncharted territory. Ang Nima had obviously been hard at work while we were up high on the mountain, and I felt immense gratitude for his efforts. If it had been just the three of us up there with no support team, we'd have been stuck having to find a way through there and never would have made it down that night.

As it was, making it down that night wasn't a sure thing anyway, since by now it had begun snowing heavily and the wind was whipping it around so much that it bit any exposed skin on our faces. A few hours earlier, we'd been roasting in the late-morning sun as we skied into Camp II, and now it felt as if I'd just gotten off the tram at Jackson Hole in the middle of the kind of storm where you can't see your hand in front of your face. Lama Geshe's prediction for "a storm on or before October 20" had come true. We were all so fatigued that we occasionally stumbled and had to remind one another to be careful.

Having left Camp IV just after we began our ski descent, Dave met us near the bottom of the icefall. The accordion closed for the final time as the four of us made it off the last ladder in the waning light. With just a half mile of horizontal distance and a few hundred vertical feet of icy, rock-strewn moraine separating us from base camp, we stopped to take our crampons off and were greeted by a Sherpa toting a thermos of warm Gatorade to welcome us.

While we drank it, I considered what other chores we might be able to tackle during this last stop. "I think we should get our headlamps out," I said.

Jimmy laughed. "No double-headlamp day!"

We hadn't started the day with headlamps, but I knew he was alluding to our long training days in the Tetons when we took pride in not using our lamps twice in a day. And if any occasion called for pride, this was it. We'd just climbed Everest and skied what we could—a little swagger was in order as we returned to base camp, even if it looked more like stumbling.

It was six o'clock when we came "home" to a blazing fire in the Berg Adventures *chorten* and, in keeping with tradition, walked around the left side of it. Most of our team was still on the mountain, but the six people remaining at base camp, including our kitchen cook/*puja* lama and Nima, who had carried the cooler of filet mignon from Lukla, all rushed out to welcome us on the other side of the monument. Wally greeted us with hugs, popped the cork on a bottle of Champagne, and poured it into plastic flutes.

Happiness coursing through me, I raised my glass. "This is the first time I've ever felt like I *deserve* Champagne!"

Actual climbing schedule—Part 3
Summit Rotation

10/12	Climbed to CII on final summit rotation. Sherpas rested at BC
10/13	Rested at CII. Sherpas returned to CII
10/14	Rest at CII for everyone. High winds. Avalanche on neighboring Pumori.
10/15	Winds were too high at 5:00 a.m., canceled move. Another day at CII
10/16	Climbed to CIII
10/17	Climbed to CIV
10/18	Summit! Second night at CIV
10/19	Descended to base camp
10/20	Other climbers arrived at BC

FREEING THE SPIRIT

I WAXED MY SKIS AND tossed them into the back of the pickup truck alongside my backpack, which was filled as tightly as a well-rolled burrito with everything I'd need up there: stove, instant coffee, sleeping bag, sleeping pad, bivy sack, down jacket, Gore-Tex jacket and pants, hat, headlamp, gloves, climbing skins, crampons, harness, rope, two ice screws, a few pieces of rock protection, two ice axes, two water bottles, and food for tomorrow. Dinner would be an actual burrito that I could order for pickup just as soon as I was done coaching a soccer game.

The younger of our two daughters, a month shy of her fourth birthday, was finally old enough to play soccer in the town's youth league, which she'd been asking to do for a year. When she'd been turned away because of a shortage of coaches for the "Minikickers" league, she was heartbroken, so I volunteered to coach a team. Thankfully, the league lasted only six weeks, from late April when we played outside in a western Wyoming snowstorm until this final game on the sunny afternoon of June 5, 2013. Many of the Minikickers, our daughter included, preferred the camaraderie of the Monday-afternoon practices over these formal Wednesday-afternoon games so much that by this last game, they refused to play at all. So while Tia stayed home, I carried out my final coaching duties with a reduced team roster and then I called the taquería and hit the road. There was a chance, albeit a slim one, that the roasted vegetables, beans, and rice would still be warm inside their foil wrapper when I stopped to eat it at high camp in a few hours.

Although I'd skied the Grand Teton five times in the past ten years, I'd never done it alone, but that's exactly what I was planning for the next day. It was out of the ordinary for me to attempt any kind of a solo ski mission, especially one that involved steep mixed snow and ice climbing, but I was mentally preparing myself and really wanted to try it alone.

My plan was to be off the mountain and back to Jackson in time to pick the kids up from school at three fifteen the next day. If I could do that, I'd feel like I was succeeding at merging motherhood and my desire to spend challenging days in the mountains. In the six years since the birth of our first daughter—a year after I'd completed the Seven Summits project with the Everest ski—it had become difficult to fit this type of big alpine day into my life.

I knew my plan was possible, even probable, but what I didn't know was if I'd really be mentally strong enough to start the climb up the ice bulges of the Stettner Couloir alone and unroped. During the past several days of weather-watching, though, I'd decided there was no reason not to try. *It's OK to turn around if you're not feeling it, but until you put yourself in that position, you'll never know.*

When I'd told Rob of my plan, he said, "Wow, if you do it, I think you might be the first woman."

I cringed. *Who cares? This isn't about being first, and it isn't about being a woman in a man's domain. I love the Grand. It's been a rite of passage for me in so many ways, and this time I want it to be just me up there. That's all.*

It was already after seven as I drove north into Grand Teton National Park, and the sun had just set over the Cathedral Range, 7,500 feet above the valley floor. I was alone on the empty roads leading to the trailhead, so I took the chance to steal long glances over my left shoulder at these mountains that I'd long called home and scan my body for whatever signals it might be sending. Go home? Just do it? At least try? I was a little shocked when everything in my senses told me, "I'm really excited to do this! I can do this! You know the way, Kit."

As I got closer, I could see up into the snowy reaches of Garnet Canyon and I thought back ten years to my first climb and ski of the Grand Teton. I'd spent the previous three winters ramping up my winter climbing skills, and when Rob and I finally skied it in 2003, I became the second woman to do it. Four years later, during my first pregnancy, I'd been afraid of becoming a mother who lost her drive to be in the mountains, so I set myself a postpartum goal of being fit enough, mentally and physically, to ski the Grand in a day. I hadn't imagined doing it alone, though, and when the time came I asked Jimmy Chin to go with me. In the end, we successfully skied from the summit and I was home by 2:00 p.m. to nurse six-month-old Grace. I'd done it—I was a mother and a mountaineer. I was thrilled and content. Jimmy, on the other hand, most definitely wasn't satisfied. The very next day, he went back up to solo climb and ski the Grand Teton and the Middle Teton—in a single day. I can remember what I thought when he humbly told me about his accomplishment: *How could he even imagine doing that? I wonder if I'll ever feel confident enough to ski the Grand alone.*

"I wonder" seems to be a theme in my life. When I read in *Seven Summits* that Dick Bass called himself a high-altitude trekker, I wondered if I could climb and ski those mountains. I wanted to explore my perceptions of limitations, and the fact that it hadn't been done posed an irresistible challenge. The road wasn't paved. And it had been wonder that led me to suggest playing "the game" with Rob as we sat cross-legged on the dingy carpet at the Boston airport. With the palpable energy of new love flowing between us, I wondered if I could marry Rob and move to Jackson within a year; if I could ski in Bhutan, spend a year in France, and earn a master's in landscape architecture within five years; if I could travel the world, have two children, and win something at some point in my life.

Fourteen years later, I've accomplished most of the things on that original list. Some of those entries have lost their priority, while newer entries such as being a good mother will remain goals for the rest of my life. Still, others appear to be completed but have actually transformed into bigger things, keeping me striving. *I wonder if I'll ever feel confident enough to ski the Grand alone.*

Confident. The state of being certain that I can do something and do it well. That's the feeling I had when Rob, Jimmy, and I started to ski down the Lhotse Face on Everest. On such extreme terrain, none of us could have predicted the outcome, but each of us went into it with complete confidence in our ability. When we arrived back at Everest base camp, though, and the immediate need for absolute focus had finally dissipated, I discovered I had conflicting emotions about our accomplishment. We'd summited during the difficult post-monsoon season with a small team, and we'd survived without injury. We'd skied from the summit, and even more amazing, we'd skied the ominous Lhotse Face direct from Camp IV. But I was struggling with the rest of what had happened—and hadn't. How could I confidently answer the question "Did you ski Mount Everest?"

Over that glass of Champagne by the light of the juniper fire burning in the stone *chorten* at base camp, Wally had smiled from ear to ear. "How does it feel?"

"It's great to be back," I said, "but we failed. We tried to make a complete ski descent and we lived through it, so that's a huge accomplishment, but we bailed. I bailed."

Wally's smile faded. "Do you guys have any idea what you did today? What you did today on the Lhotse Face—that's history. That's what this whole trip is about. It doesn't matter what happened up high. You summited, you skied from the summit, you did what you had to do, and then you kept your focus and skied the Lhotse Face!"

I saw his point and felt a little better, but while waiting for sleep to come that night, I still struggled with my doubts.

The next morning, I was obligated to call the marketing people at The North Face to let them know what they were finally allowed to say to the media. As a brand that stands strongly behind its athletes, The North Face had honored my request to not speak publicly about the expedition until it was over, even though the company had contributed significantly toward the expenses of the Everest trip. But now that it was time to break the silence on the morning of October 20, 2006, I wasn't sure what to say.

"A part of me still feels like we didn't do it," I said to Rob. "What should I say?" I was angling for his permission to share a piece of what I'd seen up there, his story. The story that would help me tell my story. Without Rob's approval, it didn't seem right to tell the world that my husband had run out of oxygen on the Hillary Step, passed out, and then somehow fallen to the bottom of the Step, all of which had scared me so much that I took my skis off and tried to help him while trying to spare myself the same fate. But Rob and I hadn't even talked about it yet, so who was I to mention it to a major media engine so soon?

"Are you serious, Kit? You skied from the summit, we ran out of oxygen and had to down-climb a bit, then we skied the Lhotse Face, which was the most amazing and difficult ski descent of our lives. That's all you have to say."

Just say what you did.

That was it then. I wandered off into the quiet snow-covered boulder fields near base camp to make the call, and when I told the vice president of marketing what we'd accomplished, I was met with over-the-top enthusiasm, accolades, and praise for our efforts. I accepted the remarks graciously but said very clearly, "We didn't make a complete ski descent, though."

"I hear you, but don't focus on that, Kit," he said. "What you did is amazing, really, and you guys should be proud. We are all very proud of you and happy for you."

It seemed to be unanimous. After I got off the phone, I realized it had been selfish to wallow in the intricacies of what constitutes a ski descent while everyone else was trying to celebrate what had clearly been a success. Until we'd arrived back at base camp, every ski turn or cramponed step of the descent had held powerful consequences, and *after* getting off the Lhotse Face, I nearly fell to my death in two crevasses within five minutes—*of course* it had been an amazing accomplishment. No step of the way had been a given, and we'd prevailed. But the fact remained—now that the fat lady had finally sang, I was hung up on the spots where she'd missed her high notes.

As it turned out, I wasn't the only one. Immediately after our return home, the naysayers began to post hate mail on Internet blogs saying things like, "Thanks for dumbing down the sport of ski mountaineering. Your ethics will allow more and more people to make wild claims about things they didn't actually do. I, for one, was getting sick of working hard and rising to the challenge of the mountains. Thanks to you, I can stay home and play video games while making all sorts of claims about my ski descents!"

I was paralyzed. My obligations to The North Face included many speaking engagements about skiing the Seven Summits—would the people who were mad at me be in the audience? All I could do was tell the truth, and that's what I did, always explaining the incomplete Everest ski descent and omitting only what didn't fit into a forty-five-minute presentation. To my surprise, each time I finished a talk, hundreds of people stood in line for the chance to chat one-on-one and tell me how inspiring they found my story to be. "When's the book coming out?" they would ask. "I want to hear more!"

I began to think about Lama Geshe's words: "You must have kindness for all beings at the root of the reason for whatever you do if you wish to have continued success." For the sake of inspiring others to challenge what they perceive to be their limitations—the reason I'd wanted to climb and ski Everest—maybe I *would* have to write a book about how I'd achieved my Seven Summits goal. If only I could find the courage to face the abusive comments sure to accompany it...

As for the other question posed so often by the people standing in those lines—"Would you go back?"—my answer came easily: "Probably not. I really feel like we barely got away with our lives. I'm not sure I want to ask Chomolungma for another chance."

But now my answer is different: "I'll go back when my daughters want to go." After Everest, instead of running back for a redo, I threw myself into bearing and raising two children, the second one born four months before I turned forty, and much in life flows from them now.

It would be denying my soul's essence to put skiing and mountaineering on hold altogether, though, and when our youngest was ready to wean at nine months, I left for a three-week ski journey in the Brooks Range of Alaska. I was part of a North Face team that achieved its goal of making self-supported first ski descents in the gigantic wilderness of the Arctic National Wildlife Refuge, and it felt great to be back in my element. It was as if I'd come home. Except that it wasn't my home anymore. I had a "real" home where two children were waiting for me, and I missed them desperately. At one point, as my last drop of breast milk spilled along with more than a few tears, I was led to wonder yet again: *I wonder if I'll ever be good at merging motherhood and a life in the mountains.*

As we skied next to polar bear and wolf tracks, I came to a realization. In the wild silence, it became clear to me that in addition to loving my daughters beyond all measure, the greatest gift I could give them was to continue to be true to myself and do what I was born to do. Like a wolf.

In 1999, the year I met Rob, he asked me to move to the Tetons, where he lived. It was a difficult decision for me to leave Ophir, but ultimately it felt like the right one, and in November, Alta and I drove up to our new home in the mountains near Jackson, Wyoming, a week before his eighth birthday. My epiphany had come true: We would either live in Ophir for a very long time or move someplace far away, like Jackson Hole.

Shortly after we arrived, Alta became lethargic, and for all of the next summer he was visibly sick. Neither of the vets we took him to could figure out the reason, though. In November 2000, a month after Rob and I married, the veterinarian finally diagnosed Alta with an inoperable tumor on his adrenal gland that was causing excess cortisol production. Cortisol is the hormone the body releases in response to stress, and the diagnosis confirmed what I'd long suspected but hadn't wanted to face: Alta was dying of a broken heart.

For the eight years that we'd lived together in the Ophir Valley, I'd happily dedicated myself to giving Alta the best life possible. Once when the most eligible bachelor in nearby Telluride had asked me out, my response was: "Yes, if the date includes a hike in Ophir with my wolf, since I'll be away from him all day while I'm at work."

My suitor couldn't contain his surprise. "Are you turning me down for your wolf?"

"Not exactly." He didn't understand that rather than turning him down, I was inviting him to come along with us because I had made a vow that I deeply enjoyed honoring. *And if he doesn't get that, then he doesn't get me and it won't work out between us anyway.*

But after meeting the man I was going to marry, I moved Alta and I from our home valley that he and I knew every inch of and where we both had a sense of belonging. Although we set off on one kind of adventure or another in our new surroundings in Wyoming almost every day, Alta's health quickly deteriorated to the point where he couldn't enjoy most of them.

When the diagnosis came, I felt sick to my stomach. After all I'd done to provide him with a good life, in the end I had failed. No one can *own* a wolf, and the truth is there's no way for a human to entirely protect a wolf from the dangers of living in a human's world. By adjusting my life to be with Rob, I was being true to my nature, just as Alta had spent his entire life being true to *his* nature, and suddenly I could see the conflict that had been inevitable all along.

The night before his death, we lay together on my bed. Rather than curling up like a wolf, Alta lay on his side across from me. After a timeless moment spent looking deeply and lovingly into each other's eyes, I was sure that the only way that such a powerful scene could end was with the final closing of his eyes, but instead he reached his leg out in front of him and laid his paw in the crook of my underarm with the same gentle pressure that lovers might use when holding hands. I smiled and moved my arm to touch him in the same place on his body. We lay like this throughout the night while Rob slept in the living room, not wanting to disturb us.

The next day while Rob was at work, I could clearly see that the pain reflected in Alta's eyes was unbearable. He hadn't drunk any water in more than twenty-four hours, and I knew it was time to take him to the vet.

"Can you come to our house after five o'clock and put him out of his misery?" I asked the vet after he'd confirmed that Alta was at the end of his life. "I'm just not ready to say goodbye, and I want it to be at our cabin in the woods."

He agreed, and then I asked him if he could give Alta something to ease the pain for the next five hours.

"Yes. I'll do my best, but you should be aware that sometimes giving them anything at this stage will be too much."

As I weighed the options, Alta's eyes rolled back in his head. "Please give him something."

After the injection, I carried him back to the car and set him on his bed in the back of our Subaru before realizing I hadn't given the vet directions to our house. I ran back inside, and as I wrote down our address for him at the front desk, he remained at the door watching Alta. "Kit, I think you need to go to him," he said. "He's standing up looking for you."

I ran outside and from across the parking lot I saw the look of confusion on Alta's face. It wasn't unlike the way he'd looked at me when I would ask him not to chase the elk. After I climbed in through the hatch, he whimpered and, despite the close quarters, tried to walk in a circle the way he often did when he was trying to find a comfortable place to lie down. In a hushed voice, I reassured him that he was OK, that I was there, and that he could go if he had to go. But he was scared and confused, and neither one of us wanted him to go. His body tense as I embraced him, we were both holding on to the amazing life we'd lived together.

Ultimately, I understood that I had to help him to be free. When the image of Alta flying off the cliff after the elk came to me, he seemed to finally relax in my embrace even though he was convulsing in pain, so I let the vision play through in my mind.

"Fly. Fly away, Alta Love Wolf," I whispered in his ear as I rocked him like a baby. "Fly off the cliff—you can do it this time."

Within moments, Alta went limp in my arms and I knew he'd left his body. Barely able to see through my tears, I drove home with him on his bed in the back of the car. At the cabin, I wrapped him in the sweater we'd worn together during his first month with me and I spent the night outside on the porch next to him. I thought his soul might need to adjust to being out of his body—my soul certainly needed to adjust. I waited till late the next day to take him back to the vet to be cremated along with his sweater.

The next summer, I took his ashes to Ophir and scattered some of them off the same cliff I'd seen him jump in his final moments. I scattered the remainder in other spots of the valley that we had both loved.

I WAS CALMLY EAGER as I stood at the base of the Grand Teton's Stettner Couloir at 5:00 a.m. on June 6, 2013. This was the moment when I could turn around—I'd given myself permission. This was the place above which a mistake could prove fatal. Strangely, turning around never crossed my mind.

I feel great. I'm here at the exact time I told myself I had to be here. The ice bulges look small. The snow looks good. Everything is perfect. I'm going to do this!

While I'd been the only woman on the Everest team, I go with *only* women on some expeditions as a conscious effort to create some sort of balance in the male-dominated sport of ski mountaineering. But as I began the technical climbing of the Stettner Couloir with my skis on my back and an ice tool in each hand, I realized that the only balance that matters comes from inside. I needed to honor both the masculine and the feminine powers within me. To blindly charge up the mountain without acknowledging my role in my family and my fear of failure, to disregard the need for my intuition and my objective to be in alignment, would have been to fail to honor the feminine. And if I didn't acknowledge the skill that allowed me to do what no woman had done before and the courage that allowed me to try, I wouldn't have been honoring the masculine.

I once drew a divination card that resonated for me even though I didn't fully understand it. I knew it wasn't a coincidence that I'd drawn it—it had been intended for me. I wrote down what it said:

> Carrying your gift of consciousness from the heart of woman, of Mother Earth, trek toward the summit of higher knowledge... The masculine God is in search of the feminine Goddess. One cannot live without the other. He brings gifts of driving force to her powers of intuitive, creative receptivity... Balance your masculine and feminine energies through meditation and awareness of when you are carrying a male or female shield. This is your struggle in life and a great source of power for you.[2]

Now I was beginning to understand. The things I've been drawn most to in life, the things that make me feel most connected to my energy source, don't fit neatly into traditional female roles. The reason I wanted to ski the Grand alone wasn't that I wanted to become the first woman to do it. My motivation was far more primal than that. I'd simply wanted to tap into my energy source, to commune with my deepest drives, to commune with one of the high places I loved so much, just as Alta had. It was the same reason I'd wanted to ski the Seven Summits and challenge my perceptions of limitations. "I wonder..." has nothing to do with gender. It's about existing on a level where masculine and feminine blur and you reach your absolute highest potential and feel more alive than anywhere else.

When I reached the summit, I looked down at the valley where my home is and thought about Lama Geshe. "The top of our head is the junction of heaven and Earth," he'd said, and here I was again at the physical junction of heaven and Earth. The kind of place where I experience higher love. And that's just what happened. I felt my heart fill with love for the planet and all her creatures—including me—and suddenly I knew it was time to finish this book.

It was almost time to pick up the kids, too, and as I skied the Grand—which in some places had consequences every bit as extreme

---

2   *Andrews, Lynn* (1991). The Power Deck: The Cards of Wisdom, *New York, HarperCollins Publishers.*

as I'd confronted on the Lhotse Face—I wondered if Lama Geshe would agree that high places are also the junction of masculine and feminine. Regardless, I felt confident in my assessment. I'd just lived it, after all.

When I got to the school just in time for pickup, Grace and Tia met me with body-wrapping hugs and unconditional love, not unlike the love of a wolf I'd once known. And in that moment, I was filled with gratitude for the direct navigating that had led me to this spot.

AFTERWORD:
FILLING IN THE GAPS
IN THE EVEREST DESCENT

By Doug Wagner

S O, WHAT EXACTLY WAS it that led to Kit's decision not to ski the 2,500-foot stretch from the Hillary Step to Camp IV on Mount Everest? What *happened* to Rob up there?

"At the summit, I'd checked my tank and I was at about two liters, and that could have lasted fifteen minutes or it could have lasted forty-five minutes," Rob says. "I didn't tell anybody because I just had this sense that I was getting really close, and I knew I had to get out of there."

After skiing from the summit to the top of the Step, Rob used the belay that guide Dave Hahn had set up to get down to and around the rock outcrop of the Step, but that's where he ran into trouble.

"I was yelling into my mask for slack, for Dave to pay out more rope so I could scoot across the traverse, but Dave couldn't hear me, so he didn't let it out quick enough. I was pulling myself forward against the backward pull of the belay and sucking wind with the exertion."

Eventually, Rob was able to clip his safety carabiner into the anchor at the top of the vertical part of the Step. "As I was untying my knot, which was extra hard because it still had tension from Dave's belay, I ran out of oxygen, and I felt myself starting to go in and out of consciousness."

He fought to gain control of his breath and remain conscious and then turned his attention to planning his next move, which included placing a second carabiner above the anchor and moving the first one to below the anchor. "The idea is that you're never without a point of contact with the rope," he says, "so on a descent you have one 'biner on the high side of the knot, then you clip another 'biner to the low side, then remove the upper one and keep going."

He figured he had to make a right-turn move that would drop him twenty vertical feet to the next anchor point in the rope, a maneuver that would amount to scraping the tips of his skis along the rock while holding the rope. And he turned out to be right, except that when he made the turn, he got caught on the highest of the two anchor points on the vertical part of the Step. He'd forgotten to take his upper carabiner off.

So he struggled to hoist himself up and unweight it, but in the process he continued to fade in and out of consciousness. That's when Mingma Ongell Sherpa, who'd helped fix the ropes up the Step that day, arrived on the scene. "I remember Mingma helping me unclip my 'biner that was still above the anchor, and then I remember a mixture of sidesliding and falling to the next anchor point."

Now hanging beneath the second anchor point, Rob had the same problem—this time because he slipped right past it. His skis were on the near-vertical rock and tangled in old fixed lines, preventing him from using an edge to self-rescue, and he was unable to climb back up to unclip his carabiner. Sonam Sherpa was the next person to arrive, and he and Mingma descended to Rob.

"When I reached him, Rob's ski was stuck with the old rope," Sonam recalls. By removing one ski and cutting away the old rope, the Sherpas freed Rob from his tangle, which allowed him to kick the toe of his boot into the mountain while also pulling himself up on the rope in an effort to climb up and unweight his carabiner. But he still wasn't able to fully unweight the carabiner, so Mingma gave Rob a boost and Sonam was able to unclip and then reclip the carabiner beneath the anchor. Rob lost consciousness almost simultaneously.

"I remember the Sherpas seeming frustrated and in a hurry," he says. "And the last thing I remember was kicking my boot into the snow and pulling on the rope. I was working so hard to climb up and unweight the rope. That must have been when I passed out and fell."

Fortunately, before that second fall, Sonam had reattached Rob's carabiner to the fixed line below the anchor, so although Rob fell about forty vertical feet below that lower anchor, he didn't plunge 8,000 feet to the Western Cwm. He came to rest lying facedown in a no-man's-land more than thirty feet beneath the climbing route on the Nepal side of the knife-edge ridge below the Hillary Step. Pulled by his weight, the fixed rope now stretched in an arc between the two closest anchor points, and it didn't allow anyone else an easy hand-line off the bottom of the Step to the ridge. Several other Sherpas arrived from above while Sonam carried Rob's ski and a pole down to the bottom of the Step.

"When I came to, Sonam was hitting me on the head with my ski pole," Rob says. As the cobwebs started to clear, he realized that he had only one of his skis on and that it was pinned under him. His heel had come free from the binding, leaving only his toe connected to the ski. As his body struggled to restart, his brain took inventory, and a voice inside coaxed him into action. After unpinning the ski, he alternately sidestepped and postholed his way twenty feet uphill through the steep sugary snow toward the ridge. Linked arm in arm with Lakpa Gelu Sherpa, who stood on the ridge, Sonam reached down to Rob and extended his ski pole to bridge the gap. Rob used a bent elbow to latch on to the whippet—in effect an ice axe attached to the handle of the pole—and the two Sherpas pulled him toward them.

Back on "safe" ground, Rob took off his ski, which Lakpa carried for him, and Sonam shared his oxygen with Rob as they made their way to the oxygen cache on the South Summit. Along the way, Rob couldn't help noticing that something was amiss.

"Even in my state, I could feel everybody's sense of urgency. The Sherpas were out of oxygen and they were scurrying by us to get to the cache. It was like on an airplane—they tell you to help yourself before you help others, and that's what the Sherpas were trained for and smart enough to do."

In Sonam's case, he went above and beyond.

"We just kept buddy-breathing till we got to the cache," Rob says. "Sonam saw that my mask was frozen, with snow and ice in it, so he changed the tank on his mask first and then tried to put that system in my backpack, but I said 'no, no, no.' I was stubborn because I wanted to keep my own mask. So we continued to buddy-breathe on his mask while Sonam cleaned mine up and screwed a new tank on for me. I can still hear him laughing about how I wanted my own so much.

"My hands were seizing up like Kit says hers had done. Sonam and another Sherpa started hitting and rubbing them for me. I thought, *They've seen this before. They know what to do.* They were very calm, and they were all business. I wasn't freaked out at all. I knew we were going to be fine at that point. With that help and the oxygen, I was good to go down."

From there it was a matter of careful foot placements with just one crampon. The other one had been lost in the fall, along with a ski pole and Rob's goggles.

At the time, Rob wasn't happy with Kit's executive decision to confiscate his skis. "I felt it would have been much easier to ski. I can sideslip pretty much anything. When I started doing ski cinematography work, I considered myself one of the world's best sideslippers," he says with a laugh. "You've got thirty pounds of camera gear, including a thirteen-pound tripod dangling off the back of that, and you sideslip some crazy stuff to get the shots. So I wasn't worried about skiing. But I knew down-climbing with one crampon was going to suck."

Hindsight offers him a different perspective on what happened. "I was incapable of making a good decision up there. It's a crazy type of hangover you get after being without oxygen and passing out. It takes time—and dropping vertical—to get over that fogginess and get your faculties back."

Faculties like your eyesight. For some period of time after regaining consciousness, Rob saw in black-and-white. When expedition partner Jimmy Chin arrived at the cache, Rob told him about it.

"He looked at me with a totally casual look on his face," Jimmy recalls, "and he said, 'Hey, do you have a pair of sunglasses?' He must have lost those in the fall, too, though I didn't see it happen. I was wearing my goggles, so I gave him my sunglasses and asked him if he was doing all right. He said, 'Well, I'm kind of only seeing in black-and-white.' I was thinking, 'Well, the sunglasses aren't really going to help.' But he put them on, and even though I could tell he was more down than I've ever seen him, he smiled this classy smile and started joking around like nothing was wrong. Classic Rob."

Though not common, what happened to Rob makes sense when you consider that the cone cells of the eye—the cells that distinguish color—require more energy to operate than the rod cells, which are responsible for monochrome vision. So it would follow that once oxygen is restored, you see the world in Technicolor again, and that's what happened in Rob's case.

Dave, Rob, and Jimmy retraced the climbing route back to the top of the Triangular Face, picking up Rob's skis where Kit had left them. During a rest at the Balcony, Rob and Jimmy told Dave they wanted to ski down from there.

"Dave said no and that he wasn't comfortable with it," Jimmy recalls. "He felt it was too late and if anything went wrong it would be too much of a risk to the Sherpas, so he asked us not to ski. Although we were disappointed, we respected his request even though it was terrain we were both very comfortable on."

The Balcony was also the place where Rob and Jimmy had their first conversation about what had happened higher on the mountain.

"How're you doing?" Jimmy asked.

"I'm fine. I just didn't see it happening like that," Rob said with tears in his eyes.

"Everything happens for a reason," Jimmy said.

Once off the steep part of the face, Rob and Jimmy again asked to ski, and Dave approved, so the two of them skied the bottom few hundred vertical feet back to Camp IV.

As for Kit's decision to start climbing down ahead of Rob, he didn't need supplemental oxygen to realize that it had been the wise course. "You just have to keep moving down," he says now. "Kit set the pace and everybody was on it. There were no questions, because everybody knew big disasters start as little problems up there. It was Kit's trip and Kit was doing the smartest thing in the world by leading down quickly. Actually, it was part of our deal, too: Don't kill yourself saving the other person. She was doing the safe thing."

Eight years later, it's *himself* he struggles not to be disappointed with.

"You work for a lot of years on a lot of mountains, and it was disappointing to go that far on the most difficult one and have it all be totally skiable and not to have it happen. It was such a magical expedition, with the harmony in the team and the connection with the mountain, the solitude of being there alone. Everything was just perfect, and the fact that we didn't ski all of it makes me sad to this day. It's hard not to feel responsible for the fact that Kit didn't make a full descent. I've lost a lot of sleep over that. On all the other mountains, Kit had pure, classic, complete descents." Besides being a world-class sideslipper, Rob is a pioneer of American extreme skiing. He's one of the fearless steep skiers and cliff jumpers who appeared in Warren Miller's early documentaries on the subject in the late 1980s and 1990s, and his resume includes plenty of major ski descents on peaks around the world. So when this accomplished athlete describes the conditions on Mount Everest as "totally skiable" on a given day, you understand that he means it's skiable for people like him and Kit and Jimmy.

But as cheated as he felt—as much as he laments having held Kit back when she was so close—he also realizes that the "What if?" cycle is an endless one. And he realizes that there may well have been a reason that things turned out as they did. Everyone survived, and he and Kit have gone on to bring two bright, shiny souls into the world: daughters Grace and Tia.

"Our life is whole," Rob says. "If things had gone differently that day, it might not be."

Jimmy concurs with that outlook. "As long as we're alive and healthy, there are no regrets. The snow we walked up and down on above the Triangular Face to the South Summit was like a hollow drum. Five days earlier, the upper flanks of Pumori, with a similar aspect, calved off in a massive avalanche that killed everyone when it ripped out the fixed lines. We were probably lucky it happened the way it did up there. The other alternatives in those kinds of scenarios are pretty bad."

Rob muses on the connectedness they had with the mountain. "Chomolungma obviously didn't want to be skied that day, or couldn't have safely been skied that day. I like to think she spared our lives in the way it all played out. I have only gratitude for her kindness and for granting us safe passage."

Any regrets aside, the truth is that the South Pillar Route of the Lhotse Face held the most difficult sustained steep skiing of the team's intended Everest descent and they skied it after everything that had happened higher up and spending a second, unplanned night at 8,000 meters. This rarely attempted climbing route has claimed the lives of several people—without skis—and it's the same one that Yuichiro Miura tumbled thousands of feet down in 1970.

"The Lhotse Face has over 5,000 vertical feet of a very steep and continuous fall line," Rob says. "The biggest extreme descents in Chamonix, South America, and Alaska have between 3,500 and 4,000 vertical feet, so a vertical mile is pretty much unheard of."

As of 2006, Miura was the only person to have tried to ski the South Pillar route on the Lhotse Face, and no one has tried it since Kit and her team's descent. The few who *have* skied below Camp IV in recent years have all skied a line along the regular climbing route, which is within range of a bailout or rescue and traverses much of the face, leaving only about half the direct vertical that Kit's team skied.

When you take everything into account, that Kit down-climbed from the Hillary Step to CIV does nothing to diminish her accomplishment. She skied about 65 percent of what is arguably the world's most extreme descent, and that 65 percent includes the summit.

As Rob puts it, "She skied off the top of Everest, saved her husband's life, skied the Lhotse Face, continues to climb and ski with great passion, and is a great mom."

All in all, more than sufficient reason for Rob to let himself off the hook.

ACKNOWLEDGEMENTS

My debt spans all seven continents of this planet, and for that I'm truly thankful.

Throughout my years of making the lifestyle choices that have led to this point, I've found that the lines between friends and family often blur. I like to call this blend of people my tribe: They've been my partners in the mountains, those who help care for our children since we live far away from grandparents, and the friends and colleagues who fit into neither of those descriptions yet land squarely in the tribe. You've all been a part of this book and I thank you.

Beyond my tribe, I have a family whom I love deeply, especially because they let me be me. My mom once told me, "Don't ever let someone tell you there is something you can't do." I guess I took that too seriously. When I called to tell my dad that I'd won the US Freeskiing Nationals, he said, "Of course you did, Kit. You seem to be the only one who didn't know that you would." To be surrounded by people who believe in me is the fuel that keeps me burning. I thank my sister, Ann, for giving me all her oxygen genes since she suffers from altitude sickness even in airplanes, and my brother, Jonathan, who was the first to show me that it can be rewarding to sit down and write for the sake of writing.

I could not have written this book without first learning to write, and I have the utmost admiration for my writing coach, Toni Robino of Windword Literary Services, who graciously led me along this many-year journey. Her "BookWalk" program taught me that the only reason a nonfiction writer gets stuck is that she doesn't have a good enough outline. And Toni herself taught me to find the place inside where I'm raw enough to laugh and cry and to write from there. Thank you, kind lady.

Windword's Doug Wagner is the reason this book was finished before the tenth anniversary of our Everest descent as well as the reason it's as well written as we like to think it is. With a gentle heart and voice, Doug taught me the nuances of transitions and the fine art of writing while he helped develop my first, second, and sometimes fifth drafts into a far more polished book than I could have done without him. Thanks for your incredible work,

Doug, and for steering me into the unknown by making me finally write about Wolfie.

Appreciation beyond words is what I feel for my private sponsor, who is the true embodiment of an angel. And he appeared at the moment I most needed one.

My corporate sponsors, especially The North Face, who for over ten years have also believed in me, deserve a round of applause. "You've got to live your life as purposefully as if you are already sponsored," is what I tell young people who ask me how to become a professional athlete. Thanks to all of you who have recognized that quality in me and in my peers.

Many people wonder what it's like to share experiences like these with one's spouse. To them I say, "Rob has always been my best partner in the mountains because I can tell him exactly how I feel, whether confident or scared, and then it's like water under the bridge. It just is." Rob, thank you for being my partner in all ways. I wouldn't have done this without you.

To our daughters, Grace and Tia, I owe my deepest gratitude. The fact that you both picked me to be your mother makes me feel like the luckiest woman on Earth.